The Fight against Book Bans

The Fight against Book Bans

Perspectives from the Field

Shannon M. Oltmann, Editor

BLOOMSBURY LIBRARIES UNLIMITED
NEW YORK • LONDON • OXFORD • NEW DELHI • SYDNEY

BLOOMSBURY LIBRARIES UNLIMITED
Bloomsbury Publishing Inc
1385 Broadway, New York, NY 10018, USA
50 Bedford Square, London, WC1B 3DP, UK
29 Earlsfort Terrace, Dublin 2, Ireland

BLOOMSBURY, BLOOMSBURY LIBRARIES UNLIMITED and the Diana logo are trademarks of Bloomsbury Publishing Plc

First published in the United States of America 2023

Library of Congress Cataloging in Publication Control Number: 2022060875

ISBN: PB: 978-1-4408-7976-0
ePDF: 978-1-4408-7977-7
eBook: 979-8-216-17148-5

Typeset by Amnet ContentSource

Printed and bound in the United States of America

To find out more about our authors and books visit www.bloomsbury.com and sign up for our newsletters.

To my parents, Duane and Melody Oltmann—they always gave me freedom to read widely, and my passion for standing up for others comes directly from them

Contents

CHAPTER ONE

The Precarious State of Libraries in the 2020s

Shannon M. Oltmann

Introduction

It is no secret that in 2021, the number of challenges of and bans on books in public and school libraries rapidly increased. For example, suburban school districts around Des Moines, Iowa, have faced demands from parents to remove certain books (Clayworth, 2022). In Utah, multiple school districts are banning books and disregarding state rules about formulating a challenge and reconsideration policy (Alberty, 2022). To overcome book bans in Oklahoma, one teacher shared a QR code with her students that would allow them to access the Brooklyn (New York) Public Library—this library has made banned and challenged books available for all teens, across the United States, online. The teacher ended up resigning after being accused of "being political" in the classroom (Hernandez, 2022). These are only a few of the more recent stories.

In 2021, the American Library Association (ALA) recorded 729 challenges against 1,597 books, more than double the previous year's figures and an all-time high since the organization began tracking challenges in 2002 (ALA, 2022). Likewise, PEN America compiled a list of book bans in school libraries by reviewing media reports, covering a period of nine months; they reported 1,586 bans during that time span.

Some have speculated that the number of book bans was reduced in 2020 due to the COVID-19 pandemic and the rise of in-home online schooling. At the same time, most public libraries shut down in-person services. Simply put, there was less exposure to the resources held in school and public libraries. Children and young adults were not browsing the shelves, and parents, guardians, and grandparents were less aware of the vast diversity of resources in most libraries.

Two other changes have occurred at roughly this same time. First, in the past decade, there has been increased diversity in children and young adult books being published. Simply put, there are *more books* with authors or protagonists who are Black, Indigenous, or people of color (BIPOC) or part of the lesbian, gay, bisexual, transgender, and/or queer/questioning (LGBTQ+) community (Flood, 2021; Grady, 2019). Books with diverse authors and/or protagonists are making their way onto library shelves and curriculum lists. (It is worth noting, of course, that the proportion of these diverse books is still woefully short of where it should be; nonetheless, there has been some improvement.) Second, there has been a steadily increasing backlash against diverse books and a more inclusive society in general (see Chow et al., 2021; Meckler & Natanson, 2021; Will & Hamilton, 2021). This backlash has complicated roots and explanations, beyond the scope of this book. Nonetheless, it is impacting libraries in meaningful (and often negative) ways.

Often, public libraries and school libraries face the most challenges and bans to books and other resources (ALA, 2013). This is, in part, because these are the most accessible to the public and because they are public institutions, funded at least partially by taxpayers. This book focuses on both types of institutions.

The Right to Read

These book challenges and bans directly contradict Americans' right to read freely. This right is drawn from the First Amendment, which states that "Congress shall make no law . . . abridging the freedom of speech" (Library of Congress, n.d.). Court cases have established that the freedom of speech includes the right to access information freely (Oltmann, 2016). Children and young adults (those under the age of eighteen) enjoy the same rights, only somewhat curtailed. Both public and school libraries are seen in the eyes of the law as government (or quasi-government) institutions, meaning that the First Amendment right to free speech applies to these libraries. Thus, from a legal perspective, public and school libraries should promote reading freely rather than restricting access to books.

The ethics and core values of librarianship echo the essential freedom of the First Amendment as well. For example, access and intellectual freedom are core values according to the ALA (ALA, 2019). The ALA states that "all information resources that are provided directly or indirectly by the library, regardless of technology, format, or methods of delivery, should be readily, equally, and equitably accessible to all library users" (para. 3). The organization defines "intellectual freedom" as

> the right of every individual to both seek and receive information from all points of view without restriction. [Intellectual freedom] provides for free access to all expressions of ideas through which any and all sides of a question, cause or movement may be explore. (ALA, 2007)

The ALA also notes that intellectual freedom is essential for our democracy. It enables people to become educated (in the broadest sense) and to form their opinions about matters important to them. Although it was last affirmed in 2004, the Freedom to Read Statement is very applicable today:

> The freedom to read is essential to our democracy. It is continuously under attack. Private groups and public authorities in various parts of the country are working to remove or limit access to reading materials, to censor content in schools, to label "controversial" views, to distribute lists of "objectionable" books or authors, and to purge libraries. These actions apparently rise from a view that our national tradition of free expression is no longer valid; that censorship and suppression are needed to counter threats to safety or national security, as well as to avoid the subversion of politics and the corruption of morals. We, as individuals devoted to reading and as librarians and publishers responsible for disseminating ideas, wish to assert the public interest in the preservation of the freedom to read. (ALA, 2004, para. 1)

This stance is generally accepted and upheld by most librarians across the United States, though it has come under some scrutiny from both the left and the right. Nonetheless, this book argues that intellectual freedom is an essential foundation of librarianship and should be vigorously defended.

Challengers and Astroturfing

Defending intellectual freedom is not always an easy task. It can be quite challenging to stand for intellectual freedom when detractors and critics are vigorously opposed. According to the ALA (2013), most challengers are patrons and parents. Since 2020, the number of challenges coming from individuals who are *not* patrons has increased; some of these, for example, do not have a library card, have not used the library, have not read the books being challenged, or do not have children in the school district.

In this same time period, we have seen challengers use a wide variety of tactics to further their agendas, sometimes at the expense of defenders of intellectual freedom. For example, there has been a rise in personal attacks and offensive language used to describe librarians and library supporters. Sometimes, vitriolic terms are misappropriated and hurled at librarians, primarily to incite further anger and challenges—but also to intimidate and harass them.

Some national groups have used the approach of "astroturfing," which *Merriam Webster* defines as

> organized activity that is intended to create a false impression of a widespread, spontaneously arising, grassroots movement in support of or in opposition to something (such as a political policy) but that is in reality initiated and controlled by a concealed group or organization.

Thus, the many seemingly unconnected, independent challenges to books often have the same origin in certain well-funded national groups.

This tends to create more pressure on local librarians, who generally do not have the resources to respond to these challenges. The ALA's Office for Intellectual Freedom (OIF) tracks these challenges and assists librarians in combatting them; state- and local-level library organizations and committees also help with resources and support. However, state and national organizations, as well as librarians themselves, were unprepared for both the onslaught of challenges and the vitriolic approaches used in recent times. The rise in challenges has, frankly, caught the profession off guard and left librarians scrambling to figure out appropriate, successful countermeasures and solutions.

Advocacy: The Future of Libraries

One thing seems clear: libraries, librarians, and their professional organizations need to become better at advocacy and explaining the mission of libraries—and quickly. The future of libraries may be at stake.

In fact, some libraries have (hopefully temporarily) closed down due to challenges, bans, and the fight about what should be on library shelves (Cantor, 2022; Migdon, 2022). Other libraries have faced reduced funding after book challenges (Carlisle, 2022). Sometimes, challenges—and comments from the public—are so difficult that library staff leaves the library or even the profession. This is occurring at the same time that other community members are using the library more often for more purposes (e.g., EveryLibrary, 2020; Jensen, 2022).

Advocacy has several components. Librarians are, naturally, better at some aspects than others. Helping library patrons is a form of implicit advocacy, as we hope that happy patrons will share their stories and, later, support the library. Friends of the library groups (which could be for public or school libraries) can formalize community support. These groups should be focused on more than an annual book sale; they should be active in the community, spreading stories about the good work of the library.

Other forms of advocacy include working with local elected and appointed officials; interacting with broader swaths of the local community; sharing the mission and values of librarianship; and ensuring the appointment of a strong board of trustees. Community members who are not currently library patrons should be considered important points of potential advocacy. Why are they not library users? What would get them in the doors or on the website? What would convince them to support the library?

Furthermore, libraries need to be more explicit about their mission and core values. Perhaps libraries should post their mission statement, the Library Bill of Rights, the Freedom to Read Statement, and/or the core values of librarianship. Maybe some programming on these topics would be useful. These statements could be printed on bookmarks, posted on the library website, or otherwise embedded in daily library practices. We have a powerful goal—to connect people with information—and we should be bold about sharing and explaining that goal to all in our communities.

Advocacy needs to be done with both passion and restraint, as we work to convince our communities about the value of libraries in people's lives. While advocacy does not come naturally to some librarians, it is time for our profession to get out of its comfort zone and into the community.

About This Book

This book is organized into five parts; most sections contain both general content and personal narratives from librarians. In the first part, several authors provide background information about the rise in book challenges across the nation. Chapter 2, by Glen Benedict, describes three characteristics of the current wave of book challenges. Chapter 3, by Andrea Jamison, focuses on supporting the intellectual freedom of youth. In chapter 4, Rene Burress, Angie Wiegers, and Amanda Harrison describe the challenges faced by school librarians in Missouri and Kansas. Chapter 5, by Jamie Gregory, is a personal narrative of challenges encountered in South Carolina.

The second part of the book focuses on the ways that challenges and bans affect librarians. Chapter 6 by Terri Lesley recounts attacks on books and programs at a library system in Wyoming, focusing on lessons learned. In chapter 7, Kelly Mayfield describes a preemptive weeding project, which removed hundreds of books before challenges even occurred. Chapter 8, by Julie Hornick, focuses on a challenge in a school library, in which the administration was not supportive of the library. Chapter 9, by Joe Schweiss, describes the emotional fallout that librarians may experience from a challenge.

In the third part of the book, the authors detail different types of external support that have been created to deal with the rise in book challenges and bans. Chapter 10, by Dorcas Hand, describes a helpline set up to provide librarians with a supportive resource. In chapter 11, Becky Calzada and Carolyn Foote provide information about a group of school librarians that came together. Matthew Noe, Amie Wright, and Moni Barrette, in chapter 12, explain how graphic novel and comics advocates have supported librarians facing challenges.

The fourth part offers advice on what librarians should do when facing challenges and bans. In chapter 13, Kristin Pekoll describes the resources of the ALA Office for Intellectual Freedom and suggests ways to handle challenges. Chapter 14, by Jenna Kammer and Mernie Maestas, reflects on the use (and nonuse) of policies in challenging situations. Chapter 15, by Cindy Welch, focuses on foundational documents and the communities we serve. In chapter 16, by Rhona Campbell, approaches to nervous parents are discussed.

The final part of the book contains advice from librarians who have faced their own challenges. In chapter 17, by Dee Ann Venuto, the author describes the similarities between an older challenge and the present day. Chapter 18, by Kerrie Lattari, recounts a challenge in a school library. Chapter 19, by Martha Hickson, explains how a librarian utilized community support to help fight a book challenge. In chapter 20, Tonya Ryals reviews the importance of advocacy in countering a public library challenge.

References

Alberty, E. (2022). *Utah schools are adapting new book-banning procedures.* Axios Salt Lake City. https://www.axios.com/local/salt-lake-city/2022/08/29/utah-schools-book-banning-procedures

American Library Association. (2004). *The freedom to read statement.* https://www.ala.org/advocacy/intfreedom/freedomreadstatement

American Library Association. (2007). *Intellectual freedom and censorship Q&A.* https://www.ala.org/advocacy/intfreedom/censorship/faq

American Library Association. (2013). *Infographics.* https://www.ala.org/advocacy/bbooks/frequentlychallengedbooks/statistics

American Library Association. (2019). *Core values of librarianship.* https://www.ala.org/advocacy/intfreedom/corevalues

American Library Association. (2022). *State of America's Libraries Report.* https://www.ala.org/news/state-americas-libraries-report-2022

Cantor, M. (2022). US library defunded after refusing to censor LGBTQ authors: "We will not ban the books." *The Guardian.* https://www.theguardian.com/books/2022/aug/05/michigan-library-book-bans-lgbtq-authors

Carlisle, M. (2022, September 7). Public libraries face threats to funding and collections as book bans surge. *Time*. https://time.com/6211350/public-libraries-book-bans/

Chow, R. M., Phillips, L. T., Lowery, B. S., & Unzueta, M. M. (2021). Fighting backlash to racial equity efforts. *MIT Sloan Management Review*. https://sloanreview.mit.edu/article/fighting-backlash-to-racial-equity-efforts/

Clayworth, J. (2022). *The books Des Moines suburbs want to ban in schools*. Axios Des Moines. https://www.axios.com/local/des-moines/2022/02/11/des-moines-suburb-districts-book-ban-requests

EveryLibrary. (2020). *Why we need libraries now more than ever.* Medium. https://medium.com/everylibrary/why-we-need-libraries-now-more-than-ever-2118019cebe0

Flood, A. (2021). Report shows fourfold rise in minority ethnic characters in UK children's books. *The Guardian*. https://www.theguardian.com/books/2021/nov/04/report-shows-fourfold-rise-in-minority-ethnic-characters-in-uk-childrens-books

Grady, C. (2019). *Diversity in children's books has increased exponentially over the past 10 years*. Vox. https://www.vox.com/culture/2019/12/28/21039014/childrens-books-little-women

Hernandez, J. (2022). *An Oklahoma teacher gave her students access to banned books: Now she's under scrutiny.* NPR. https://www.npr.org/2022/09/01/1120576731/an-oklahoma-teacher-gave-her-students-access-to-banned-books-now-shes-under-scru

Jensen, K. (2022). *Libraries are more popular than ever and library workers don't earn a livable wage: The state of U.S. public libraries*. BookRiot. https://bookriot.com/libraries-are-more-popular-than-ever/

Library of Congress. (n.d.). *Constitution of the United States: First Amendment*. https://constitution.congress.gov/constitution/amendment-1/

Meckler, L., & Natanson, H. (2021). As schools expand racial equity work, conservatives see a new threat in critical race theory. *The Washington Post*. https://www.washingtonpost.com/education/2021/05/03/critical-race-theory-backlash/

Migdon, B. (2022). Library temporarily closes after resignations over LGBTQ+ book challenges. *The Hill*. https://thehill.com/changing-america/respect/diversity-inclusion/3567597-library-temporarily-closes-after-resignations-over-lgbtq-book-challenges/

Oltmann, S. M. (2016). Intellectual freedom and freedom of speech: Three theoretical perspectives. *Library Quarterly, 86*(2), 153–171.

Will, P., & Hamilton, O. S. (2021). *Is political correctness holding back progress on diversity, equity, and inclusion?* LSE Blog. https://blogs.lse.ac.uk/businessreview/2021/09/06/is-political-correctness-holding-back-progress-on-diversity-equity-and-inclusion/

PART 1

The Rise in Book Challenges across the Nation

CHAPTER TWO

It's Not Just the Quantity: Book Challenges in 2021 and Beyond

Glen J. Benedict

> "It's a volume of challenges I've never seen in my time at the ALA—the last 20 years. We've never had a time when we've gotten four or five reports a day for days on end, sometimes as many as eight in a day," says ALA [Office for Intellectual Freedom] director Deborah Caldwell-Stone. "Social media is amplifying local challenges and they're going viral, but we've also been observing a number of organizations activating local members to go to school board meetings and challenge books. We're seeing what appears to be a campaign to remove books, particularly books dealing with LGBTQIA themes and books dealing with racism."
>
> —Flood (2021, para. 2)

Increase in Volume of Challenges

The American Library Association's (ALA) Office for Intellectual Freedom (OIF) collects data on book challenges and bans. This information is released in ALA's annual State of the Libraries reports in the spring and during Banned Books Week in the fall. The numbers released for 2021 are startling.

In 2021, both the total number of challenges (729) and books targeted (1,597) represent a dramatic increase over the 2020 numbers—156 and 273, respectively. While it is true that reported challenges were down in 2020 due to COVID-19, the 2021 statistics mark a sharp departure from pre-pandemic trends (ALA OIF, 2013) (please refer to figure 2.1 for more details).

Other findings from ALA include an increased focus by censors on books about race and racism. In 2019, only two of the Top 10 Challenged Books (*The Handmaid's Tale* by Margaret Atwood and the *Harry Potter* series by J. K. Rowling) were not targeted for lesbian, gay, bisexual, transgender, queer/questioning, intersex, and asexual (LGBTQIA+) content. In 2020, as a reaction to the June protests following the murder of George Floyd and the accompanying increased focus on race relations and police brutality in the United States, five of the Top 10 were challenged for "political content" and "anti-police views." In 2021, these two trends combined as every title in the Top 10 either had so-called anti-police views, LGBTQIA+ content, or a label of "sexually explicit."

PEN America (2022), a nonprofit organization formed to support First Amendment rights for writers, created their own Index of School Book Bans by reviewing newspaper articles and interviewing educators, covering July 1, 2021, through March 31, 2022. The index only covers instances where a book was removed from a classroom or library for at least one day but still reports 1,586 bans covering 1,145 titles. Like ALA OIF's report, PEN America found recurring subjects in the titles banned: "race and racism in

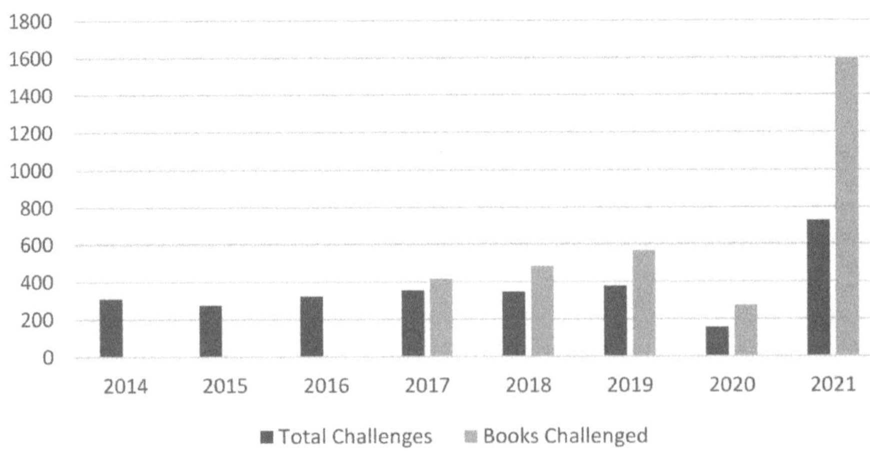

Figure 2.1 Book Challenges Over Time. (Source: ALA Office for Intellectual Freedom, 2013)

American history, LGBTQ+ identities, and sexual education in schools" (PEN America, 2022, para. 10).

An investigation into book bans and challenges in almost one hundred school districts in Texas found an increase in formal challenges over previous years, with several districts reporting more challenges in January of 2022 than in the previous two decades combined (Hixenbaugh, 2022). Most of these challenges "targeted books dealing with racism or sexuality, the majority of them featuring LGBTQ characters and explicit descriptions of sex" (para. 8).

Grassroots or Astroturf?

The term "grassroots" refers to political activity that is organic, originating from citizens, and independent from interests of political or cultural elites—"bottom-up" rather than "top-down." Being portrayed as grassroots is important to a variety of populist ideologies for the rhetorical value the label can imbue (Yenerall, 2017). Groups working to organize book challenges and bans are no different.

In contrast, astroturfing, as a concept, refers to the use of grassroots aesthetics in political organizing to pose an illusion of organic, unprompted, or populist support. Three major organizations, Moms for Liberty (MFL, 2022), No Left Turn in Education (2021b), and Parents Defending Education (2022a), each refer to themselves as a grassroots organization or movement. However, a closer look at each reveals deep connections to powerful political figures and institutions.

Moms for Liberty

MFL was founded in 2020 and incorporated in 2021 with a mission to expand what they see as parental rights in education, initially in opposition to mask mandates during the COVID-19 pandemic (Craig, 2021). As of February 2022, it was reported that MFL had over seventy thousand members across 165 chapters (Skolnik, 2022). While masking has continued to be an important topic for the group, it has expanded its remit to include opposition to critical race theory (CRT) (Craig, 2021) and protections for LGBTQ students (Jenkins, 2021).

Although two of the initial cofounders of MFL were former school board members, the third cofounder and initial codirector was Bridget Ziegler, the wife of Christian Ziegler, vice chairman of the Florida Republican Party (Little, 2021). Neither Ziegler is mentioned on the "Who We Are" section of MFL's (2022) website, which does include the other two cofounders and the current executive board.

The executive director of program development at MFL was formerly an employee of Republican Florida state representative Randy Fine (Skolnik,

2022). Fine once posted the personal telephone number of a Brevard County School Board member on his Facebook page, urging his followers to call her regarding an upcoming vote on mask mandates (Little, 2021). That board member was Jennifer Jenkins, who won her position by unseating Tina Descovich; Tina would later become one of the cofounders of MFL. Jenkins (2021) has described harrowing acts of retaliation and intimidation, including threats, vandalism, and a false report of child abuse to the Florida Department of Children and Families following protests organized by MFL. The continuing symbiotic link between the organization and lawmakers creates the possibility of further implicitly state-sanctioned harassment of libraries and library workers.

No Left Turn in Education

No Left Turn in Education (2021a) boasts a similar scope—thirty chapters in twenty-three states—and mission as MFL. It also features similar close ties to elite Republican power players, including David A. Clarke (a former spokesperson and senior advisor to Donald Trump's America First Action super PAC), the National Rifle Association, Family Watch International, and the Heritage Foundation (Skolnik, 2022). Unlike MFL, which generally only refers to vague terms such as "liberty" or "parental rights" on their website, No Left Turn in Education (2021b) is very explicit about the subjects that concern them, including CRT, the 1619 Project, sex education, and "Woke Education."

The No Left Turn in Education website also includes example letters and petitions, offering these templates for use in crafting book challenges. To assist in these challenges, a book list is maintained with ratings for explicit sexual content. Some titles have expanded "book reports," which consist of e-reader screenshots with profanity highlighted. A concluding page summarizes the amount of profanity, along with any topics that make it "not appropriate literary content for K-12 schools." While No Left Turn in Education (2021b) claims to believe "education should be free from indoctrination and politicization," it is hard to take that claim seriously when their Recommended Titles page (No Left Turn in Education, n.d.) includes *Amy Coney Barrett—A Justice and Mother* (2021) and *Black Eye for America: How Critical Race Theory Is Burning Down the House* (2021).

Parents Defending Education

Parents Defending Education (2022a) is another organization that dubiously promises "the restoration of a healthy, non-political education." President Nicole Neily was previously the president of Speech First, another nonprofit that could be described as "astroturfing," with connections to the Koch Brothers and (via their legal and web-hosting teams) Donald Trump and the National Republican Senate Committee (Moattar, 2018). Neily also served with other Koch-funded institutions, including the Cato Institute (Skolnik, 2022).

Resources provided by Parents Defending Education (2022b) include instructions on filing a Freedom of Information Act request, running for school boards, and creating Gmail and Instagram accounts with the usernames "Woke At [name of municipality]." These otherwise anonymous social media accounts are then used to present out-of-context material that the organization finds objectionable, to rally local parents into supporting censorship efforts (Cunningham, 2022). An *IndoctriNation Map* provides links to parent organizations and incidents (2022d). Parents Defending Education not only opposes books that it claims contains CRT or gender/queer theory, but it also ties the two concepts together, defining the latter as "critical race theory translated to gender and sexuality" (2022c).

State-elected officials

PEN America (2022) found that 41 percent of the bans in their Index of School Book Bans could be directly traced to political pressure and directives from politicians in Georgia, South Carolina, and Texas. Book bans played a role in the 2021 gubernatorial election of Glenn Youngkin in Virginia (Shephard, 2021). Florida, home to both MFL and Governor Ron DeSantis, made national headlines over the Parental Rights in Education Bill, also known as the "Don't Say Gay" bill (Skolnik, 2022). The actions of these politicians have led to worries about a "chilling effect" (Hixenbaugh, 2022), which has historically involved soft- or self-censorship (Yorio, 2020).

Florida

Florida governor Ron DeSantis signed legislation in 2021 that requires colleges and universities to survey students, faculty, and staff on indoctrination, using the language of "intellectual freedom." That same week, DeSantis signed a bill requiring that high schoolers "receive instruction on the evils of communism and totalitarian ideologies" (Villarreal, 2021). In April 2022, the Florida Education Department rejected 41 percent of math textbooks for referencing racism, social-emotional learning, climate change, and vaccines (Balingit, 2022). However, nothing has entered the national discourse as strongly as the "Don't Say Gay" bill, signed by DeSantis in March 2022.

The law bans discussion of LGBTQ issues until fourth grade and opens schools to lawsuits from parents over what is being taught (Phillips, 2022). DeSantis's press secretary, Christina Pushaw (2022), posted to her Twitter that the "Don't Say Gay" bill is an "Anti-Grooming Bill" and stated, "If you're against the Anti-Grooming Bill, you are probably a groomer or at least you don't denounce the grooming of 4–8 year old children," accusing Democrats and other political opponents of being either active child molesters or complicit in the sexual abuse of children. Prior to the bill becoming law on July 1, 2022, activists and other critics of the bill noted that it was already impacting LGBTQ students and educators, including a teacher who was fired for sharing elements of her personal life with students (Atterbury, 2022), a concern that straight and gender-conforming teachers do not experience.

Georgia

In Forsyth County, Georgia, the local school district revised its book challenge policy to reduce the time allotted for reviews from forty-five to thirty days and created a process by which a book that contains "explicit material" can be removed from the entire district's schools rather than only one individual media center (Kerns, 2022). Governor Brian Kemp signed several bills in April 2022, collectively limiting schools' ability to teach concepts related to race and racism, revising the process for challenging "obscene" materials (Tagami, 2022), and establishing a commission that could—and probably will—ban trans girls and women from competing in high school sports (Burnside & Cole, 2022).

South Carolina

Following letters sent by state officials in Texas (see below), Henry McMaster, the governor of South Carolina, sent a similar missive to the state Department of Education regarding Maia Kobabe's 2019 graphic novel *Gender Queer: A Memoir.* He called the work "pornographic" and pledged to prevent similar works from showing up at schools (Lavietes, 2021). In April 2022, a proposed amendment to the South Carolina Senate's budget was introduced, which would ban "explicitly sexual" books from the children's sections of public libraries. South Carolina Democrats and librarians noted that the language in the proposal was so vague as to possibly exclude *The Scarlet Letter* (by Nathaniel Hawthorne) and the Bible (Adcox, 2022).

Texas

In October, State Representative Matt Krause, chair of the Texas House of Representatives Committee on General Investigating, sent a letter to the Texas Education Agency and some school district superintendents with an attached list of 850 book titles, demanding to know the number of copies held, the amount spent on those copies, and any other titles owned that cover similar material. An analysis of the books on Krause's list found that approximately 63 percent of titles were on LGBTQ topics, 14 percent covered sex education, and 8 percent discussed race and racism; some of the 15 percent remaining titles included books on the legal rights of teenagers (Ellis, 2021). Others have noted the "haphazard" nature of the list (Sarappo, 2021), including the presence of an academic text that "is deeply critical of leftist academic theorizing, including critical race theory" (Powell, 2021, para. 22).

Following Krause's letter, Texas governor Greg Abbott released a similar letter to the commissioner of the Texas Education Agency alleging that obscene books, including pornography, had been found in Texas schools. Some librarians in Texas have expressed concern to reporters that they could be targeted on social media or formally accused of a crime (Hixenbaugh, 2022). This may not be an unfounded concern, as Abbott has also targeted gender-affirming care for trans youth as "child abuse," directing the Texas Department of Family and Protective Services to investigate parents and medical professionals for potential prosecution (Alfonseca, 2022).

Virginia

As a gubernatorial candidate, Glenn Youngkin invoked the specter of Toni Morrison's 1987 novel *Beloved* in campaign ads during the last weeks of the 2021 Virginia election (Lutz, 2021). Once elected, in his inaugural address, Youngkin promised that "political" topics would be removed from schools, followed by signing an executive order banning CRT from being taught in schools (Schneider & Vozzella, 2022). Some school board members have advocated for burning books that have been removed following challenges (Uphaus-Conner, 2021).

Conclusion

While challenges to books are not new, the current epidemic of book challenges and bans is unique. Growing out of frustrations over COVID-19 restrictions, exacerbated by "parental rights" groups, and stoked by opportunistic politicians, the current crisis has added CRT to perennial boogeymen such as LGBTQIA+ acceptance and sex education. The misuse of the term "CRT" as a blanket for any material that discusses race, racism, or the lived experience of Black authors and characters mirrors the frequent excoriation of queer content, regardless of intended audience, as sexual, explicit, or obscene.

Seemingly not content with limiting their reactionary overreach to public schools and libraries, recent news stories indicate that this movement is expanding to target e-reader apps (Ingram, 2022), private booksellers (Natanson, 2022), and children's television programing (Lavietes, 2022). Following electoral and legislative victories, conservatives believe they have found a winning issue and are planning on riding this wave through the 2022 and 2024 election cycles. It is vitally important for libraries, library workers, and their patrons to understand how these censors operate so that they can maintain their personal and communal freedoms.

References

Adcox, S. (2022, April 29). SC public library leaders fight proposal banning sexual books from children's sections. *The Post and Courier.* https://www.postandcourier.com/politics/sc-public-library-leaders-fight-proposal-banning-sexual-books-from-childrens-sections/article_f50dfc0e-c7d2-11ec-96ba-778a31117f0f.html

ALA Office for Intellectual Freedom. (2013). *Top 10 most challenged books lists.* https://www.ala.org/advocacy/bbooks/frequentlychallengedbooks/top10

Alfonseca, K. (2022, March 3). *Texas court halts investigation into family's gender-affirming care amid ACLU lawsuit.* ABC News. https://abcnews.go.com/US/texas-governor-sued-aclu-directive-investigate-parents-transgender/story?id=83184486

Atterbury, A. (2022, May 17). *Florida's fight over "don't say gay" is getting more heated: And it hasn't even gone into effect yet.* Politico. https://www.politico.com/news/2022/05/17/florida-fight-dont-say-gay-00032512

Balingit, M. (2022, May 9). DeSantis accused textbooks of "indoctrination": Here's what he meant. *The Washington Post.* https://www.washingtonpost.com/education/2022/05/09/florida-banned-textbooks-math-desantis/

Burnside, T., & Cole, D. (2022, April 28). *Georgia Gov. Kemp signs bill into law that limits discussions about race in classrooms.* CNN. https://www.cnn.com/2022/04/28/politics/georgia-bill-limits-race-discussions-classrooms/index.html

Craig, T. (2021, October 15). Moms for Liberty has turned "parental rights" into a rallying cry for conservative parents. *The Washington Post.* https://www.washingtonpost.com/national/moms-for-liberty-parents-rights/2021/10/14/bf3d9ccc-286a-11ec-8831-a31e7b3de188_story.html

Cunningham, M. (2022, June 4). *Right wing dark money targets Wellesley.* WGBH. https://www.wgbh.org/news/commentary/2021/06/04/right-wing-dark-money-targets-wellesley

Ellis, D. (2021, November 5). *All 850 books Texas lawmaker Matt Krause wants to ban: An analysis.* Book Riot. https://bookriot.com/texas-book-ban-list/

Flood, A. (2021, November 25). US libraries report spike in organised attempts to ban books in schools. *The Guardian.* https://www.theguardian.com

/books/2021/nov/25/us-libraries-report-spike-in-organised-attempts-to-ban-books-in-schools

Hixenbaugh, M. (2022, February 1). *Banned: Books on race and sexuality are disappearing from Texas schools in record numbers.* NBC News. https://www.nbcnews.com/news/us-news/texas-books-race-sexuality-schools-rcna13886

Ingram, D. (2022, May 12). *Conservative parents take aim at library apps meant to expand access to books.* NBC News. https://www.nbcnews.com/tech/tech-news/library-apps-book-ban-schools-conservative-parents-rcna26103

Jenkins, J. (2021, October 20). I'm a Florida school board member: This is how protesters come after me. *The Washington Post.* https://www.washingtonpost.com/outlook/2021/10/20/jennifer-jenkins-brevard-school-board-masks-threats/

Kerns, S. (2022, March 11). Forsyth County Schools planning for changes to media centers, book challenges in 2022–23 year. *Forsyth County News.* https://www.forsythnews.com/news/education/forsyth-county-schools-planning-changes-media-centers-book-challenges-2022-23-year/

Lavietes, M. (2021, November 12). *South Carolina governor calls for LGBTQ book to be banned in schools.* NBC News. https://www.nbcnews.com/nbc-out/out-politics-and-policy/south-carolina-governor-calls-lgbtq-book-banned-schools-rcna5409

Lavietes, M. (2022, May 9). *GOP senators urge TV ratings board to warn viewers of "disturbing" LGBTQ content.* NBC News. https://www.nbcnews.com/nbc-out/out-politics-and-policy/gop-senators-urge-tv-ratings-board-warn-viewers-disturbing-lgbtq-conte-rcna27934

Little, O. (2021, November 12). *Unmasking Moms for Liberty.* Media Matters for America. https://www.mediamatters.org/critical-race-theory/unmasking-moms-liberty

Lutz, E. (2021, October 26). Glenn Youngkin assures Virginia voters he'll protect them from Toni Morrison books. *Vanity Fair.* https://www.vanityfair.com/news/2021/10/glenn-youngkin-assures-virginia-voters-hell-protect-them-from-toni-morrison-books

Moattar, D. (2018, July 9). The dark money behind campus speech wars. *The Nation.* https://www.thenation.com/article/archive/dark-money-behind-campus-speech-wars/

Moms for Liberty. (2022). *Careers.* https://www.momsforliberty.org/careers/

Natanson, H. (2022, May 20). Va. Republicans seek to limit sale of 2 books in Barnes & Noble for "obscenity." *The Washington Post.* https://www.washingtonpost.com/education/2022/05/20/gender-queer-barnes-and-noble/

No Left Turn in Education. (n.d.). *Recommended books.* https://bwentzel6.wixsite.com/website-7/nlte

No Left Turn in Education. (2021a). *Information by state.* https://www.noleftturn.us/state-information/

No Left Turn in Education. (2021b). *Missions, goals, & objectives.* https://www.noleftturn.us/mission-goals-objectives/

Parents Defending Education. (2022a). *About.* https://defendinged.org/about/

Parents Defending Education. (2022b). *Engage.* https://defendinged.org/engage/

Parents Defending Education. (2022c). *Following the books.* https://defendinged.org/resources/following-the-books-how-did-the-indoctrination-happen/

Parents Defending Education. (2022d). *IndoctriNation Map.* https://defendinged.org/map/

PEN America. (2022). *Banned in the USA: Rising school book bans threaten free expression and students' first amendment rights.* https://pen.org/banned-in-the-usa/

Phillips, A. (2022, April 22). Florida's law limiting LGBTQ discussion in schools, explained. *The Washington Post.* https://www.washingtonpost.com/politics/2022/04/01/what-is-florida-dont-say-gay-bill/

Powell, M. (2021, December 10). In Texas, a battle over what can be taught, and what books can be read. *The New York Times.* https://www.nytimes.com/2021/12/10/us/texas-critical-race-theory-ban-books.html

Pushaw, C. [@ChristinaPushaw]. (2022, March 4). *If you're against the Anti-Grooming Bill, you are probably a groomer or at least you don't denounce the grooming of* [Tweet]. Twitter. https://twitter.com/ChristinaPushaw/status/1499890719691051008

Sarappo, E. (2021, December 8). This is a shakedown. *The Atlantic.* https://www.theatlantic.com/culture/archive/2021/12/texas-book-ban-between-the-world-and-me/620938/

Schneider, G. S., & Vozzella, L. (2022, January 15). Glenn Youngkin, first Republican to win statewide in Virginia since 2009, takes office. *The Washington Post.*https://www.washingtonpost.com/dc-md-va/2022/01/15/youngkin-inauguration-virginia-governor/

Shephard, A. (2021, October 26). Glenn Youngkin wants to ban Toni Morrison's *Beloved. The New Republic.* https://newrepublic.com/article/164163/youngkin-ban-toni-morrisons-beloved

Skolnik, J. (2022, February 8). *What's behind the right-wing book-ban frenzy? Big money, and a long-term plan.* Salon. https://www.salon.com/2022/02/08/whats-behind-the-right-wing-book-ban-frenzy-big-money-and-a-long-term-plan/

Tagami, T. (2022, March 30). Georgia Legislature approves new process for banning books in schools. *The Atlanta Journal-Constitution.* https://www.ajc.com/education/georgia-legislature-approves-new-process-for-banning-books-in-schools/4EQV5OCTQFCYTOW56CN3RNCSZY/

Uphaus-Conner, A. (2021, November 9). Spotsylvania School Board orders libraries to remove "sexually explicit" books. *The Free Lance-Star.* https://fredericksburg.com/news/local/education/spotsylvania-school-board-orders-libraries-to-remove-sexually-explicit-books/article_6c54507a-6383-534d-89b9-c2deb1f6ba17.html

Villarreal, A. (2021, June 6). Backlash after Florida governor signs bill against "indoctrination" at colleges. *The Guardian*. https://www.theguardian.com/us-news/2021/jun/24/ron-desantis-florida-governor-bill-indoctrination-colleges

Yenerall, K. M. (2017). Grassroots politics. In M. A. H. Genovese & Lori Cox (Eds.), *Encyclopedia of American government and civics* (2nd ed.). Facts on File.

Yorio, K. (2020, February 4). Not quite banned: Soft censorship that makes LGBTQIA+ stories disappear. *School Library Journal*. https://www.slj.com/story/not-quite-banned-soft-censorship-makes-LGBTQIA-stories-disappear-libraries

Books Discussed in This Chapter

Atwood, M. (1985). *The handmaid's tale*. McClelland and Stewart.

Claiborne-West, J. (2021). *Amy Coney Barrett—A justice and mother.* Heroes of Liberty.

Hawthorne, N. (1850). *The scarlet letter.* Ticknor, Reed & Fields.

Kobabe, M. (2019). *Gender queer: A memoir.* Oni Press.

Morrison, T. (1987). *Beloved*. Alfred A. Knopf.

Rowling, J. K. (1997–2007). *Harry Potter* series. Bloomsbury Publishing.

Swain, C. M., & Schorr, C. J. (2021). *Black eye for America: How critical race theory is burning down the house.* Carol Swain Enterprises, LLC.

CHAPTER THREE

Preserving Equity for Young Adult Readers

Andrea Jamison

Introduction

Book challengers have long opposed young adult books with social justice themes, lamenting indoctrination of critical race theories, anti-police sentiments, sexual immorality, or obscenity. Challenged, and in some cases banned, young adult books often seek to promote the voice(s) of marginalized communities by highlighting their experiences with social or racial injustice. For example, *The Hate U Give* (2017) by Angie Thomas was challenged for promoting anti-police sentiments. However, this book acclimates readers to incidents of police brutality from an African American perspective. *All Boys Aren't Blue* (2020) by George M. Johnson was challenged for its lesbian, gay, bisexual, transgender, queer/questioning, intersex, and asexual (LGBTQIA+) content. Similarly, *Melissa* (2015) by Alex Gino was challenged and banned for its transgender content and *Lawn Boy* (2008) by Jonathan Evison was banned for depicting same-sex relationships. Yet, as of 2020, nearly 2,000,000 youth between the ages of thirteen and seventeen identify as lesbian, gay, bisexual, or transgender (Conron, 2020), and these books underscore some of the challenges that LGBTQIA+ youth encounter. *Stamped: Racism, Antiracism, and You* (2020) by Jason Reynolds and Ibram X. Kendi was challenged and banned for theories about race. However, books on racism written by members of marginalized communities provide counternarratives to mainstream narratives that have romanticized and whitewashed the history of slavery and racism in America (Cook, 2016).

Book challenges have been increasing in number in recent years and have also spurred an increase in proposed legislation designed to prevent some schools or school libraries from making specific titles accessible to young adults. An example of recent legislation is Oklahoma's Senate Bill 1142. This bill was introduced to prohibit public schools and school libraries from carrying books related to the study of sex, sexual preference, sex-based classifications, sexual identity, or gender identity. According to the bill, if a school were to receive a parental request to have a title removed from its library, it would have thirty days to remove the title or face paying daily fines of $10,000 for noncompliance. Tennessee's House Bill 800 proposes similar legislation by prohibiting public schools from using books that reference LGBT lifestyles. Then there are bills such as Florida's HB 7, which prohibits instruction related to critical race theory or that espouses the idea that people are privileged or oppressed due to their race or sex (Avila, n.d.).

These legislative bills have reignited concerns about the rise in self-censorship due to fear. Self-censorship or self-censoring occurs when librarians intentionally suppress information or resources due to their personal preferences, beliefs, ideologies, or fears. Self-censoring behaviors among librarians were evidenced in a 2008 survey conducted by the *School Library Journal* (*SLJ*). A significant number of librarians admitted that they purposefully omitted certain books and content from their respective library collections due to personal bias or fear of conflict. *SLJ* surveyed 653 school librarians; many indicated a tendency to avoid books with "sexual content (87%), language (61%), violence (51%), [and] homosexuality (47%)" (Whelan, 2009, p. 28). Today, librarians are not the only self-censors of library books. School administrators have begun preemptively removing book titles from their school libraries, making self-censorship a more menacing exclusion act.

When libraries refuse to provide access to books because they may be deemed controversial, especially books with LGBTQIA+ or race-based themes, it is a form of discrimination. Self-censors not only engage in discriminatory acts against authors but also discriminate against Black, Indigenous, and people of color (BIPOC) and LGBTQIA+ students who may have an interest in reading books that reflect their identities and experience. When books representing specific communities are absent from library shelves, it reaffirms harmful messages of inferiority and marginalization for the omitted groups. When specific authors are excluded, it can exacerbate existing publishing inequities for minoritized communities as publishers may financially disinvest in their work. Self-censorship also reflects negatively on the entire profession—librarianship cannot be viewed as a profession dedicated to equity when some members do not adhere to its core values or professional responsibilities.

Uniform Adherence to the Library Bill of Rights

To ensure equity for all youth, librarians need to have consistent practices that are visible across all types of library organizations (public, school, academic, and special). A lack of such practices can potentially lead to professional disunity akin to the Jim Crow era. It was during this time that Northern and Southern librarians clashed over the maltreatment of African Americans in the South. Southern librarians refused service to African Americans due to ideologies that were inherently racist. Leaders of the American Library Association (ALA), one of the largest and oldest library organizations in the world, were slow to respond to this discord. As a result, the field of librarianship was heavily criticized by civil rights leaders not only because of the undemocratic practices of Southern librarians and the silence of library leaders, but also because of the professional discord among librarians. Some librarians visibly supported the civil rights of African Americans, while others championed the continuance of discriminatory practices. This discord discredited the work of libraries in general, given that there was no message about the function of libraries in a democratic society.

In 1939, the ALA published its first iteration of the Library Bill of Rights (LBR) as an attempt to make clear the value of libraries and to address social intolerance (ALA, 2006c). However, because the LBR was written to only provide guidance and not regulation to librarians, it did little to end discriminatory practices in the South. These practices continued and eventually placed libraries at the center of the civil rights movement, along with other institutions that refused to honor the civil rights of all people. Given this history, it is imperative that all librarians fully represent the values of a democratic society by aligning their practices to core librarian values articulated by the ALA.

Today's ALA strongly condemns all forms of censorship, citing it as a danger to democracy. Librarians of today are thought of as gatekeepers of democratic values. These values do not apply to *some*; they apply to *all* people. Continued censorship will upend the civil liberties of minoritized communities and prevent youth from having access to books that foster inclusion. However, librarians can preserve equity for youth by aligning their practices with two core library documents: the LBR and the ALA's Freedom to Read Statement.

The current iteration of the LBR is an extensive list of ethical propositions that provide guidance on how the First Amendment of the Constitution of the United States applies to library settings. These propositions attempt to demystify the relationship between free speech and access for all within libraries. According to the LBR's "Access to Library Resources and Services for Minors: An Interpretation of the LBR," young adults undeniably have First Amendment rights within libraries, which means that they should have access to a variety of perspectives through books and other resources (ALA, 2006a). Parents do have the right to limit access to certain content, but for their child only. Therefore, librarians should turn to specific LBR language when defending against book challenges.

Similar to the LBR, the Freedom to Read Statement is also a set of ethical propositions that reaffirms the rights of all users to have access to a variety of resources (ALA, 2006b). Librarians, therefore, have a professional obligation to make these types of diverse resources available. Both the LBR and the Freedom to Read Statement should be used when drafting policies and communicating to wider audiences about the mission and purpose of school libraries. By doing so, librarians will share strong messages about preserving First Amendment rights that apply equally to all libraries. Librarians cannot preserve equity for young adults if they fail to apply these tenets uniformly to censorship challenges.

Understanding the Value of Diverse Books for Young Adults

Since diverse books are often at the center of censorship challenges, it is important to know how these books support the development of young adults. Diverse books benefit young adults in many ways. They provide them with opportunities to learn about themselves and the world around them. Rudine Sims Bishop (1990) notes that diverse books are affirming because youth can see their reflection mirrored back to them through characters with similar identities or experiences. Through these mirror images, they can develop a positive sense of self and feel they belong in the world. Diverse books can help young adults not only find acceptance for their own lives but also learn about the lives and experiences of dissimilar groups. Such exposure has the propensity to foster cross-cultural understanding and mutual respect. It allows young adults to gain insight into the perspectives and worldviews of communities outside of their own. While young adults may not fully understand or agree with these differing perspectives, they can still learn empathy and value for the diversity of thought. For example, books such as Angie Thomas's *The Hate U Give* present protagonists who experience the world through the lens of being Black in America. While frequently challenged and banned for anti-police sentiments, it provides a counter worldview from the perspective of cultural insiders. Books such as *Black Flamingo* by Dean Atta and *All Boys Aren't Blue* by George M. Johnson can help outside communities understand the experiences and perspectives of individuals with LGBTQIA+ identities. Overall, books like these prepare young adults for their adult roles in society by helping them understand democratic values.

Therefore, banning books that represent a multiplicity of experiences within society is undemocratic. It can create social stigmas for youth. Young adults whose lives and images are absent from literature or library shelves may develop a sense of inferiority and view their lives as less important than those of predominantly represented groups. It can also perpetuate existing stereotypes by not giving diverse authors space and visibility to provide counternarratives to historical inaccuracies. These inaccuracies, if unchallenged, can continue to control narratives about marginalized communities that may be psychologically, socially, or emotionally damaging. Furthermore, when censors challenge the appropriateness of diverse books for young adult authors, it trivializes the experiences of the young adults whose real lives may match many of the themes presented in diverse books.

Young adults undergo physiological and psychosocial changes before entering adulthood. These changes impact their level of autonomy, ability to make rational decisions, peer relations, emotions, cognition, and motivation. Therefore, another benefit of diverse books is that they can help support young adults during specific stages of their psychosocial development. According to Erikson's theory (Orenstein & Lewis, 2021), there are eight stages of psychosocial development. At each stage, individuals encounter conflict that they must resolve. Erikson viewed these conflicts as crises. Crises are moments when one's individual and/or psychological needs conflict with those of the world around them. How one responds to existing crises determines how one will respond to crises during later stages of development. If an individual resolves conflict in a way that produces positive outcomes, it will provide them with the requisite dispositions needed to resolve conflicts positively during future stages. Thus, positive outcomes produced at one stage are considered indicators of a future progression of more of the same and the development of a healthy personality. Conversely, negative outcomes at any stage will set a trajectory for more negative outcomes and will lead to the development of unhealthy personality traits.

Given that adolescents between the ages of twelve and eighteen are considered to be in the "Identify vs. Confusion" stage of their psychosocial development, they need access to information and resources to help them resolve identity conflict. During this stage, adolescents ponder questions about their identity and life's purpose. They are self-discovering and experimenting with multiple identities, including discovering their sexual, physical, and social selves. Crises occur when young adults' ability to self-discover is met with pressure to conform to the ideologies of adults or peers around them. Such pressures can either lead to weak responses, resulting in role confusion, or positive, self-affirming responses, resulting in a keen sense of identity and fidelity. Therefore, during this stage, young adults need to explore various ways to resolve crises positively. They need opportunities to think through multiple outcomes to determine which path makes the most sense to them. Diverse books provide young adults with these types of options. They provide opportunities for young adults from various backgrounds to explore the choices and outcomes of fictitious characters that represent a wide range of identities. The young adult can view these outcomes as cautionary or inspirational. Further, they can think critically about the characters in these stories and the lessons learned and use these narratives to help them resolve their own crises in a positive manner.

It is also important to understand the types of conflict that adolescents may experience during this stage of development. They may experience conflict or crises at a micro (individual, interpersonal, or family), mezzo (community or neighborhood), or macro (societal) level (Bender et al., 2021; Samsanovich, 2021). At the micro level, adolescents may experience conflict associated with gender identity, sexuality, dating, abuse, or substance use. At the mezzo level, they may experience conflict associated with segregation or community attitudes toward gender identity or sexuality (Bender et al., 2021). At the macro level, they may experience factors associated with racism, unfair laws, political conflict, or war. By considering the potential types of conflict that adolescents may face during this stage of development, librarians can provide book challengers with a rationale for selecting diverse narratives with these types of themes.

Diverse books are also important because they can be used to support learning acquisition. When school librarians select books, they do so to meet the needs and interests of students. They also choose books to support the educational mission and goals of the school. Books with protagonists from culturally and socially diverse backgrounds mirror marginalized young adults' real-world experiences and identities. This parallel structure makes diverse books more relatable and engaging (Hickey & Hopenwasser, 2013; Wood & Jocius, 2013). They have increased engagement because culture matters in terms of knowledge acquisition, since learning is a social process (Ouimet, 2011). Adolescents build knowledge through their interactions with the physical and social worlds (Daniels & Shumow, 2003; Ouimet, 2011).

When young adults find books that are of interest to them, they are more inclined to engage in the process of deep reading. Deep reading refers to a process of critical thinking that stimulates comprehension through inferential and deductive reasoning, analogical skills, critical analysis, reflection, and insight (Wolf et al., 2009). Both teachers and librarians can leverage young adults' engagement with diverse books by facilitating conversations that invite the young adult mind to explore character motives, question value systems, identify problems and solutions, make connections to their own lives, interpret meaning, make comparisons across multiple texts and personal experiences, and evaluate themes. Having these types of discussions will improve the literacies of young adults. They can learn how to think deeply about different experiences and better understand the world.

Radically Inclusive Collection Development Policies

Collection development policies are significant to the work of librarians because they guide the selection and removal of library resources. They also serve as a framework for ensuring alignment with institutional goals and can provide clear guidelines on how to build library collections that are fair, equitable, and aligned with core librarian values (Lukenbill, 2002; Woolls & Coatney, 2017). Given that an increased number of book challenges seek to suppress the experiences of marginalized communities, school librarians must create collection development policies that clearly articulate a commitment to equity, diversity, inclusion, and access. These types of policies can serve two purposes. First, they can provide transparency regarding the scope of library materials made accessible through the school library. Second, they can be used to defend against book challenges by highlighting selection protocols and how those protocols adhere to professional best practices.

Below are some recommendations for creating inclusive collection development policies:

1. When developing policies, it is important for policy writers to understand that words have meaning and that the meaning of words is made clear through context and the relationship that words have with other words (Stemler, 2000; White & Marsh, 2006). Therefore, the meaning of "diversity" needs to be clearly defined within library policies. In and of itself, "diversity" is a broad term that denotes a variety of experiences. It is often considered a "catch-all phrase" because it refers to any of the following: issues of race, gender, socioeconomic status, political views, ideas, expression, education, ability, language, literacy, geography, and sexual orientation (Boyd et al., 2015; Jaeger et al., 2015; Williams & Deyoe, 2014), or the "mix of individual characteristics (for example, race, gender, social class, and ability) present in groups, organizations, or societies" (Morales et al., 2014, p. 440). Diversity within libraries can also mean material format or diversity of ideas. It is not enough for libraries to indicate that they have a "diverse" collection. Specificity is needed to clarify what diversity within this context means, particularly in relation to people's diversity. Diverse collections could mean diversity of thought or formats. This message can be clearly articulated by naming the diverse communities represented within the collection. For example, a policy may state that "ABC library has an expansive collection of diverse books reflective of a pluralistic society. We intentionally collect books within our collection to give voice to a multiplicity of and that represents diverse experiences, including books that reflect BIPOC communities, individuals with exceptionalities, and members of the LGBTQIA community." The goal here is to be transparent so parents are not surprised about what is accessible in the library.

2. If diversity is central to a library's service, that library should make that value known in policies. However, it is common for policy writers to articulate diversity values through a statement of diversity. Imagine reading a collection development policy that prominently features a diversity statement, but then diversity is not mentioned anywhere else in the policy document, which may be ten or more pages long. Having the statement of diversity there does not have any real value. How can diversity be operationalized when it is not enumerated anywhere in the policy or when it is barely discussed? Since policies guide practice, policy creators need to ensure that language about diversity commitments is interwoven throughout policies. Librarians can accomplish this by articulating a commitment to diversity, naming the diverse communities represented within the collection, highlighting how diverse resources are selected, and discussing resources used to learn about and acquire diverse resources.
3. Many books are being challenged because some deem the content inappropriate or controversial. Often, these challenges, if successful, will further marginalize minoritized communities. Therefore, policy writers must align the language within their policies with language written in ALA's "Access to Library Resources and Services for Minors: An Interpretation of the Library Bill of Rights," the LBR, and the Freedom to Read Statement.
4. School librarians must also include a process for reconsideration in their policy. This process should reference or reiterate why and how certain books are selected. The selection process becomes significantly important during reconsideration. Here is where librarians can have an oversight committee determine whether certain materials were selected according to policy.
5. School librarians must also consider how language is phrased. Does the language positively affirm the communities or experiences discussed? School librarians should avoid using derogatory language that can further marginalize communities.

Conclusion

In conclusion, it is important that all librarians protect the First Amendment rights of youth by critically examining the important role that libraries play in a democratic society and by implementing practices that promote inclusion. Librarians must also understand that conversations about diversity must extend beyond narratives that only seek to increase representation on library shelves. The diversity conversation of today needs to morph into larger conversations about protecting the intellectual freedom rights of minoritized communities. Book challengers are making concerted efforts to minimize diversity in libraries by erasing narratives that do not align with the viewpoints or values of certain groups. As such, librarians must employ standardized practices that bolster inclusion and clearly communicate the role of libraries in a democratic society.

References

American Library Association. (2006a). *Access to library resources and services for minors: An interpretation of the Library Bill of Rights.* https://www.ala.org/advocacy/intfreedom/librarybill/interpretations/minors

American Library Association. (2006b). *The Freedom to Read statement.* https://www.ala.org/advocacy/intfreedom/freedomreadstatement

American Library Association. (2006c). *Library Bill of Rights.* https://www.ala.org/advocacy/intfreedom/librarybill

Avila, B. (n.d.). *The Florida Senate.* House Bill 7 (2022)—The Florida Senate. Retrieved July 6, 2022, from https://www.flsenate.gov/Session/Bill/2022/7

Bender, A. K., Koegler, E., Johnson, S. D., Murugan, V., & Wamser-Nanney, R. (2021). Guns and intimate partner violence among adolescents: A scoping review. *Journal of Family Violence, 36*(5), 605–617.

Bishop, R. S. (1990, March). Windows and mirrors: Children's books and parallel cultures. In *California State University reading conference: 14th annual conference proceedings* (pp. 3–12). California State University.

Boyd, F. B., Causey, L. L., & Galda, L. (2015). Culturally diverse literature. *Reading Teacher, 68*(5), 378–387. https://doi-org.dom.idm.oclc.org/10.1002/trtr.1326

Conron, K. (2020, September). *LGBT youth population in the United States.* Williams Institute School of Law. http://williamsinstitute.law.ucla.edu/wp-content/uploads/LGBT-Youth-US-Pop-Sep-2020.pdf

Cook, M. R. (2016). Counter-narratives of slavery in the Deep South: The politics of empathy along and beyond River Road. *Journal of Heritage Tourism, 11*(3), 290–308.

Daniels, D. H., & Shumow, L. (2003). Child development and classroom teaching: A review of the literature and implications for educating teachers. *Journal of Applied Developmental Psychology, 23*(5), 495–526.

Hickey, P. J., & Hopenwasser, C. B. (2013). Lingua Anglia: Bridging language and learners: Engaging Miguel: Culturally relevant YA literature. *The English Journal, 103*(2), 105–107.

Jaeger, P. T., Sarin, L. C., & Peterson, K. J. (2015). Diversity, inclusion, and library and information science: An ongoing imperative (or why we still desperately need to have discussions about diversity and inclusion). *The Library Quarterly, 85*(2), 127–132.

Lukenbill, W. B. (2002). *Collection development for a new century in the school library media center.* Libraries Unlimited.

Morales, M., Knowles, E. C., & Bourg, C. (2014). Diversity, social justice, and the future of libraries. *Libraries and the Academy, 14*(3), 439–451.

Orenstein, G. A., & Lewis, L. (2021). Erikson's stages of psychosocial development. In *StatPearls [Internet]*. StatPearls Publishing.

Ouimet, A. (2011). *Culturally relevant literature how to identify and use culturally relevant literature*. Fisher Digital Publications. https://fisherpub.sjf.edu/education_ETD_masters/15/

Samsanovich, A. (2021). *Theory and diversity: A descriptive study of Erikson's psychosocial development stages* [Master's thesis]. https://scholarworks.lib.csusb.edu/etd/1230

Stemler, S. (2000). An overview of content analysis. *Practical Assessment, Research, and Evaluation, 7*(1), 17.

Whelan, D. L. (2009). SLJ self-censorship survey. *School Library Journal, 55*(2), 27–30.

White, M. D., & Marsh, E. E. (2006). Content analysis: A flexible methodology. *Library Trends, 55*(1), 22–23, 27–34, 36–45. http://dx.doi.org/10.1353/lib.2006.0053

Williams, V. K., & Deyoe, N. (2014). Diverse population, diverse collection? Youth collections in the United States. *Technical Services Quarterly, 31*(2), 97–121.

Wolf, M., Barzillai, M., & Dunne, J. (2009). The importance of deep reading. *Challenging the Whole Child: Reflections on Best Practices in Learning, Teaching, and Leadership, 130*, 21.

Wood, S., & Jocius, R. (2013). Combating "I hate this stupid book!": Black males and critical literacy. *The Reading Teacher, 66*(8), 661–669.

Woolls, B., & Coatney, S. (2017). *The school library manager: Surviving and thriving*. ABC-CLIO.

Books Discussed in This Chapter

Atta, D. (2019). *The black flamingo*. Hachette Children's.

Evison, J. (2008). *Lawn boy*. Algonquin Books.

Gino, A. (2015). *Melissa (previously published as GEORGE)*. Scholastic.

Johnson, G. M. (2020). *All boys aren't blue: A memoir-manifesto*. Farrar, Straus and Giroux (BYR).

Reynolds, J., & Kendi, I. X. (2020). *Stamped: Racism, antiracism, and you: A remix of the national book award-winning stamped from the beginning*. Little, Brown Books for Young Readers.

Thomas, A. (2017). *The hate u give*. Gyldendal A/S.

CHAPTER FOUR

Missouri and Kansas School Librarians Face Unprecedented Community Concern

Rene Burress, Angie Wiegers, and Amanda Harrison

> I am not asking for this book to be banned in the state of Missouri or even in our country. But a book like this, it doesn't belong in any public school.
>
> —Sandy Garber, school board director, Wentzville School Board meeting, February 25, 2022

Attacks on the First Amendment

On February 25, 2022, during a specially called board meeting, the Wentzville School District Board of Education held a twelve-minute meeting specifically to discuss an action they had taken during their previous regular board meeting. This special board meeting was held ten days after the American Civil Liberties Union (ACLU) filed a suit against the Wentzville School Board in response to decisions made by the school board at their regularly scheduled meeting on January 20, 2022. In that meeting, the school board voted to ban *The Bluest Eye* by Toni Morrison.

During the February 25 meeting, school board vice president Dan Brice made the motion to rescind the decision not to retain *The Bluest Eye*. The school board members had a discussion, and then a roll call vote was recorded. Voting in favor were Dan Brice, Erin Abbott, Jason Goodson, Shannon Stolle, and Betsy Bates; voting against were Dale Schaper and Sandy Garber.

Vice president Brice made a second motion—to accept the recommendation of the Challenged Materials Committee to retain *The Bluest Eye*. As part of the discussion prior to the vote, board member Sandy Garber stated:

> If you want your child to read the book, go and buy the book. I am not asking for this book to be banned in the state of Missouri or even in our country. But a book like this, it doesn't belong in any public school, in any state in our country. It doesn't belong there. These are minor children, and we have laws on the books that are going to protect these children. (WSDvideo, 2022b, 10:50–11:19 minutes)

A few minutes later, Garber voted "Absolutely not" in response to the motion to accept the recommendation of the Challenged Materials Committee. However, despite Garber's opposition, the motion did pass.

Back during the January 20, 2022, meeting, school board member Shannon Stolle made the motion to move *The Bluest Eye* to the restricted list for Advanced Placement (AP) classes only, with a parent opt-in requirement. If the novel became part of the curriculum or a supplement, parental opt-in would again apply. Vice president Dan Brice seconded the motion.

During the discussion before the vote, school board member Erin Abbott said, "President Bates, I have a question. Will this be discriminating against the students who want to read it but are not in AP classes?" This question received applause from the audience (WSDvideo, 2022a, 3:10–3:11 minutes). After further discussion, a roll call vote was recorded with Betsy Bates, Shannon Stolle, and Jason Goodson supporting the motion to move the book to a restricted list, while Erin Abbott, Sandy Garber, Dale Schaper, and Dan Brice voted against the motion. The motion failed.

Immediately following the failed vote, school board secretary Dale Schaper made the motion to not retain the book. Sandy Garber, Shannon Stolle, and Dan Brice supported this motion, while Erin Abbott, Betsy Bates, and Jason Goodson voted against it. However, with a vote of four to not retain and three to retain, the school board had banned the book from the school library.

These scenes join many others in the states of Missouri and Kansas during the 2021–22 school year. In the fall of 2021, members of the public started showing up at school board meetings across the Kansas City region, in both Missouri and Kansas schools, and during public comment times, they read out passages of books they deemed offensive and inappropriate. They also started filling out book challenge forms. This resulted in unprecedented amounts of book challenges and parent communication to school librarians about what their children could and could not check out from the libraries.

In the Kansas City, Missouri, area, a group called the Northland Parent Association (NPA) organized themselves with a Facebook group and created a Google Sheet with a list of allegedly offensive books. The spreadsheet is organized by category such as HS pornography, HS Violence Sexual, and MS Sexual Inappropriate (*sic*). Each category has lists of titles and page numbers with "offensive" content. They also searched the Online Public Access Catalogs of school libraries for phrases and keywords and listed how many hard and digital copies each school library had. The NPA, along with other groups in Kansas, continuously queried librarians.

In the McPherson Unified School District in Kansas, a school librarian noted that while previous searches in the high school library catalog had been minimal, the search traffic greatly increased in mid- to late April 2022. Searches included the terms "equity," "sexual grooming," "homosexuals," "pedophilia," and "diversity," along with more specific titles and author requests (A. Harrison, personal communication, March 7, 2022). This uptick in searches occurred around the same time that a local recall group was attempting to unseat three school board members. On the website of the recall group, a list of library books in the district was posted along with this statement: "These library books are one of MANY concerns with our district. The school board is responsible for what goes on in our district" (418 Recall, 2022).

Likewise, even when books were not being challenged, an unprecedented number of complaints undermined other, traditional library duties. For example, during a Scholastic Book Fair at a school in Kansas, complaints were fielded regarding the books available from the company, and its "woke ideology" and "anti-American" themes, along with claims that 90 percent of the books "that they are advertising are transgender/alternative sexual preferences/climate change/anti-American sentiments/indoctrination" (A. Harrison, personal communication, March 7, 2022). This complainant followed up with the request that the district no longer uses Scholastic for any sort of book fair or book fundraising.

Students Take a Stand

The ACLU of Missouri filed a lawsuit in federal court on behalf of the students and their families in Wentzville, saying the students have "a First Amendment right to be free from official conduct that was intended to suppress the ideas and viewpoints expressed in the Banned Books." The plaintiffs in the suit were two students from the Wentzville School District.

In response to the NPA, four students formed the Northland Student Association. They started a petition to advocate for books to remain in school libraries, attended school board meetings themselves, and spoke out against censorship. Due to their work, two of the four students who formed the group were the recipients of the 2022 Intellectual Freedom Award from the Missouri Association of School Libraries (MASL) in April of that year. They were the first-ever student recipients of the award.

Support in Challenging Times

It is important to note that librarians are not alone in dealing with these challenges. District administrators, building administrators, staff, students, community members, and national organizations stood for school librarians and offered their support in many different ways. School librarians and district library coordinators in North Kansas City, Liberty, Rockwood, and Wentzville School Districts discussed their experiences with challenges. It is our hope that this information will demonstrate that by working with administrators at the building and district levels, staff, students, community, and national organizations, challenges can have a more positive outcome.

One of the most important forms of support for librarians within these challenges is the assurance that the districts support school libraries. In North Kansas City School District (NKCSD), the district coordinator was assured that the district would work with librarians to handle complaints and challenges. As in so many other districts, misinformation pertaining to certain book titles was spread at school board meetings. The library coordinator, the assistant superintendent in charge of academic services, and the school lawyer met several times to discuss policies, procedures, and First Amendment rights. In NKCSD, the assistant superintendent in charge of academic services met with librarians as a group twice during the challenges to give assurances, answer questions, and keep them informed.

Librarians within that district worked together in a committee to research court cases, create material to present to the board and a talking points document that librarians could use moving forward, and attend board meetings in support of student organizations speaking out against censorship. These librarians also contacted the ACLU, the American Library Association Office for Intellectual Freedom (ALA OIF), and the National Coalition Against Censorship to assure students that they would work with these organizations toward the best possible outcome. These organizations reassured the NKCSD school librarians that they would write letters in support of intellectual freedom and the First Amendment. State and local library organizations, MASL, and the Greater Kansas City Association of School Librarians also wrote letters in support of the freedom to read and the First Amendment within the NKCSD. Building administrators within the district, specifically at Staley High School, where the complaints originated, were vocal about their support for the library and took time within their day to check on librarians and see if there were any needs. The building administrator at North Kansas City High School congratulated students who spoke against censorship at board meetings on a job well done.

In the Liberty School District, the library coordinator Andrea Sumy met with her superintendent and assistant superintendent of instructional design many times. She had assurances that the district was working with her. The center of their conversations was always about following board-approved policies. She also had the opportunity to meet with the school lawyer who reassured her.

In Rockwood School District, the district superintendents followed policy and regulations and supported intellectual freedom. They even put a plan in place to improve policy. According to Margaret Sullivan, the lead librarian in Rockwood, administrators are always part of the review committee, and they are committed to intellectual freedom. Furthermore, the principal at Rockwood was supportive and trusted librarians to handle challenges. Parents in the Rockwood district spoke out at board meetings in support of libraries, letting the board know that books should not be restricted. Staff members offered words of encouragement, and students asked questions and read more widely than ever before.

In the Wentzville School District, the assistant superintendent in charge of curriculum was pro-libraries, according to their lead librarian Mernie Maestas. The assistant superintendent advocated for programming, financial support, and purchases programs to assist libraries. The superintendent and the assistant superintendent in this district supported intellectual freedom, and the principal at the high school was supportive and on one of the review committees.

Throughout the challenge processes, communication was key. In NKCSD, librarians informed their building administration in formal or informal meetings about policy and procedure for selection as well as challenges. Students and staff at each building had questions that the librarian helped to answer. Students wrote articles in school newspapers to inform peers and discussed censorship within social media groups. The district communications department informed parents of steps that librarians took, including the reminder that parents had the right to censor their children by contacting the school librarian and requesting that students be restricted from the specific titles. Parents and community members were invited to suggest books on a digital form provided at each school.

The school lawyer assisted by informing the board about policies and procedures. This was a helpful reminder that the district needed to follow board-approved policy. Staff and students were notified through information provided by the communications department and the school librarian. The community, teachers, administration, and the assistant superintendent were informed of the selection policy and procedure in a formal presentation.

Students informed the community, parents, and the board about the importance of a diverse collection and why titles and topics of all types were necessary in a school library. This was an excellent opportunity to inform all stakeholders about intellectual freedom and First Amendment rights.

In the Liberty School District, the communications director sent information to families explaining the board-approved policies that were in place, gave options for parents to restrict their students from individual titles, and provided information about committees that were meeting on book challenges. The library coordinator met with principals, superintendents, and assistant superintendents to keep stakeholders informed. Building administrators fielded parent questions. When students and staff wanted more information, the librarians provided that, along with the challenged books. At subsequent board meetings, parents, students, and the community spoke to the board about the importance of having diverse books in school libraries.

In the Rockwood School District, Margaret Sullivan, the lead librarian, worked with the communications department and an assistant superintendent to craft a response to the community, explaining the process and procedure of selecting books, including relying on professional reviews. The assistant superintendent has, in turn, spoken with the media and local newspaper regarding the challenges.

In the Wentzville School District, the district office sent out newsletters and put information on the district website stating that librarians were happy to work with parents regarding their students' reading habits. The assistant superintendent maintained constant communication with librarians and the review committees.

Interestingly, in many of the school districts, there seemed to be some levels of protection. In NKCSD, the superintendent fielded calls from lawmakers and parents as did the assistant superintendent of academic services and the library coordinator. The building administration fielded e-mails from concerned parents and worked with librarians in forming communication responses. Students created a petition to form their own organization to respond to parents who believed in censoring them.

In the Liberty School District, building administrators fielded parent phone calls and e-mails. Librarians reported that in this district there was parent support for a diversified collection and parents were grateful for the work librarians were doing. The library coordinator was able to report those positive voices back to the district administration.

In the Rockwood School District, the assistant superintendent spoke with the media and local newspaper. The lead librarian took parent phone calls and transferred them to the assistant superintendent if they were not satisfied with her answers.

In the Wentzville School District, the assistant superintendent wanted librarians to know that the events were not an attack on librarians. She also told them the challenges were coming from an isolated view with a loud voice. The assistant superintendent shielded librarians from the challenges by asking them not to attend the board meetings because they were so vicious. She supported the high school librarian when the police were called out to the high school library in a complaint that they were distributing child pornography. When librarians faced a Facebook smear campaign from community members in Wentzville, the assistant superintendent let librarians and review committee members know what was happening and continued to support and advocate for libraries and librarians. She has also shielded them from the school board because working with its members has been challenging.

Resolutions within the different districts were diverse. In the Liberty School District, the library coordinator and her team of librarians created a "rights and responsibilities of a reader" document, which was presented to the community. They also updated their district library page, which discusses parent and student rights.

In the Wentzville and Rockwood School Districts, the resolution has been in revisions of policy and procedures. The challenges have opened up dialogue about intellectual freedom and reinforced the concept that the library is not assigned reading but about free choice reading and access to materials. The conversations have touched on the freedom to read, the library as a choice, how students are encouraged to use the library to broaden their minds, and the power of reading. Wentzville learned that the policy must be ironclad; there can be no loopholes because of the way things are worded.

District support, communication, protection, and resolutions have been key to facing these challenges across the state. In every district interviewed—North Kansas City, Liberty, Rockwood, and Wentzville—districts demonstrated the importance of support, communication to staff, students, and community members, and protection that the administration is putting in place to assist and advocate for libraries. These key resolutions support our libraries and listen to our community concerns. Part of this work relies on not seeing members of the community who disagree as the enemy, but listening to their concerns and figuring out a way to coach, teach, and possibly come to a resolution.

State Legislation

While many book challenges have resulted in district employees and school boards working together in many states, Missouri and Kansas included, educators have watched the progress of numerous state bills designed to alter the framework of local education. In spring 2022, in Kansas, the Committee on K–12 Education Budget advanced SB 58, also known as the parents' bill of rights, which would require boards of education to create policies for parents to "challenge the material or educational benefit of any book, magazine, or other material available to students in the school library, the successful result of which would lead to the removal of the item from the school" (Parents' Bill of Rights, 2022). Working drafts of the bill included language that parents should not just be allowed to view materials but be informed of what those materials are. Ultimately, Governor Laura Kelly vetoed this bill on April 15, 2022, and the Kansas House was unable to find enough votes to successfully override (Kelly, 2022).

Numerous bills were also introduced in Missouri during the 2022 legislature session, including HB 1474, which was combined with HB Bill 1995, which "provides for protections for parental rights and transparency in public schools" (Parental Rights in Public Schools, 2022). In addition, a Missouri constitutional amendment was proposed, HJR 110, that would give parents "the right to transparent access to school and school district curricula and lesson plans, made available in an electronically searchable format and available at all times online on the home page of the website hosted by the district" (House Joint Resolution no. 110, 2022). This constitutional amendment was defeated in the House on May 9, 2022 (Missouri House of Representatives, 2022). Overall, the Kansas and Missouri bills, designed to enhance a parent's rights over their child's education, mirror those that have been introduced or prefiled in more than thirty-five different states this year, according to the news website the 19th (Nittle, 2022).

Conclusion

A well-trained and certified school librarian, who has taken master's level coursework in collection development, has been prepared to fight against challenges like the ones described here. For reasons such as this, school districts would be wise to require their librarians to have a master's degree in library science. Furthermore, districts such as Rockwood are providing additional training to all district librarians on topics such as collection development. School librarians need to be prepared to help school boards and district administrators write policies and procedures. State associations such as MASL stand ready to send letters and continue to provide professional development for new and experienced librarians on topics of intellectual freedom and other areas of interest.

Despite the support of district administrators, building administrators, staff, students, community members, and national organizations, these challenges to school libraries in Missouri and Kansas are likely not over. In April 2022, school board elections in Missouri and Kansas did result in the election of many school board candidates who promised to continue banning efforts similar to what was seen in Wentzville. In Springfield, Missouri, for example, the community elected Kelly Bryne to their school board. When Bryne was running, he stated that "banning books from schools is not a freedom of speech or First Amendment issue. We're not talking about banning them from society but we're talking about within our public school system. We are talking about minors here" (Riley, 2022).

In Nixa, Missouri, on May 12, 2022, during the first meeting of a newly elected school board, the board of education voted to ban *Fun Home: A Family Tragicomic* (2006) by Alison Bechdel and *All Boys Aren't Blue: A Memoir-Manifesto* (2020) by George M. Johnson and restrict *Homegoing* (2016) by Yaa Gyasi. According to the publicly available board agenda, all three items went through the review committee process, and the complainant was not satisfied with the committee recommendation; therefore, it was now up to the school board to decide (Nixa Public Schools, 2022). The board voted after two hours of public comment, which included statements from students asking the board not to restrict books (Sullender, 2022a). The ACLU has sent a notice to Nixa Public Schools about pending actions, however. Carissa Corson wrote on Facebook, "Two books were voted to be removed. . . . We expect the ACLU will sue Nixa. We have retained free legal counsel. Please continue to pray for our district and the board to remain strong!!!" (Sullender, 2022b).

It is clear that librarians can no longer sit back and believe that everything will be fine. Censorship attempts will not disappear. The hope is that school boards are now more prepared because they better understand library policy and procedures. They have reviewed First Amendment rights. They understand that defending intellectual freedom is important. It is important for librarians to be knowledgeable and vigilant about what is happening in parent organizations such as the NPA. Librarians must continue to be aware of what is happening related to intellectual freedom across the state and the nation. It is beneficial to have a library coordinator or lead librarian to help work with librarians, administrators, the school lawyer, the community, and national organizations. Finally, one of the most important factors is that we can work together for a more positive outcome.

References

418 Recall. (2022, May 5). *Library books of concern*. USD 418 School Board Recall. https://418info.com/library-books-of-concern

House Joint Resolution no. 110, 101st Gen. Ass. 2nd reg. sess. (Mo. 2022). https://house.mo.gov/billtracking/bills221/hlrbillspdf/4504H.01I.pdf

Kelly, L. (2022). Message from the governor regarding veto of Senate Bill 58. *The Governor's Office*. http://www.kslegislature.org/li/b2021_22/measures/documents/sb58_enrolled.pdf

Missouri House of Representatives. (2022). *HJR 110*. https://house.mo.gov/Bill.aspx?bill=HJR110&year=2022&code=R

Nittle, N. (2022, March 25). Parental rights bills have been introduced in most states: Teachers are pushing back. *The 19th*. https://19thnews.org/2022/03/parental-rights-bills-teachers/

Nixa Public Schools. (2022, May 12). *May 12, 2022—Regular board meeting: New business: Reconsideration of materials*. http://go.boarddocs.com/mo/nixa/Board.nsf/goto?open&id=CE7N975ECCCA

Parental Rights in Public Schools, HB 1995, 2nd sess. (Mo. 2022). https://house.mo.gov/billtracking/bills221/hlrbillspdf/4504H.01I.pdf

Parents' Bill of Rights, S.B. 58. (Ks. 2022). 2022 reg. sess. http://www.kslegislature.org/li/b2021_22/measures/documents/summary_sb_58_2022

Riley, C. (2022, March 3). How Springfield school board candidates view efforts to ban books from schools. *Springfield News Leader*. https://www.news-leader.com/story/news/education/2022/03/21/banned-books-list-2022-springfield-public-school-board-sps-candidates/7119979001/

Sullender, A. (2022a, May 12). Nixa school board bans books amid contentious meeting. *Springfield News Leader*. https://www.news-leader.com/story/news/education/2022/05/12/nixa-school-board-bans-books-amid-contentious-meeting/9708200002/

Sullender, A. (2022b, May 17). ACLU tells Nixa schools to preserve evidence, warns of possible lawsuit over book bannings. *Springfield News Leader*. https://www.news-leader.com/story/news/education/2022/05/17/after-book-bannings-nixa-aclu-signals-possible-lawsuit-coming-preserve-evidence-litigation-ban/9811928002/

WSDvideo. (2022a, January 20). *Board of education meeting: January 20, 2022* [Video file]. YouTube. https://www.youtube.com/watch?v=NhCJAP_GuzA&t=9571s

WSDvideo. (2022b, February 25). *Board of education meeting: February 25, 2022* [Video file]. YouTube. https://www.youtube.com/watch?v=Q4RHMuq-K_c

Books Discussed in This Chapter

Bechdel, A. (2006). *Fun home: A family tragicomic*. Houghton Mifflin Harcourt.

Gyasi, Y. (2016). *Homegoing*. Alfred A. Knopf.

Johnson, G. M. (2020). *All boys aren't blue: A memoir-manifesto*. Farrar, Straus and Giroux.

Morrison, T. (1970). *The bluest eye*. Holt, Rinehart and Winston.

CHAPTER FIVE

Reclaiming the Right to Learn: Combating New Censorship Tactics

Jamie Gregory

Introduction

The rise of censorship efforts across the United States gaining national momentum throughout 2021 did not come as a complete surprise. In education, increased research and initiatives throughout the 2010s on diversity, equity, and inclusion encouraged new efforts to critically examine educational institutions. The 2010s also saw books such as *Melissa* by Alex Gino (2015; originally published as *George*) and *The Hate U Give* by Angie Thomas (2017) first appearing on the American Library Association's Office for Intellectual Freedom's (ALA OIF) annual top challenged books lists. However, no one could know these diversity initiatives would directly clash with anti-truth sentiments surrounding the 2016 and 2020 presidential elections, the racial unrest of the summer of 2020, and COVID-19. As a result, some legislators, governors, organizations, and other community leaders have generally labeled any diversity initiative as critical race theory (CRT), a pejorative rebranding of a legitimate legal framework, a tactic first initiated by Christopher Rufo of the Manhattan Institute (Wallace-Wells, 2021) as a way to centralize a conservative response against diversity initiatives they characterize as "divisive."

According to PEN America's report "Banned in the USA," 1,586 instances of book banning occurred in schools from July 1, 2021, to March 31, 2022, alone (PEN America, 2022). About half of the books challenged featured characters of color, and roughly 33 percent featured lesbian, gay, bisexual, transgender, or queer/questioning (LGBTQ+) characters or topics. In a departure from past trends, 41 percent of these occurrences were initiated by state officials or elected lawmakers instead of community members. These coordinated government efforts are not limited to book censorship but also seek to limit curriculum that portrays a negative view of the American founding or states that multiple gender identities exist (Schwartz & Pendharkar, 2022). This chapter examines specific censorship efforts in South Carolina going beyond traditional book challenges and how school librarians can meet these challenges through educational programming.

South Carolina Joins the "Banned" Wagon

It all began in South Carolina's (SC) Fort Mill School District. After a parent complained about *Gender Queer: A Memoir* by Maia Kobabe (2019), the book was removed from the district's three high school libraries, pending a review by the administration—which was not the process laid out in the district policy. This book has since been permanently removed from school libraries in the district. In a statement released to the press, a district spokesperson explained, "The decision to permanently remove the book from our high school collections was based on the inclusion of visual imagery that is not age appropriate for our students" (Carden & Tablone, 2021).

Just as quickly, this seemingly local issue gained a spotlight at the state level. South Carolina's Republican governor Henry McMaster issued a letter to South Carolina superintendent of education Molly Spearman, in which he stated his displeasure with the appearance of *Gender Queer* on school library shelves. He tasked her with "investigating" how the book ended up in school libraries and whether or not that would be a criminal offense. Furthermore, he asked her to direct the SC Department of Education to "develop—or, if existing, obviously improve upon—a transparent statewide process and procedure to review and approve the books and other materials that are available to students," with no mention of the school librarian profession.

Spearman's response also did not include the role of the school librarian in library material selection, stating that "schools and districts should not rely solely on publishers' vetting," but it did acknowledge that individual school districts have their own processes by which local texts are adopted. She outlined a three-step plan: conduct a review of current selection policies in districts, identify best practices, and draft a model policy.

Spearman's response prompted leaders from the South Carolina Association of School Librarians—President Katherine Malmquist, President-Elect

Tamara Cox, and Intellectual Freedom Chair Jill Tyner—to meet with Spearman to explain how school librarians are professionally trained in collection development. They emphasized the importance of the First Amendment and shared examples of selection and reconsideration policies currently used by some South Carolina school librarians. Cox said that Spearman wanted feedback on the model policies her staff was compiling, and she invited school librarians to the next state school board meeting. Cox encouraged SC librarians to watch and read the relevant education legislation.

According to the *Greenville News*, Greenville County School District officials removed *Gender Queer* from one of its high school libraries not because a complaint was filed and a committee recommended removal but because officials merely heard of the controversy in other schools. District spokesperson Tim Waller is quoted as saying,

> This particular non-fiction memoir was on a list recommended for school libraries by the *School Library Journal*, which makes it clear to us that the individuals who review books for this source do not share our community's values around what is appropriate for school-age children. We are extremely disappointed that the *School Library Journal*, a publication that should be a reliable resource for our media specialists, recommended this text. (Merryman, 2021, para. 9)

How did a complaint, which led to an attack on the foundation of the school library profession, arise about a book that had hardly ever been checked out?

Part of the answer lies in examining the so-called anti-CRT copycat legislation that severely limits teachers' abilities to incorporate media and news literacy education into classrooms, as well as addressing diversity, equity, and inclusion. In 2021, South Carolina joined several other states in introducing this type of legislation, beginning with five bills that were condensed into one. For example, one bill stated, "A teacher or student of history, civics, U.S. government and politics, social studies, or similar subject areas, may not be compelled by a policy of a state agency, school district, or school administration to discuss current events or widely debated and currently controversial issues of public policy or social affairs" (H4799). The same bill would prohibit students learning about or engaging "in lobbying for legislation at the local, state, or federal level, or in social or public policy advocacy; or lobbying for legislation at the local, state, or federal level, or a practicum, or like activity, involving social or public policy advocacy" (H4799). While none of those five bills passed, the House Education and Public Works Committee proposed a new bill, H5183, which essentially condensed the previous five. Titled the "South Carolina Transparency and Integrity in Education Act," it would prohibit mandatory diversity training and inclusion of the role of oppression in U.S. history in instruction. It further dictated that "library and media center material, both printed and electronically accessible, must be age appropriate and grade appropriate." At the time of publication, H5183 had passed in the House but did not advance further.

Media and News Literacy Censorship

Another part of the answer can be found by examining the influence of national grassroots[1] organizations in local communities. When I became aware that the organization South Carolina Parents Involved in Education (the state branch of United States Parents Involved in Education) would be hosting a meeting in my area, I knew I had to attend. I previously became aware of this group's role in spreading disinformation about teachers, school librarians, and diversity education, so I knew I needed to try to understand their claims to better advocate for intellectual freedom. This group actively hosts meetings across the state explaining why "anti-CRT" legislation should be passed, and one of the founders, Sheri Few, even tried to run for the South Carolina superintendent of education position. I attended the meeting, taking notes and pictures, and was taken aback when the presenters attacked media and news literacy, even specifically showing information about the News Literacy Project. The presenters suggested that educators are using "media literacy" as a cover for "critical media literacy," requiring students to utilize only "progressive" sources of information that the presenters view as "fake news" and untrustworthy, extending this egregious misinterpretation to news literacy initiatives as well. I followed up by requesting an interview with Few. She shared her presentation slides with me, and I submitted the interview as one of my monthly blog posts for the Office for Intellectual Freedom (Gregory, 2021). The fear, paranoia, and disinformation this group spreads are difficult to overstate. Members accuse educators who include diversity, equity, and inclusion principles into their curricula, or teach media and news literacy skills, of Marxist indoctrination. In addition, the organization consistently argues that pornography is available in school libraries through diverse books that are otherwise uniformly recognized as excellent writing in children's and teen literature.

I have also sent several letters and e-mails to the representatives serving on my state legislature's education committee, pointing out the mis- and disinformation spread by these political groups that are trying to restrict students' and teachers' rights. I traveled to my state capital in February 2022 to meet with my state representative and senator in order to advocate against this pending education legislation, which would unlawfully restrict students' access to information, thus negatively impacting educators' abilities to teach vital news literacy skills and concepts. I discussed examples from my school library and classroom to illustrate how teaching news literacy does not constitute indoctrination; in fact, news literacy *strengthens* a teacher's ability to promote free speech and inquiry. Teaching news literacy concepts does not mean I only allow students to use a very narrow set of prescribed news sources; rather, I design learning opportunities for students to discover a wide variety of news sources, comparing and contrasting them. They learn how newsrooms function, the history of the freedom of the press, and the watchdog role of journalism in a democracy. I explained that media literacy does not refer to how some ominously utilize the phrase "the media" but rather simply means any nonprint source of information. Can students interpret the messages of images and videos? Can they analyze the techniques used to create images or videos, and how those impact the intended purpose? Whether or not some version of H5183 passes in South Carolina, I have already shown students, administrators, parents, and legislators how valuable it is for students to freely learn about controversial issues that directly affect them, without fear of indoctrination by me. In this way, I have connected media and news literacy education and book censorship with students' intellectual freedom rights.

When Censorship Came for Me

While I have been an active defender of students' First Amendment rights to read through my OIF blog posts and other actions for many years, I had not personally faced threats of censorship and other consequences until March 2022, when I was announced the winner of the South Carolina School Librarian of the Year Award by the South Carolina Association of School Librarians (SCASL). Around the same time, *Greenville News* reporter Krys Merryman included some of my comments in a news article updating the community on actions taken by the local school district related to CRT. A local radio talk show host seized on these comments, as well as some of my Twitter posts defending the book *Gender Queer*, to make slanderous claims about me and my professional work. Some of my colleagues and acquaintances heard these radio show segments, and the SCASL president informed me that the organization received a few e-mails complaining about my award.

Because of this tension, SC state senator Josh Kimbrell sent a letter to the SCASL leadership expressing his disapproval of my selection as the award's recipient because I defended books such as *Gender Queer*. Kimbrell posted a thread about me on his Facebook account, directly accusing me of being a pedophile and a leftist groomer, and some people responded with threatening comments, encouraging each other to contact my school. I even received threats of violence. Although I e-mailed him and called his office more than once, the only conversation we had was through Facebook Messenger. He never apologized for spreading lies about my professional work and my character, although several days later he did take down the Facebook thread.

A similar situation happened with SC state representative Steven Long, in which he posted the same defamatory statements. He did eventually apologize to me and take down his Facebook thread. However, both officials told me they could not be held responsible for other people's comments on social media and that they highly disagreed with my defense of books such as *Gender Queer.*

Thankfully, my school leadership did assure me of their support, although the marketing team removed the school's social media posts celebrating my award, due to the volume of negative and threatening comments posted. While I knew I had done nothing wrong, and certainly nothing illegal or harmful, this level of attack did take an emotional toll. Knowing that people in the community were questioning me and accusing me of a criminal offense because of rumors and disinformation was frustrating. It is easy to feel exasperated when people who misunderstand the librarian profession deliberately misrepresent what we do and have no desire to consider viewpoints different from their own. However, there is a way to counter these narratives: education.

Fighting Back: Intellectual Freedom Programming

According to the ALA's *Intellectual Freedom Manual* (Garnar & Magi, 2021), educating the American public, including library staff, on the value of intellectual freedom is fundamental to the mission of libraries of all types. When libraries guarantee physical access to information, they foster awareness of intellectual freedom rights within the context of educational programs and instruction in essential information skills. In short, the answer to disinformation is education. Indeed, when I interact with legislators and community members, they generally have no working knowledge of the ethical foundation of the American library system and how it relates to the First Amendment.

The National School Library Standards (American Association of School Librarians [AASL], 2018) give school librarians specific guidance for the inclusion of intellectual freedom principles in lessons. Adapting school library standards into reflective questions is one effective strategy. For example, under Shared Foundation Include, the Create Domain, students should "evaluat[e] a variety of perspectives during learning activities [and] represent diverse perspectives during learning activities." After a lesson, students can ponder the following questions as an exit slip or a piece of reflective writing: "Did I evaluate a variety of perspectives today? Did they represent diverse perspectives? Did I participate in class today? If so, was my participation informed by accurate, reliable information? When I engaged in inquiry, did I seek out diverse perspectives? Did I question my own assumptions and misconceptions?"

By extension, school librarians can complete a similar self-reflection: "Did I model respect for diverse perspectives? Did I advocate for including diverse perspectives in my school's learning opportunities? Did my learning activity provide students with the opportunity to learn from others who are diverse? Did my learning activity give students the chance to access a wide range of information sources? Did my learning activity require students to evaluate a variety of perspectives?"

In January 2022, I presented a webinar "Protecting a student's right to read in a hyper-partisan environment," sponsored by the University of South Carolina School of Information, about current attempts to censor education. I shared information about how would-be censors target media and news literacy education as being inappropriate, controversial, and divisive, and I gave advice for responding in support of this education. One example I shared involved analyzing state education standards to find elements of disinformation based on what I learned from the News Literacy Project's infographic on types of mis/disinformation. It is critical for educators to closely follow their own state legislatures to be aware of efforts to limit intellectual freedom rights. I also shared learning activities that promote critical thinking and respect for various diverse perspectives on controversial current events, such as creating argumentative thesis statements to represent a variety of viewpoints. Students can also learn about important court cases that provide guidance on their legal rights to intellectual freedom.

Since October 2020, I have presented three additional webinars through the South Carolina Association of School Librarians related to media and news literacy: "Information literacy and elections," "Journalism and the school library: Embedding news literacy skills across the curriculum," and "The new basics: Practical approaches to media & news literacy." In all three, I shared examples from my school library and classroom of how to incorporate media and news literacy into all areas of instruction and ability levels, in ways that promote free inquiry and the exploration of multiple viewpoints, teaching skills instead of forcing a point of view on students. For example, I created a breakout box game in collaboration with a social studies teacher to introduce concepts and strategies related to disinformation found online before the teacher assigned the class to find news articles related to current events. When I collaborated with an English teacher on a voice of protest unit, students investigated recent examples of book burnings in the United States and analyzed videos and images, and read local newspaper articles. Then, I introduced books I was able to purchase by winning a Freedom to Read Foundation grant, and students formed book clubs based on their interests. One class wrote editorials defending their book selections. Utilizing editorial writing also encourages students to become active citizens.

I presented a session called "Not-so-scary intellectual freedom programming" at the South Carolina Association of School Librarians' annual conference in March 2022. I included an instructional example from my journalism classroom to illustrate how news literacy instruction can be implemented without indoctrination or bias. After the news story broke last fall about Instagram's negative effects on young female users (Feiner, 2021), I asked my students to find examples of unbiased, straight news, opinion pieces, and biased sources of information, which they posted on a shared Google Doc. I also utilized news articles to teach students how to write argumentative thesis statements in preparation for an opinion writing opportunity; students had to write statements strongly agreeing, strongly disagreeing, somewhat agreeing, or somewhat disagreeing with some of the claims that appeared in the articles they had already shared with each other. This activity was adapted from the News Literacy Project's lesson plan bank. My students completed a similar activity during the 2020–21 school year, analyzing examples of COVID-19 information found in news articles, infographics, videos, and user-generated content. I did not tell students what to think about the COVID-19 vaccine but rather asked them to evaluate a wide range of viewpoints found in various pieces of media.

I have also made a connection between news literacy and intellectual freedom rights in my journalism newspaper class. I shared local newspaper articles that were being published about pending CRT-related legislation, which interested my students because the censorship of instructional materials (including library books) and current events directly impacts them. We engaged in discussions about how the reporters used certain wording to remain neutral, which words perhaps showed some bias, and whose voices were left out of the reporting. I noticed that some of these articles were written by the same reporter, so I reached out to her. After suggesting that she interview some school librarians in order to give voice to all stakeholders in her articles, we set up a time for her to be a guest speaker in my class. The students had already read several of her articles, so they were able to ask pertinent questions, both as students affected by what she was covering and as student journalists. It was an incredible learning experience, connecting news literacy curriculum with a practicing reporter on a topic that affected them as students. She even interviewed me as a result of my initial e-mail conversation with her, and she included my remarks in a recent story following developments in the ongoing censorship attempts, which allowed me to advocate not only for my profession but also for my students. Being able to involve my students in this entire process, letting them observe me move through the process of reading articles, contacting the reporter, establishing a relationship, inviting her into the classroom, and being interviewed to provide a voice that had been ignored was the most hands-on, relevant learning experience I could have imagined. Sharing this learning experience with others created an opportunity for me to advocate for news literacy by making clear just how valuable this learning experience was.

School and public libraries can also utilize other methods of education, such as interactive bulletin boards, trivia contests, writing contests, and bookmark design contests to promote awareness of intellectual freedom rights. Make available black armbands on the anniversary of *Tinker v. Des Moines* (1969); schedule a virtual visit with an author whose works have been challenged; host a "Freedom to Read" night during Banned Books Week, offering a history of book censorship throughout American history. Designing educational experiences for students and patrons to explore America's rich history and tradition of intellectual freedom may surprise them, encouraging citizens to realize the complex nature of such rights and freedoms.

As stated in the National School Library Standards,

> Not everything a learner hears will be accurate or beneficial, so honing critical and analytical skills is crucial to growth as an informed global citizen. When learners articulate the cultural relevancy of varying viewpoints and perspectives, and appreciate others' unique contributions, they better understand their own placement within larger learning communities. (AASL, 2018, p. 78)

Conclusion

The goal of education is not to protect students from harmful or inaccurate information; with the rapid evolution of technology, that would be impossible. Rather, the goal is to equip students with the skills necessary to navigate a world full of information. Furthermore, in a democracy, students should develop the ability to respectfully consider a variety of viewpoints and understand why people hold those viewpoints.

Note

1. Organizations such as United States Parents Involved in Education have established local branches across the country in an effort to effect change at grassroots levels, which are nonetheless spearheaded on a national level (Yousef, 2022).

References

American Association of School Librarians. (2018). *National School Library Standards for learners, school librarians, and school libraries*. ALA Editions.

Carden, C., & Tablone, E. (2021, November 16). *Fort Mill School District wraps up administrative review of book that caused statewide review of libraries*. WCNC

Charlotte. https://www.wcnc.com/article/news/education/fort-mill-schools-south-carolina-statewide-review-book/275-db1b55e0-6572-41dd-82f4-2be160a3bd0a

Feiner, L. (2021, September 15). *Lawmakers demand answers from Zuckerberg after investigation finds Instagram is toxic for teen girls.* CNBC. https://www.cnbc.com/2021/09/15/lawmakers-demand-facebook-answer-how-it-impacts-kids-mental-health.html

Garnar, M., & Magi, T. (Eds.). (2021). *Intellectual freedom manual.* ALA Editions.

Gregory, J. (2021, December 28). *South Carolina Parents Involved in Education (SCPIE) hosting meetings across state, demanding censorship.* Intellectual Freedom Blog. https://www.oif.ala.org/oif/south-carolina-parents-involved-in-education-scpie-hosting-meetings-across-state-demanding-censorship/

Merryman, K. (2021, November 11). Greenville County Schools reviewing books after McMaster calls for statewide investigation. *The Greenville News.* https://www.greenvilleonline.com/story/news/local/south-carolina/2021/11/11/sc-greenville-county-schools-gov-mcmaster-investigation-illustrated-novels-library/6386302001/

PEN America. (2022). *Banned in the USA: Rising school book bans threaten free expression and students' First Amendment rights.* https://pen.org/banned-in-the-usa/

Schwartz, S., & Pendharkar, E. (2022, February 2). Here's the long list of topics Republicans want banned from the classroom. *Education Week.* https://www.edweek.org/policy-politics/heres-the-long-list-of-topics-republicans-want-banned-from-the-classroom/2022/02

Wallace-Wells, B. (2021, June 18). How a conservative activist invented the conflict over critical race theory. *The New Yorker.* https://www.newyorker.com/news/annals-of-inquiry/how-a-conservative-activist-invented-the-conflict-over-critical-race-theory

Yousef, O. (2022). *Book bans and the threat of censorship rev up political activism in the suburbs.* NPR. https://www.npr.org/2022/03/21/1087000890/book-bans-and-the-threat-of-censorship-rev-up-political-activism-in-the-suburbs

Books Discussed in This Chapter

Gino, A. (2015). *Melissa.* Scholastic.

Kobabe, M. (2019). *Gender queer: A memoir.* Oni Press.

Thomas, A. (2017). *The hate u give.* Balzer + Bray.

PART 2

How Challenges and Bans Affect Librarians

CHAPTER SIX

Riding Shotgun for Intellectual Freedom

Terri L. Lesley

The Catalyst

Born and raised in Wyoming, and having lived most of my life in a boomtown melting pot of ranchers, coal miners, oilfield workers, and support workers, I had always loved the hard-working cowboy spirit and the live-and-let-live philosophy of my town and my state. Comfortably happy in my role as the executive director of Campbell County Public Library (CCPL), I was unprepared for the storm of 2021.

It all began with a Facebook post. At home for the evening on June 28, 2021, I received a text from the library's public relations coordinator advising me that a county commissioner had made a comment on a library Facebook post. The post read:

> *Library*: June is pride month and Rainbow Book Month. For this month's Teen Room blog, a staff member writes about a few titles you can check out from your library that will connect you with the LGBTQIA+ collection at CCPL. (The post linked to the Teen Blog)

Commissioner 1 commented that he did not believe Pride Month or Rainbow Book Month had been designated by the county.

I discussed the matter immediately with the library's public relations coordinator. We considered whether to delete the post or maybe add the word "National" to clarify that Pride Month and Rainbow Book Month were national designations. I considered the people I knew who belonged to the lesbian, gay, bisexual, transgender, and/or queer/questioning (LGBTQ+) community—family, friends, and acquaintances—good people who were not always treated kindly, who had been bullied, and who were not always accepted by their families or their community. I thought about our duty as a public library and the First Amendment's protection of the individual right to read and access information. I also considered our mission to serve all citizens of our community and decided the post would remain with no edits. I also chose not to respond as there was nothing to be gained by arguing the point on social media. Instead, I decided to reach out personally to the commissioner the following day.

The next morning, before I could respond, I received e-mails from two county commissioners.

The first e-mail from Commissioner 1 stated he was "disturbed" by the library's recent LGBTQ post on social media. He indicated the county had not designated a month as "Pride Month" or "Rainbow Book Month." He felt the post sent a false message to county residents and that teaching this kind of behavior to underaged residents is up to parents, not the government. He went on to say the post implies the county is giving special treatment to a particular group, and that since the Wyoming Constitution says "all people are created equal," this special recognition would suggest otherwise. He concluded by asking me to forward his e-mail to the library board.

My response:

RE: LGBTQ post on social media

Commissioner,

This is an unexpected, unintended interpretation that the County has designated a Pride Month or Rainbow Book Month. These are national designations. The post supports the library mission to provide diverse cultural opportunities for reading, learning and entertainment to all citizens of our community. As you requested, I passed your email onto the Library Board.

The second e-mail from Commissioner 2 referenced the Teen Room Blog. She advised me that she was out of town but had received communication about the teen room promotion of Pride Month and Rainbow Book Month. She stated the perception was that this was something the county had established. She relayed the public concern about teens being minors and stated her belief that this topic and related information be a conversation between parents/families. She also asked me to share her e-mail with the board and let me know she would be back in town the following week if I wanted to further discuss the matter with her.

I responded to the second commissioner and then forwarded her e-mail to the library board as well. I then contacted library board members to ensure there were no concerns from the board and was relieved by the supportive feedback. In Wyoming, county commissioners are charged with appointing library board members and setting the library's budget. The library board sets the policy and appoints a library director; therefore, county commissioners typically are not involved in the daily operations of the library. I did not receive any other e-mails, and so I hoped the matter would be dropped.

The Attack

At 8:30 a.m. on July 7, I was contacted by a third county commissioner and told to come to the 9 a.m. Board of Commissioners meeting "ASAP," as a crowd had gathered to complain about the Facebook post.

I arrived at the courthouse to see a room packed full of people. A well-organized group spoke heatedly during the public comment session, which lasted for over an hour. The speakers shared their religious opinions and beliefs, spoke against a variety of books with LGBTQ+ and teen fantasy themes that they had checked out from the library, and asked that the books be removed. One of the protestors stated that he had been seeing a demoralization of America and that the library promotes immorality and perversion to kids. Another protestor demanded that the library board be removed and suggested a parent board be implemented to review youth books before they could be added to the collection. None of the people who spoke against the library books had approached me or my staff to discuss their concerns.

I was then asked to address the commissioners regarding the concerns from the public comment session. I explained the ordering process for library collections as outlined in our collection development policy. I reviewed the process patrons could use to challenge a book to the library board and stated that the information was readily available on the library website. I spoke further about the library's mission to serve all people of the community and the need for a balanced collection that does not take sides on social issues. Commissioner 1, who had e-mailed me about the Facebook post, asked me if we have a "straight" section in the library. He then read the e-mail he sent me to the audience and stated that if the library is not going to promote a straight pride month, then it should not promote a gay pride month.

Later that day, I received another e-mail from Commissioner 1. The situation had evolved from attacking books to attacking programs.

His e-mail referenced magic show performances scheduled for the following week. He had conducted online research on the magician and determined the show was a transgender act. He thought hosting the magician was a bad idea and that spending taxpayer funds on this type of show would cause further distress to the taxpayers of the county.

I researched his claim and learned that the program was simply a magic act geared toward children and nothing more. I responded to the commissioner to reassure him there was no cause for concern.

From me:

Commissioner,

When we book summer reading shows, we rely on professional recommendations from a network of other libraries. I want to reassure you that I've looked into this thoroughly, and I am confident that this grant-funded program is strictly a magician's show. The program was professionally recommended to us, highly reviewed, and the magician has performed for children at libraries all across the Midwest—on countless occasions—with no issues.

I did not get a response, but the chaos of the day continued when a staff member advised me that a local pastor and former state representative had posted a Facebook message about the magician program on Facebook. The post was widely read and shared. This was the catalyst for additional angry posts all over social media. Community posts included numerous anti-LBGTQ+ comments as well as comments defending the library and the magician.

The pastor's long post invited readers to guess what was being promoted to teens at the Public Library and then stated it was a transgender magic show. He added that this marketing effort followed on the heels of a month where the library had actively advanced sexual topics to teenagers. He pointed out that typically there is nothing wrong with a magic show unless the event, disguised as a fun and entertaining program, is intended to glorify something sinister and hurtful. He had questions, from the viewpoint of a pastor and a parent, on whether the event was an entertaining magic program or was instead a shield for the magician to talk about sexual matters with teens. He repeated that he did not have issues with a magic show, but that he certainly had issues with using youth events to expose kids to a sexual agenda, such as the library had been doing over the past month.

He then went on to list characteristics he felt separated humans from animals, including "faith, integrity, perseverance, justice, wisdom, fortitude, self-control, a positive attitude, gratitude, and humility." He felt that we, as human beings, should encourage and seek these advanced virtues. He then focused on sex, stating it was a base, animal, biological instinct experienced by all living things. He added that while all animals have sex, humans were made in the image of God and not simple animals. He wondered why the library was promoting the base things of life instead of higher virtues, and he also questioned why the human race was being downgraded to an animal state. He concluded the library owed the public answers and accountability.

This post also referred to a YouTube video of the magician discussing her personal transgender experience. The video was not located on her professional website but had been discovered by the protestors. I still do not know why local community members were inspired to investigate the background of this library performer.

On July 11, an "unnamed informant" passed around screenshots of an online chat held by several members of the community, including the two commissioners who had contacted me and the pastor who made the Facebook post, as well as the people who spoke against the library at the county commissioners meeting. The screenshots of this secret collaboration outlined the plan for the verbal attack on the library at the July 7 Commissioners' meeting. The transcript also discussed the transgender status of the magician. Three commissioners who also received the transcripts expressed frustration with the other two commissioners for being blindsided by protestors without any forewarning.

Tensions Rise

The period from July 11 to July 13 became a time of increasing tensions. Social media posts, both good and bad, focused on the magician program. Supporters and detractors sent e-mails and letters and also called library officials and the county commissioners to voice their opinion. The youth services librarian and I discussed whether to cancel the magician program. As I debated the best course of action, I knew that if I canceled this program, I would be sending the wrong message to the LGBTQ+ community, which deserved better from its public library. I decided not to cancel the program if the magician wanted to proceed. The youth librarian advised the magician about the controversy, and the magician decided that she would still perform as planned.

A protest was organized by the anti-library crowd and shared on social media, and Facebook blew up with disinformation and misinformation, as well as feuds between supporters and detractors. No amount of reassurance from library officials about the program being a magician program took hold with the protestors. Community tension was increasing, and so I contacted the police department to make security arrangements for the magician program.

The next evening, front desk staff received a threat from an unknown person who parked at the curb, came in, and warned circulation staff that people were angry and that staff should close the library for the magician program or they would "be sorry." The chairman of the county commission also left me a message that he had received a threatening phone call. I reported the threats to law enforcement.

On July 13, the day before the magic performance, the magician canceled due to anonymous telephone threats she received. She expressed worry about her safety and the safety of the audience. The youth services librarian and I talked to the magician in a conference call and extended our heartfelt apologies. I then sent a press release reporting the program was canceled due to safety concerns for the performer, staff, and patrons.

On the day the magician had been scheduled to perform, the anti-LGBTQ+ crowd still protested at the library with numerous picket signs such as "Don't Trans Our Kids" and "Your Library OK's LGBTQ." This protest received national attention. The actions of the protestors increased awareness and inspired many people, locally, statewide, and at the national level to reach out with support for the library.

The director of Wyoming Equality also arrived in Gillette to support LGBTQ+ residents. She arranged for an LGBTQ+ teen ambassador to talk to County Commissioner 1. He met with the teen ambassador in the library Teen Room, where she talked about why LGBTQ+ books were important to her. Commissioner 1 was initially favorably influenced by the meeting but ultimately did not back down on his stance toward the library books.

The protestors and a group of library supporters attended the next county commissioner meeting on July 20. The protestors continued to speak heatedly about LGBTQ+ people, the magician program, the library, and library books. Library advocates also spoke at the meeting, denouncing censorship and supporting the magician, the LGBTQ+ community, and the rights of all citizens to choose reading material. At the end of the public comment session, Commissioner 2, who helped plan the original attack on the library, spoke against the magician and advocated for protecting the children.

On July 26, the library board held its regular monthly meeting. The collection development policy and request for reconsideration process were reviewed to assist the public to use the library's process for challenging library materials. This process allows patrons to request that an item be moved or removed from the collection. The director and a library manager review the book and determine whether the item meets the guidelines in the collection development policy. A decision by the director to retain the challenged item may be appealed to the library board.

The anti-library crowd showed up in force, with similar intensity but with more hostility than demonstrated at the county commission meetings. One protestor accused the library board and director of purposefully corrupting the youth and grooming them to accept sexual practices. Another protestor accused a board member of child indoctrination, stating it was child endangerment and pedophilia. The state librarian and many library directors from other counties were also in the audience in a show of support.

MassResistance

During the first part of August, I became aware of an organization called MassResistance. The Southern Poverty Law Center has designated

MassResistance as a national LGBTQ hate group (Anti-LGBTQ | Southern Poverty Law Center, splcenter.org). This organization, among other things, has challenged school district anti-bullying rules on the grounds that such rules are part of the LGBTQ+ agenda. I was informed about a local car sales publication that was produced by one of the anti-library protestors. It contained an article about the cancelation of the magician show and the writer's efforts in making that happen. The writer stated that MassResistance had helped him organize against certain library books and to cancel the magician show. I soon became aware that there was a MassResistance playbook that discredits leadership, goes after supporters, targets particular books, and more.

By mid-August, the anti-library crowd became more open about their association with MassResistance. They even had a booth at the county fair displaying a MassResistance banner suggesting particular books be banned, including many books that were not in the library collection. They tried recruiting people to attend a parent meeting and also tried to get fair attendees to protest against the Campbell County Public Library and library books.

Request for Reconsideration

Our next hurdle was to persuade protestors to use the library's Request for Reconsideration process. Although we had presented the information at the July meeting, no challenges had been submitted. It took a Special Joint Meeting of the Library Board and County Commissioners on August 12 to persuade the crowd to use the reconsideration process.

Over the course of the next seven months, we would receive fifty-seven requests for reconsideration forms from seventeen unique challengers on twenty-nine unique titles. In comparison, we had received three written challenges, with no appeals, since I became the director nine years ago. Two of the twenty-nine titles were moved by the manager and director from the young adult graphic novel collection to the adult graphic novel collection as a result of these challenges. Otherwise, all other items were retained in the same area of the library's collections. The library board upheld the decision of the director on the ten titles that were appealed to the library board.

Library board decisions took into consideration the First Amendment, which does not allow governmental bodies to restrict freedom of speech. This encompasses talking, writing, printing, and other forms of expression. The board was also influenced by case law in *Sund v. City of Wichita Falls, Texas* (2000). In this case, the city of Wichita Falls enacted a resolution that involved the forced relocation of books from the children's department to the adult area. The court found that moving books from the children's part of the library to the adult area placed a significant burden on a library patron's ability to gain access to those books and therefore was unconstitutional under the First and Fourteenth Amendments.

Our time frame for processing challenges did not consider the time needed to manage a large number of challenges in a short time period. Many of the challengers did not have children and did not even have a library card. One challenger lived in another city. We also began to realize that many of the challengers had not read the book they were challenging, but had instead seen screenshots of particular sections of the book. The challengers used the screenshots to provide information about the book on their request for reconsideration forms. It became increasingly obvious that we needed to rework our policy and processes to address some of these problems.

More Attacks

The September 27 library board meeting was another joint meeting with the commissioners. We focused on educating the public on the role of public libraries, the parenting collection, and parental responsibility for what their children were reading and on correcting misinformation about how long it takes to challenge and appeal a book to the library board. The commissioners were split between supporting and opposing the library. Commissioner 1 threatened to defund the library. Around the same time, the local MassResistance chapter placed ads on electronic billboards located all over the city, with statements such as "STOP LGBTQ indoctrination at our library" and "Warning! Inappropriate youth books at library."

A few days after the board meeting, I received a call from the county attorney's office informing me that citizens had gone to the sheriff's office to press charges against me and the Campbell County Public Library for violating child sex laws. Five books were named in the complaint:

1. *Dating and Sex: A Guide for the 21st Century Teen Boy* (2016), by Andrew P. Smiler
2. *Doing It! Let's Talk about Sex* (2018), by Hannah Witton
3. *Sex Is a Funny Word: A Book about Bodies, Feelings, and You* (2015), by Cory Silverberg and Fiona Smith
4. *How Do You Make a Baby?* (2020), by Anna Fiske
5. *This Book Is Gay* (2014), by Juno Dawson

One citizen insisted I should be arrested for obscenity and soliciting sex from a minor. The sheriff passed the complaint to the county attorney to see if it was a legitimate charge, and the county attorney hired an independent attorney to render an opinion on whether the charge had any validity. One of the people pressing charges claimed that library books were "horrible, vile, erotic porn that belongs in an adult bookstore." Another person who filed the complaint said the titles were "hard-core pornography to children" and that carrying them was "felony behavior."

It would take nearly two months to receive a decision on these charges.

At some point the protestors changed their tactics. They stopped demanding that books be removed from the library, instead asking that the books be moved to the adult collection. They still, however, continued to speak loudly and angrily at county commissioner and library board meetings. They cherry-picked passages from teen sex education books and read them out loud. The group also began bringing protest signs to meetings with statements such as "Fire Terri Lesley" and "The library indoctrinates children." Over a year later, public comment on this controversy continues at commissioner and library board meetings.

Many patrons were curious about the challenged books and wanted to see the books for themselves. Several of the books were checked out or are being used by librarians to process challenges. The Friends of the Library agreed to purchase the challenged books, and the library created a display in the adult area so patrons could access the books. The protestors were infuriated by this action. Social media blew up again, and library board members were harassed with angry and threatening phone calls. The fervor was so potent that I moved the books to the administration office in an attempt to calm things down. Patrons could still see the books, but they were no longer on public display.

On October 27, the special prosecutor from Weston County sent out an opinion on the library case, declining to prosecute the library and the library director. This document was circulated to every library director in Wyoming.

Conclusion: Impacts on Staff and Board

Throughout the controversy, staff endured personal attacks, in person and via social media. The staff was in the business of helping people and was not accustomed to harsh public pressure and criticism. I invited staff to strategic meetings, held venting sessions, and encouraged vacations, but it was not enough. When I found myself comforting staff members who were in tears, it became necessary to bring counseling services in to help them cope with the stress.

The controversy was hard on the library board too. Board members received numerous abusive comments at board meetings and were called and harassed at home. One member was convinced a commissioner had given out her private number, and she eventually resigned in early February. Another member was understandably struggling with anxiety, and so we created a barrier between the library board seating and the public to help her feel safe.

Although the words and actions of protestors have been difficult to endure, the support that the library staff and the board received over the course of this controversy has been phenomenal. Libraries across the state sent regular care packages to the staff to express their support and concern. Residents and businesses also delivered food items, inspiring letters, flowers, and more to express support. These actions have been key in helping boost the fortitude and morale of the board and staff.

As I reflect on this experience in intellectual freedom, the image of the protestors' vehemence for their cause will forever be imprinted on my mind. Brené Brown speaks to this in her Ted Talk "The Power of Vulnerability." Brown talks about how we, as a society, have become numb by wanting certainty in our lives. She says, "Religion has gone from a belief in faith and mystery to certainty. 'I'm right. You're wrong. Shut up!'" (Brown, 2010). In their righteousness, and despite valid information to the contrary, the protestors have consistently insisted that the challenged books harm children. I disagree. Poverty, neglect, abuse, lack of acceptance from parents and family, bullying, substance abuse—these are examples of things that harm our youth.

In the avalanche of communication I have received, an e-mail from an LGBTQ+ person stands out. He thanked me for standing strong and said he wished he had had access to these books as a teenager, as it would have saved him from years of self-destructive behavior. Books eventually helped him turn his life around. I received multiple similar stories and phone calls from other LGBTQ+ individuals. Yes. Books really do save lives.

References

Brown, B. (2010, October). *The power of vulnerability* [Video]. TED Conferences. https://www.youtube.com/watch?v=X4Qm9cGRub0

Sund v. City of Wichita Falls, Texas. (2000). 121 F.Supp.2d 530.

Books Discussed in This Chapter

Dawson, J. (2014). *This book is gay.* Sourcebooks Fire.

Fiske, A. (2020). *How do you make a baby?* Gecko Press.

Silverberg, C., & Smith, F. (2015). *Sex is a funny word: A book about bodies, feelings, and you.* Seven Stories Press.

Smiler, A. P. (2016). *Dating and sex: A guide for the 21st century teen boy.* Magination Press.

Witton, H. (2018). *Doing it! Let's talk about sex.* Sourcebooks Fire.

CHAPTER SEVEN

A Library without Controversy

Kelly Mayfield

The Inappropriate Book Removal Project

A few years ago, I accepted a part-time job as the school librarian at a private religiously affiliated K–8 school. I had no prior library experience, but as has become common across the United States, the school administration was eager to save money by replacing the full-time credentialed teacher librarian with a paraprofessional. In my meeting with the principal, she mentioned in passing that she was starting a project to cull "inappropriate" books from the collection. She said,

> We want our library to be a place where parents can trust that their child will be reading books that will help them to grow in faith and understanding. Of course, it's good to challenge students, but our goal for the library collection is moderation rather than controversy. I'd like to particularly focus on expanding and updating our nonfiction collection.

This sounded reasonable to me at that time. A private school library does not have the same budget as a metropolitan public library where you could buy dozens of copies of a popular title that few will still be reading after a year or two. I assumed in this setting "inappropriate" meant graphic descriptions of sex or violence, anything touching on sexuality or sexual identity, and probably too much profanity. Although the school was religiously affiliated, it was not fundamentalist. Promisingly, I had noticed multiple copies of the *Harry Potter* series prominently displayed across the top of the fantasy section during my tour of the library. I had no idea what I was getting into.

The principal had designated someone to read and evaluate the library collection. At first, the books that disappeared were ones that seemed to meet the criteria I had understood. *The Martian* (2014) had too much profanity, and *The Hunger Games* (2008) was too violent. As for *The Hitchhiker's Guide to the Galaxy* (1979), well, "It's quite zany, but more appropriate for high school," the designated evaluator told me with a straight face. After a few months, the science fiction section had shrunk so much that I moved it to a smaller bookcase.

I tried to look at this as a good opportunity to add some great new titles to a collection that was really quite dated. However, this also did not go as planned. The principal required me to submit a list of titles for her approval prior to ordering them. She would return the list to me with titles marked through to signal her rejection. This was how I learned that the principal had a "no replacement" policy regarding the Harry Potter books (which had erroneously given the impression of a moderate administration to me during my interview), so that she could avoid any objections that might be made by parents if she removed them outright. I spent a lot of time taping and gluing the volumes together to delay their removal.

There was never a time when a proposed purchase list was returned to me with everything approved, despite my best efforts to find books that I thought would be appropriate according to the principal's standards. "Could you help me to understand why *A Unicorn Named Sparkle* was not approved? I'm not sure I understand what is inappropriate about it," I e-mailed after getting one such purchase list returned. The K–2 girls kept asking me for unicorn picture books, but we had hardly any in the library. I was told that I could purchase *Sparkle* after all, but in the future, I should try to avoid frivolous fantasy creatures and focus more on nonfiction. Ironically, in the story, Sparkle is actually a goat and not a unicorn.

By this time, I had begun to understand that "inappropriate" is not nearly as objective or easy to define as I thought it would be. I started writing little notes on my purchase lists to justify the books so that they would not be so arbitrarily refused by someone who did not know anything about them. "Very positive portrayal of a loving family" I wrote by Karina Yan Glaser's *The Vanderbeekers* (2017). "Graphic novel history books really get the middle schoolers interested in history," I wrote to pitch Nathan Hale's *Hazardous Tales*. I was mostly successful with that one. *Donner Dinner Party* (2013) was too morbid to be approved, even if it was nonfiction.

In addition to strategies to maximize my purchase approvals, I began a stealth campaign to stem the flow of culled books. I avoided drawing attention to any books that I thought might be considered suspect by not putting them on display. Instead, I recommended these books directly to students if

I thought they might be interested. Also, while the designated book evaluator had full authority, she did sometimes ask my opinion, and so I had opportunities to defend titles. One day, she approached me holding Scott Westerfeld's *Leviathan* (2009). "There's nothing objectionable in this series" she began, "It's quite good. But the main character is a girl disguised as a boy for most of the series. Do you think it's supposed to be introducing kids to transgender?" Suddenly inspired, I replied that the woman-disguised-as-a-man plot device is so old that Shakespeare used it in *As You Like It*, and that it would be a shame to discard a good series by reading too much into it. *Leviathan* was saved.

The older students did notice the inappropriate book removal project as time went by. When I first started working in the library, students would ask, "Where is *The Hunger Games*?" in a tone of expectation. Later, questions sounded more like "We probably don't have *Maze Runner*, right?" The students who read a lot started depending more on trips to the public library to meet their needs, while the marginal readers stopped checking out books altogether. You can create a library full of inoffensive books, but you cannot make kids interested in reading them.

Defining "Inappropriate"

One day I found Ben Hatke's *Mighty Jack* (2016) in my school mailbox with a note from the principal saying I should remove it due to profanity. I did not remember there being profanity in this beautifully drawn and squeaky-clean graphic novel series. Turning to the marked page, I saw that one character says to another, "Don't be an ass!" Every year around Easter the students at this school all listened to the story of Jesus riding into Jerusalem on the back of an ass. I was confident the students knew the word ass could mean donkey. I also remembered that Tinker Bell calls Peter Pan an ass multiple times in J. M. Barrie's original story, of which we had a couple of copies available on the shelf. I decided not to point this out in case *Peter Pan* (1911) ended up being removed, too. The evaluator had presumed *Peter Pan* was fine.

This was a dichotomy that I began to see clearly as more and more books were removed from the shelves. Anything "classic" was above reproach, while anything "modern" was suspect. A young woman disguised as a man is fine if Shakespeare does it but not if Scott Westerfeld does. The last volume in C. S. Lewis's *Narnia* series (*The Last Battle*) (2005) features a unicorn who is both frivolously fantastic and kills people by stabbing them with his horn during battle, but Narnia's credentials as Christian fantasy are too well established for it to be questioned. *The Inheritance Cycle* (2005) by Christopher Paolini, a homeschool graduate, was removed for being "too new-aged," while Tolkien's *The Lord of the Rings* (2022/1954), which Paolini cited as an influence, was kept.

I think one reason why so many of the books considered classic children's literature were assumed to be unobjectionable is because hardly anyone has read them—or they do not remember the details. People are usually only familiar with the sanitized Disney versions. For example, practically the first thing Pinocchio does in the original book is kill Jiminy Cricket. Later, he and his juvenile delinquent friends are all turned into jackas–er, donkeys, in one of the milder episodes of a book full of one disturbing image after another. *Peter Pan* involves runaway children and pirates continually murdering one another. Tinker Bell attempts to murder Wendy several times. Yet, it is only the Indigenous "Piccaninny" tribe that is described as wily, bloodthirsty, and savage. The blatant racism in these books, including the *Narnia* and *The Lord of the Rings* series, is also always given a pass.

I began to ask myself questions about appropriateness and censorship. Because the library collection was quite old, I found a number of picture books that had not-so-thinly-veiled racist messages or featured racial stereotypes. My inclination was to remove them so that they would not influence the children, but was that not the exact motivation given for removing what was snowballing into hundreds of books from the library? I had never before questioned the idea that children should be protected from words that conveyed ideas or images that might harm them. With every book that was removed from the library, however, I had to continually face the consequences of that.

While pondering this question, I continued to try to add more diverse books to our collection. When I called the principal's attention to the fact that according to our Christmas section only white people and animals celebrated the holiday, I was given a little extra money to add some titles, because that is the sort of thing that sounds great when you are trying to promote your school as inclusive and diverse. Getting some shiny new books just in time for December, I read Lara Hawthorne's *Silent Night* (2018) to the younger grades, where each time a student brought up the dark color of Mary and Joseph's skin in the illustrations. We had a great discussion about that, and I briefly felt I was making a real difference in my work at the library.

However, like most token efforts at diversity, that feeling was short-lived. One day, I noticed that every Walter Dean Myers book had been removed from the library. When I asked why, I was told that his work dealt with "too many mature themes." "Inappropriate" can apparently mean "an idea which makes us uncomfortable." Most of my proposed books by authors of color were declined for the same reason. Other than a handful of contemporary fiction such as Jason Reynolds's *Track Series* (2016) and *The Crossover* (2014) by Kwame Alexander, authors of color were relegated to historical fiction. The term "historical fiction" began to seem ironic to me. Believing that any problems related to race were in the past is a kind of historical fiction that was being perpetuated in this library. Stories that centered around racism, which is still in existence, disappeared from the library, so that the primarily white student population would not question the fiction that racism has disappeared from modern society.

Books that dealt with contemporary social issues often fell into this section of the inappropriate designation. Even books that touched on the most mundane social issues were scrutinized. The book evaluator came to see me holding a copy of Gary Paulsen's *Hatchet* (1987). "I'm thinking this should be marked YA," she said, referring to the designation that would limit access to the book to only sixth to eighth graders. "The main character's parents are divorced so I'm not sure it's appropriate for the younger grades." I blinked, multiple thoughts running through my mind. I thought of how many of the elementary school students at this school had divorced parents. I remembered how I read *Dear Mr. Henshaw* by Beverly Cleary (1983) multiple times during elementary school after my parents divorced because it was the only book I could find in the school library that mentioned divorce. I decided to defend *Hatchet* by explaining that it was part of the fifth-grade reading curriculum, and so it seemed pointless to limit it to the upper grades. She pursed her lips, apparently unhappy to learn that all fifth graders were reading it, but she conceded, and *Hatchet* remained available for students of any grade to read.

The Greater Impact of Book Removal

Books that mentioned suicide; books that mentioned addiction; books that mentioned abuse—they all disappeared. The realistic fiction section, which I thought of as the "real life problem story" section, was full of happy family tales such as *The Penderwicks* by Jeanne Birdsall (2005). Although *The Penderwicks* happens to mention both divorce and the death of a parent in the first book, I guess it was brief enough to pass the review. Mild school bullying, having to move, and the death of a grandparent were acceptable life problems for the students at this school. For children, reading about characters who are grappling with the same life issues as themselves can be an important part of how they process what is going on in their lives. It can also help them to feel that they are not the only person who has ever had that experience in their lives. Removing books that had stories that dealt with hard issues did not mean those things would never happen in the lives of the students. It simply took away stories they might use to help process those events.

When I had initially agreed that inappropriate books should be removed, I had not grasped exactly how much of an impact it would have. Each book might be judged individually, but the collection as a whole was transformed by these actions. I did not realize that entire groups of people would have their voices silenced because it was uncomfortable. Or that removing these voices meant you were left with the books that held outdated caricatures to inform the young minds of what those groups of people were like. Books are supposed to be a gateway to the world, but our collection had become a gateway to a very specific kind of fantasy world where a lot of different kinds of people and problems had been erased.

A library without controversial books sounds simple. However, labeling topics as "inappropriate" is pronouncing a judgment on things that people experience in real life. Take the subject of racial profiling and police-involved shootings, for example. The school where I worked is located in the suburbs of a metropolitan area where five Black minors have been killed by the police in the past six years. Books touching on this issue would help students to consider other points of view and understand how different people can have different experiences in their lives. For the handful of Black students at that school, not having any books on that topic sends a strong message that not only is their perspective unnecessary but also their lives and experiences are somehow "inappropriate."

The time of year for the fifth-grade biography project rolled around, and I turned my attention to what was available in that section. It clearly had not had new additions in quite a few years. Once again, I submitted a list of books I hoped to purchase to add more biographies of people who were contemporary and not white males. Simone Biles, an Ohio native, was an easy approval. Hilary Rodham Clinton and Ruth Bader Ginsberg were a much harder sell. When given a denial, I responded that they were women of historical significance. I was told that they held political positions contrary to what the church affiliated with the school taught. This seemed like some new arbitrary standard created for those specific women. The biography section was full of books about people who were historically significant but who did or believed in any number of immoral things in their lives. I pointed out that we had over a dozen biographies of Thomas Jefferson, who owned slaves, which is also contrary to the moral teaching of that church. But, of course, that was glossed over in those biographies because it is an uncomfortable part of history.

I suppose it is appropriate, then, that I was able to purchase biographies of Hilary Rodham Clinton and Ruth Bader Ginsburg, which only spoke vaguely of their support for "women's rights," without ever using controversial words such as "abortion." But Ruth Bader Ginsburg's biography (*Ruth Bader Ginsburg: The case of R.B.G. vs. inequality* by Jonah Winter, 2017) did not stay on the shelf for very long. I had selected a picture-book biography that focused on her hardships in getting an education and going to law school. It was removed from the library for being "too derogatory about men." I was left speechless.

The purpose of a library is to give people access to information. A school library has a specific role in the education of children. Students should have access to materials that can help them to learn about significant people and events in history, science, or any other field. The type of broad censorship that was practiced at this library seemed to me to be a missed opportunity. Rather than denying the existence of people like Hilary Rodham Clinton or Ruth Bader Ginsburg, the school could be giving students access to the information and helping them understand how to evaluate it using critical thinking. Learning about different perspectives, putting information in context, and evaluating information for validity are all essential skills that schools are supposed to be teaching students. A school library that contains no controversial material is forfeiting the chance to prompt conversations between the students and their teachers or parents as they try to process and understand the information.

You are probably wondering which of these things was the turning point for me. The point where my departure became imminent was actually Halloween. The denomination this school was affiliated with had no issue with Halloween. Teachers and students alike checked out armloads of Halloween books. But the principal did not like it. She once vetoed a local author I had proposed for an author visit, simply because he had written a Halloween picture book.

One morning in October, I came in to find a strongly worded reprimand from the principal in my e-mail inbox. It said that she and the pastor had come by the library over the weekend and were dismayed to find a book promoting witchcraft prominently displayed on the front desk. They had taken the opportunity to go through the Halloween section and remove books that glorified evil, along with a few others in the library that had seemed inappropriate. She said I would find the barcodes in an envelope in my mailbox so that I could remove them from the system.

I was mystified as to which book could be the problem. I would not have been foolish enough to display anything but the most mundane books. I glanced over at the Harry Potter section, but it was still intact. Fetching the envelope, I began to go through the contents. I found my error. It was Roald Dahl's *The Witches* (1983), a book that was inaccurately filed under "classic" in my brain. I looked up the other offending books. Forty-five books had been removed, but they had nothing in common. The removal of *Ohio Ghost Hunter Guide* (2015) I could understand as it was probably too occult for the principal's standards, but *Frankenstein* (1818) was simply a fictional monster from Mary Shelley's imagination. Even books such as *Which Witch Is Which?* (1989) or *Haunted House Jokes* (1999), which were full of Halloween puns, had been removed.

I responded, giving some pushback on the issue. I said that I thought it was poor use of our resources to throw out that many books with no regard for content, especially since I had not been given sufficient funding to replace them with books that might have better content. I said that I thought most of the books removed fell into the moderation category that the principal had said was our goal. I asked for written standards, preferably developed with input from teachers and families, to guide the selection of books for the collection. I pointed out the haphazardness and subjectivity of the current process. Why was *The Witches* unacceptable but *The Wonderful Wizard of Oz* (1900) and *The Lion, the Witch, and the Wardrobe* (1950) fine? All three contain evil witch characters.

Predictably, nothing came from my protests except that I could no longer fly under the radar while committing petty acts of rebellion. Neither the principal nor the pastor was interested in developing a written set of standards for the collection. I was told that employees were expected to obey directives from the administration. I began to look at openings at area public libraries thinking that moving to a less-restrictive library environment after the end of the school year might be for the best. However, the pandemic put an end to my school library career even before the school year ended. The principal took advantage of the pandemic to let me know that my services were no longer needed.

Conclusion

Late in the summer, I was able to go back to the school library for a day to check in and reshelve books that had been returned by a drop-off event hastily organized at the close of the school year. It was the height of the pandemic, and it would be months before I ran across any of the students in person. This last day in the library was closure that I needed. I had so many great memories in that library: the books I had read aloud to the younger children, the student who had memorized my extremely erratic schedule so he could come up to check out extra books between classes, and the time Mo Willem's Pigeon books had won the March Madness Battle of the Books voting—an event that had the entire student body arguing over a bracket full of book titles for several weeks.

I checked in all of the books that had been left in piles on the floor and which were covering every flat surface. I took down the displays that had been set up so long ago back in March. I wanted the library to be left in a condition that showed how I had lovingly cared for it. Before I shut down the computer system one last time, I ran an audit on the difference in inventory during the three years I had worked there. Three thousand books had been removed. There is a lot less imagination and fantasy than there used to be. There is no profanity, no sex, no violence. There are also no hard real-life problems, no challenges, and no uncomfortable truths. It is now a library without controversy.

Books Discussed in This Chapter

Adams, D. (2007/1979). *The hitchhiker's guide to the galaxy*. Del Ray.

Alexander, K. (2014). *The crossover*. Houghton Mifflin Harcourt.

Barrie, J. M. (2003/1911). *Peter Pan*. Henry Holt and Co.

Baum, L. F. (1995/1900). *The wonderful wizard of Oz*. Penguin.

Birdsall, J. (2007/2005). *The Penderwicks: A summer tale of four sisters, two rabbits, and a very interesting boy*. Yearling.

Cleary, B. (2000/1983). *Dear Mr. Henshaw*. HarperTrophy.

Collins, S. (2008). *The hunger games*. Scholastic Press.

Collodi, C. (1996/1883). *Pinocchio*. Puffin Books.

Dahl, R. (1997/1983). *The witches*. Scholastic.

Dashner, J. (2009). *The maze runner*. Delacorte Press.

Glaser, K. Y. (2017). *The Vanderbeekers of 141st Street*. Houghton Mifflin Harcourt.

Hale, N. (2013). *Donner dinner party*. Amulet Books.

Hale, N. (n.d.). *Hazardous Tales* series. Harry N. Abrams.

Hatke, B. (2016). *Mighty Jack*. First Second Books.

Hawthorne, L. (2018). *Silent night*. Frances Lincoln Children's Books.

Hutchins, P. (1989). *Which witch is which?* Greenwillow Books.

Lewis, C. S. (2005). *The last battle*. HarperCollins Publishers.

Lewis, C. S. *The Narnia* series. HarperCollins Publishers.

Paolini, C. *The inheritance cycle* series. Alfred A. Knopf.

Paulsen, G. (2000/1987). *Hatchet*. Atheneum Books for Young Readers/Richard Jackson Books.

Phillips, L. (1999). *Haunted house jokes*. Puffin Books.

Quackenbush, J. (2015). *Ohio ghost hunter guide III*. 21 Crows Dusk to Dawn Publishing.

Reynolds, J. *Track* series. Atheneum Books/Caitlyn Dlouhy Books.

Shakespeare, W. (2011/1599). *As you like it*. Simon Schuster.

Shelley, M. W. (2018/1818). *Frankenstein*. Penguin Classics.

Tolkein, J. R. R. *Lord of the Rings* series. William Morrow.

Weir, A. (2014). *The Martian*. Ballantine Books.

Westerfeld, S. (2009). *Leviathan*. Simon Schuster Books for Young Readers.

Winter, J. (2017). *Ruth Bader Ginsburg: The case of R.B.G. vs. inequality*. Harry N. Abrams.

Young, A. (2016). *A unicorn named Sparkle*. Farrar, Straus and Giroux.

CHAPTER EIGHT

A Middle School Challenge: Championing Cabot's *Princess on the Brink*

Julie N. Hornick

Preparation

As a student in the School of Library and Information Science at the University of South Carolina in the early 2000s, I learned about and embraced the American Library Association's (ALA) core value of intellectual freedom. I also learned that, as a school librarian, there might be points of tension between my role as a school employee and my profession that would test my ability to adhere to that value. For instance, I knew I might be asked to walk a fine line between intellectual freedom and the rights of parents to access their children's school records, of which library records could be considered a part. The possibility of book challenges also loomed large. I had read about challenges and how school librarians had dealt with them, and I had learned that a strong collection policy and clear procedures to deal with challenges were the best approach. When I secured my first position as a school librarian, I looked into best practices and recommendations for building policies and procedures and felt prepared to deal with a challenge if one came my way.

After graduation, I worked for two years in a rural elementary school and then for two more in an elementary school in a suburban setting in South Carolina. During my time in the elementary schools, I assiduously read *Booklist* and *Kirkus* reviews when making decisions about adding to my collection. I also consulted the South Carolina Book Award and Wilson's lists, as well as other states, ALA, and recommended book lists. Additionally, I had robust challenge policies at each of the libraries and could have leaned on the district policy for dealing with challenges in my second school. Thankfully, no one ever called on me to implement the process.

After four years in elementary school libraries, I learned that the district I was in was building a new middle school. Having worked with middle school students in a previous job, I knew I enjoyed working with students that age. I notified the district I was interested in making the move to the new school and, after an interview with the principal, I was hired. As the librarian for the new school, part of my responsibility was to build the collection with nonfiction, reference, and video resources to support the curriculum, in addition to a fiction section that not only represented the classics but also, I hoped, would be of interest to a diverse population of middle school–aged students. I spent months working with my Follett representative, reading professional materials, and poring over the Follett Titlewave database to find just the right balance of books. My goal was to build as robust a collection as I could, understanding that middle school librarians have a challenging task. With students ranging in age from young ten-year-olds in fifth grade to students who have not yet aged out of eighth grade in their mid-teens, the middle school library needs to have a collection that appeals to different interests, abilities, and ages. I tried to keep this in mind as I was compiling lists of thousands of titles for the new library shelves.

In building the collection, I wanted above all to ensure that all students would find something on the shelves that would mirror their experiences and speak to who they were. In fiction, classics and award winners had a home on the shelves. Popular books by current authors were also represented. I especially wanted to make sure that students of color, Latinx students, and lesbian, gay, bisexual, queer/questioning, intersex, and asexual (LGBTQIA+) students would also find books that spoke to them. I further hoped that any student could pick up a book on any topic and find in it a window through which to view and come to an understanding of experiences different from their own.

Additionally, school librarians know that not all students come from secure home situations; they deal with things that we typically wish kids did not have to: pregnancy, violence, drugs, and suicide, to name just a few. Books have the potential to help students navigate these situations in their own lives. By reading about how characters in books negotiate similar circumstances, children can learn how to respond if they ever find themselves in a similar situation. This was always in the back of my mind as I chose books whose storylines did not shy away from difficult topics.

Did I think some of the titles I chose had the potential to cause controversy? Absolutely. The old adage says a good library has something in it to offend everyone. While I do not agree 100 percent with the sentiment, there is a kernel of truth there for school libraries. If a school library is truly meeting the educational, social, and emotional needs of its student users, some books will contain material that will offend certain sensibilities. My hope, admittedly idealistic, was that the stakeholders of my new school would be less offended and more accepting of titles that could be controversial.

As any seasoned school librarian knows, though, the potential always exists for someone to raise an objection to a title. Keeping this in mind, as in my previous library positions, I had a library policy manual specific to my school. I also made sure that I was familiar with the sections of the district handbook that dealt with challenges to materials and kept my fingers crossed that I would not have to use the information. When the school opened its doors, I was ready to welcome students, teachers, and parents to the library.

Facing the Challenge

One afternoon, at the end of the school day, a couple of months after the school opened in the fall of 2007, a parent came into the library and began to peruse the shelves. I thought nothing of it—all school stakeholders were welcome. I even had a section of parenting books that I hoped would bring teachers and parents into a space most viewed as mainly for students. I realized there was a problem, though, when the parent, a mother of an eighth-grade student, brought Meg Cabot's novel *Princess on the Brink* (2007) to me. She told me that her daughter had brought it home, and she had been shocked when she opened it up and read passages that she felt were offensive and inappropriate for any child to read. She then said she thought I might want to consider removing the book from the library. I was surprised. Of all the books in the library, I would not have picked one of Cabot's Princess Diaries books as the one most likely to face a challenge.

My mind began to race. Was this really going to be my first challenge? I tried to calm the adrenaline rush that set my heart racing and, as calmly as I could, replied that I would not be able to just remove a book. Knowing the policy, I told her that if she wished to bring a formal objection to the book, I could get her the form that she would need to fill out and submit. When she requested it, I made a copy for her, and she left the library. What was the likelihood that this parent would pursue this to the end? I hoped, as I had heard was often the case, that this would be the end of the matter; of course, it was not.

When the parent returned the form, on which she detailed her objections to the book's portrayal of a teenaged girl contemplating initiating a sexual relationship with her boyfriend, the challenge process began. This meant convening a school-level committee that included a school administrator, teachers from the building, a school library media specialist from another middle school in the district, and community members. As per the district policy, the committee read the book and scheduled a hearing of the arguments from both sides for either removing the book from the shelves or retaining it.

As the school librarian, I was charged with presenting the argument in favor of retention. To prepare for the hearing, I read articles on other book challenges around the country and combed through the information provided by the ALA on intellectual freedom, the freedom to read, and book challenges. I read up on pertinent court cases and submitted a challenge report to the Office for Intellectual Freedom.[1] I hoped that the matter would be resolved at the school level, but I was preparing myself in case the outcome was not favorable. Further, I frequently spent time asking myself how far I would be willing to take the fight for this book. I knew that I would be willing to fight this within the school district, but if the district voted to remove it, would I be willing to pursue it beyond the district? Would I be willing to risk my job over the issue by refusing to accede to censorship? In those early days of the process, I could not come to a satisfactory answer.

In my statement, I presented the merits of the book, including the popularity of the Princess Diaries series, the fact that the main character, Mia, ultimately decides *against* entering into a sexual relationship with her boyfriend because she does not feel emotionally ready to do so, and the fact that the local public library was planning an event to celebrate this newly published book. Further, as a librarian committed to the freedom to read and to the Library Bill of Rights, I grounded my argument in the belief that "materials should not be proscribed or removed because of partisan or doctrinal disapproval" and that "libraries should challenge censorship in the fulfillment of their responsibility to provide information and enlightenment" (ALA, 2019). In my statement, I agreed that this parent had the right to limit what her child could read, but I argued that one parent should not have the power to dictate what every student in the school could access.

On the day the committee met, I presented the statement I had prepared and waited, hopefully, for the verdict. I assumed that the administrator and the other district librarian on the committee would fight as hard as I to stop the challenge. I was severely disappointed, then, when I learned that the committee had voted to remove the book from the library. I later found out that the administrator had tried to argue for retaining the book but had been overruled—even the other media specialist had not stood up for the book.

Rather than give in to discouragement, my disappointment galvanized me, and I chose to pursue the matter to the next level. At the time, district policy clearly stated that any party who disagreed with the school-level decision could request that the book be reviewed by a district-level Citizen's Review Committee. Believing strongly that allowing the ban to stand might eventually embolden other parents, stakeholders, or community members to target other books whose content they did not agree with, I determined that I would request a review of the decision and informed my principal that I would be taking that next step.

Unfortunately, my principal made it clear to me that they would prefer I not pursue the matter any further. I did not feel, however, that I could in good conscience step away from the fight. I knew there were books in the collection that others might consider even more controversial than the most recent installment of the Princess Diaries series, and I felt allowing this ban to stand without fighting for this book would open the door to other challenges. So, against the wishes of my principal, I informed the district that I would like to pursue the matter at the next level, and a review committee was formed.

As part of preparing myself to face whatever might come, I drafted a letter to author Meg Cabot to let her know that the school had decided to remove *Princess on the Brink*. As a bolster to my argument, I also asked who she felt the target audience was for the book. She wrote back to me to thank me for fighting for her book and told me that she had intended it for middle school students. After receiving my letter, she wrote a blog post about the challenge that celebrated the fact that she had written something that was being banned for encouraging "young girls to be strong, independent thinkers in today's society," and that portrayed one female instructing "another not to accept the traditional gender roles that have been thrust upon them for centuries by men" (Cabot, 2008). Apparently, the parent who had brought the challenge did not appreciate being memorialized in Cabot's blog, because, after being contacted by the parent who had read Cabot's post, my principal came to talk to me. They expressed concern that I had written to Cabot without checking with them, but, as I noted, I was within my rights to speak to others about the issue, and nothing more came of the parent's complaint.

For the next month or so I played the waiting game. I knew the committee was pursuing its task because I had to make sure that all members had a copy of the book to read. The title was new enough that there were only a couple of copies at any of the schools in the district, so, ironically, more were purchased for the committee's use. There was little more I could do except run the library program at my school and wait for the school board to meet.

As that meeting drew closer, I was approached by a reporter from the local newspaper who was seeking more information about the book challenge. Not wanting to take a misstep, I contacted the school district's information officer before speaking with the reporter, to see if there were any limitations on what I could say as an employee of the district. I was assured that the district would not prohibit me from speaking freely to the press if I chose to do so. I called the reporter back and provided what information I could about the challenge and how I felt about it. I mentioned that I could, if required to do so, flag the catalog record for the book so sixth-grade students would know that the book contained material that might be considered too mature. This would codify, for this particular title, what my practice already was; that is, whenever a younger student wanted to check out a book that contained more mature themes, I typically let them know about the content and told them if they were unsure, they should check with their parents before reading the title. I never, however, refused to check the book out to them, nor did I ever tell them they should not read it.

On the evening of the school board meeting, in front of a large gathering, the review committee recommended that the book be retained on the shelves of the school library, and the board voted to accept their recommendation. It was a relief, for me, to know that the process had worked—that one family would not get to determine what all other students in the school or district could access. The reporter from *The Post and Courier* approached me to ask how I felt about the decision, and I told her that I felt they had made the right choice (Hagen, 2008). I went to work the next day and put the book back on the shelf with all of Cabot's other Princess Diaries books. The district policy stated that the decision of the school board would be final and could not be revisited, and so I assumed that would be the end of it.

Conclusion: Aftermath

Not long after the school board meeting, my principal came to the library along with a district administrator. They asked to talk to me privately, and when we went into my office, they told me the parent had attended a meeting of school principals and was continuing to pursue her cause. They told me they wanted me to put the book behind the circulation desk and add a note to the catalog telling students to ask at the desk if they wanted to check it out. Additionally, they wanted me to draft a permission form that would need to be signed by a parent or guardian before the student could check out the book. I knew enough about the browsing habits of my students to know that if the book were not on the shelf, they would not know it was available. The further barrier of a permission form would virtually guarantee that students would simply not bother to try to check it out.

In essence, this was a back-alley way of effectively removing the book from circulation. I told the principal and administrator that it seemed like they were going against the spirit of the school board's decision; that it was just another way to censor the book. They assured me their intent was not to censor, but I explained that regardless of their *intent*, censorship was the net result. I had to make a decision, though, and I capitulated, but told them I was doing it under heavy protest. I have regretted, in the years that followed, that I gave in so quickly. I knew, though, that working in a state with little to no union presence left me vulnerable to termination for whatever reason the school or district felt was just cause. I assumed that insubordination on that level would almost certainly be viewed as a justifiable reason for me to lose my job.

After they left, I went to the shelf, pulled the two copies we had, and put them in a drawer at the circulation desk. That afternoon I drafted a permission form, made several copies, and placed them with the book. All the positive feelings I had after the school board meeting were gone, and my personal relationship with the school principal, which had been cordial, never recovered. All of my trust in their ability to "do the right thing" and support me in my work were gone. I remained at that school for eight more years, through two more principals. In those years, *Princess on the Brink* was never again checked out.

I think often of this episode, and even more so in recent years, as the freedom to read has been under attack by political groups who seek to limit children's access to reading material and ideas that challenge the narrow worldview of those groups. For readers of this chapter who may face challenges, and there will be too many who do, I wish that I had fought harder, that I had stood my ground when I was told I needed to restrict access to the book. I was not sure at the time, though, in only my fifth year as a school librarian, if I wanted to risk unemployment. Later, after several more years at the middle school, I promised myself if I were ever in the same position again, I would take that extra step.

Students need to know that school librarians support them, in all their diversity, with everything in their power. The library can be a place of acceptance and refuge for children and young adults who may not get the support they need from their peers and families. But it cannot be such a place if they know the librarian is willing to remove books whose characters look like them and share similar life experiences; books that tell the truth of the world as they know it; or books that show them how to navigate the always difficult waters of adolescence in honest ways. Be that safe space for the students you serve.

Note

1. The resources that were available at that time may be viewed on the pages from the American Library Association's website via the Internet Archive Wayback Machine.

References

American Library Association. (2019, January 29). *Library Bill of Rights.* https://www.ala.org/advocacy/intfreedom/librarybill

Cabot, M. (2008, January 7). *Banned in the USA*. Meg Cabot. https://www.megcabot.com/2008/01/banned-in-the-usa

Hagen, M. B. (2008, February 12). Contract extended for Dorchester 2 chief schools' Pye gets positive rating: School to keep challenged book. *The Post and Courier.*

Book Discussed in This Chapter

Cabot, M. (2007). *Princess on the brink*. Harper Teen.

CHAPTER NINE

Beyond the Paperwork: The Hidden Impact of a Title Challenge

Joe Schweiss

Introduction

In the fall of 2021, the Bullitt County Public Library received a challenge to the graphic novel *Gender Queer: A Memoir* (2020). I was the library director for the system at the time, and while almost everyone at the library was expecting a challenge to come someday soon, I did not anticipate how this one would come to be. One of the state legislators representing Bullitt County, presumably informed by little more than three screenshots from the work in question and the list of approximately 850 titles that Texas state representative Matt Krause had recently called into question (Chappell, 2021), took to social media to rile up his followers and encourage them to take on the task of getting the title removed from the library's shelves. The call to action post would later be deleted, but the staff and administration at Bullitt County Public Library had been closely monitoring the situation and were keenly aware that this would not be a traditional request.

What followed was not just the filing of a reconsideration request but also a stream of e-mails carbon copied to state legislators and a conservative watchdog group (No Left Turn In Education), an open records request looking for names of staff responsible for selecting particular titles, and additional social media posturing. We had prepared to defend the inclusion of the title to our collection, but we had not prepared for the impacts that would be brought on by the intimidation tactics being utilized alongside the challenge. What follows is a breakdown of what to expect, how to deal with the negative impacts, and how to pull positive things out of a bad situation.

I really thought I was prepared for a challenge.

As a director for a suburban library system that had not recently received a challenge, I was confident that the majority of others in my position and I had done everything necessary to stay ahead of the curve. Many of us had done the big work to ready our libraries for a challenge. We had followed the news stories, reviewed and revised our collection development policies, and identified the titles most likely to receive requests for reconsideration (anything on a Pride display or by a BIPOC [Black, Indigenous, and person of color] author, sadly). We had told ourselves it was a matter of when, not if.

I did all of that, but I was not fully prepared for the challenge.

Policies and procedures tend to remove real-world messiness from challenge events, leaving out the surrounding drama, and instead creating a mental image of something more akin to a reference transaction. A lone, unhappy patron will come in, item in hand, upset after starting in on the title and having found something objectionable, wanting to understand why the library owns this material, but also fully willing to engage in discussion and listen to the reasons the library believes that an item is worth keeping on the shelves. Instead, as with many actual reference transactions, the experience is far more complicated when it exits the theoretical realm.

When my library found out a challenge was imminent, I would love to say that the worst thing that happened was that we all rolled our eyes too hard and hurt ourselves holding back chortles. In my mind, I thought my board members, my library's staff, and I would all high five each other and recite our collection development policy from memory in unison while filling out reconsideration request response forms. I would love to say that I did not have a twenty-minute phone call in the parking lot of a liquor store on a Saturday morning at 9:30, having left a different liquor store just prior to taking the call. It would be a better story to say that I led a march to the county offices for my library to receive a letter of commendation as a token of appreciation for our awesomeness, instead of admitting that I actually spent much of the day responding to frantic texts, watching events unfold on Facebook, and dreading what might happen next.

When a challenge happens, the feelings that arise are not nearly as much fun as what some of us envision. In reality, the psychological impacts are far less jolly and will be felt at every level of the organization. Emotions will run high, fear and uncertainty chief among them. There will be doubt and anger.

Regret and remorse will make multiple appearances. None of these things should be given the opportunity to limit the positive impacts that can come from the experience, which can be achieved by using it as an opportunity to learn, upgrade, and boost team dynamics.

Negative Impacts of a Challenge

Challenges are not always the domain of the lone patron working independently. Many challenges are now the product of "grassroots" campaigns being pushed by national political strategists, think tanks, and elected officials and acted upon by "average citizens" with aligned values. Social media efforts drum up outrage using screenshots and excerpts taken completely out of context, requests are made for taxpayers to go to their libraries to complain, and a layer of separation provides an opportunity for the influencers and masterminds to pretend like the uprising and outrage is coming directly from the public.

Staff and board members can rightly experience a little bit of fear when facing a seemingly swirling maelstrom of public outrage over a title. In my experience, the combination of social media prompting by a public official and screenshots pulled to make a legitimate work of art look potentially pornographic can make normally rational people suddenly develop irrational concerns. Could we be sued today? Could we be sued in the future by someone claiming emotional damages from having read the title as a child? What are we currently doing to keep child pornography off our shelves? Is our collection development policy too liberal?

Some of the fears that arise are legitimate modern concerns. Will I be publicly named for being involved in the material review? What is the fallout if we bow to pressure? What is the fallout if we fight the challenge? Fears over the outcome are destined to arise, and voicing those fears can easily lead to arguments and resentment.

Doubts are also a byproduct of a material challenge. There will be doubts about the policy and procedures in place about how the library handles challenges. There will be doubts about the process the library uses to select titles to add to the collection. Doubters will advise you to keep your head down and not try to tell your side of the story. Saddest of all, there will be doubts that the library should offer titles that are in any way controversial.

Originally issued in 1953, the American Library Association's (ALA) Freedom to Read Statement (ALA, 2004) was in part a direct response to McCarthyism, a movement that attacked anything that was viewed as unusual or subversive by utilizing questionable tactics meant to suppress opposition. The obvious parallels to recent attacks on "unusual" titles should bolster the importance of a document that proposes "it is in the public interest for publishers and librarians to make available the widest diversity of views and expressions, including those that are unorthodox, unpopular, or considered dangerous by the majority," but a public and vocal attack on a single or small group of titles is designed to have a psychological impact to undermine one's certainty. The tactic can plant a seed of doubt that leads to second-guessing our procedures, policies, and values. Even the most resolute person may wonder if the library's beliefs are too far outside of those of its community.

Another likely outcome of an aggressive challenge is anger. Many of the recently challenged titles are targeted at members of our community whose rights are tenuous and who already feel marginalized by the majority. The materials in question contain highly personal stories that provide something relatable to people who often feel actively shunned by society. So many of our patrons have found acceptance and a sense of community through books and other items on our shelves that they have not been able to find elsewhere. When these titles come under attack, it can rightfully feel like an attack on our most vulnerable populations. When the attacks come based on out-of-context passages or panels that ignore the work as a whole, it feels like a slap in the face. Anger toward the patron filing the challenge and even society at large is a natural response.

Anger can also occur among the staff and board if there are differences in opinion regarding a challenge. An issue like this hits a nerve that is directly related to why many of us got into this field: providing access to essential materials for folks in need. Even the slightest show of doubt can spike tensions when tensions are already heightened. Wavering or outright suggesting that we act against our core beliefs will undoubtedly trigger some arguments and regrettable statements. Disagreements that come from within can cause very difficult situations that will ripple long term if not addressed properly.

Depending on one's level of preparation, regret over what was not done in advance of a challenge can easily be felt. This may be easy to deal with in isolation, but when combined with other negative feelings, this regret can be substantial and detrimental. Time that would be better spent on dealing with the situation might instead be spent on beating oneself up or, worse yet, pointing fingers at others over what else could have been done to improve policies and procedures in advance of a challenge. A form that is slightly out of date or an incomplete review procedure might cause someone to spiral, especially if that person is already experiencing any form of imposter syndrome. It is easy to lose track of a library's accomplishments and focus on perceived negatives in a moment of crisis.

Positive Impacts of a Challenge

Despite that long list of negative issues mentioned above, there are positive things that come from a challenge. How many positives can be extracted from such an event depends on the overall health of the organization. A staff and board in alignment with a system's objectives and policies can come out of this experience with far more positives than negatives. A system with issues can also come out stronger than at the start of the process, but success will depend on its ability to take advantage of the opportunities a challenge provides.

One big step toward turning the experience into something beneficial is to come to terms with the situation and accept that it is happening. This might sound like an obvious bit of self-help, but accepting the situation makes it far easier to deal with the challenge instead of fighting against the circumstances. Accept that the process is already in motion and that much can be gained or lost. Accept that, regardless of how well your library prepared for this, your library needs to deal with this and continue to provide materials that meet the needs of your patrons. Accept the fact that this might be the first crisis that many in your library staff have faced, and they might have some initial panic-induced responses that will improve as things proceed. Most importantly, unless this challenge was filed by a huge group of your community members, accept that the challenge does not necessarily accurately represent how your patrons collectively feel about your library and the title or titles in question.

That last piece of acceptance can be the hardest to achieve, thanks primarily to social media. Social media is not a major factor in every event, but there are good chances that it was involved in prompting the challenge you are experiencing or in attempts by the challenger to drum up support for their actions. Either way, one hundred angry voices on social media sharing their opinions on what does and does not belong in a library can be both intimidating and heartbreaking. All of the comments can make it seem like the entire community wants to pull every book off the shelves and lock the doors forever, especially in the initial wave. Two amazing things can happen given some time to let things simmer. First, there is an excellent chance that members of your community will act as the voice of reason and voice opinions that fall in line with the Freedom to Read Statement. Second, you will hopefully be able to come to the conclusion that these voices, loud as they may be, make up only a sliver of your community. This is not to say that libraries should ignore the voices of minority groups; instead, this is to say that someone or some group being loud and angry does not necessarily equate to being right.

A challenge is a great event to prompt some learning opportunities that will help the organization and the staff. Even the threat of a challenge or just the desire to be ready for one is a great reason to learn more about applicable laws and regulations. Depending on your location, challenges can be accompanied by open records requests. Not every request is something that needs to be answered, and it is better to know the law rather than assume every request is completely legitimate. In many states, there are no requirements to create new records if they do not already exist. If your library is creating records that do not preserve the anonymity of the staff, consider changing them to protect their privacy. If there are records being created that are nothing more than a byproduct of "that's the way we have always done it," then consider stopping their creation entirely.

Take some time to learn the shortcomings of your challenge process. Now is a wonderful time to start making upgrades. Are your challenge forms on your website, and can they be submitted online? Consider making the process difficult to spam, or make interested patrons request the forms before they can access them. All it takes is for the link to your challenge form to get shared online, and you might find yourself sifting through a multitude of illegitimate requests. Does the process set unrealistic expectations for when the challenger can expect a response? Is the wording able to account for holidays or illness? Are there limitations in place for how frequently a title will go through the reconsideration process? What happens to all of the copies of a title during the challenge process? Make whatever changes necessary to limit the ability of people in the community to effectively remove a title from circulation by filing successive challenges on it.

After reviewing your challenge filing documents and procedures, take your internal, staff-focused challenge procedures and documents under consideration. How will people be selected to serve on the reconsideration committee? Using a random selection tool will help keep the process fair and unbiased. What can you utilize to preserve anonymity of the reviewers? Focus on processes that do not create a lot of identifiable paper trails. Phone conversations are recommended, as are the use of anonymous online survey tools to collect individual reviews from the reviewers. Members of the administration, who should be acting as the point of contact for these events, can compile the reviews into a report that goes to the person that filed the challenge. The report should include only information related to the review of the material and overall conclusion. This sustains a fair process without putting library staff at immediate risk of intimidation or exposure by having their names on a report. While this may seem a bit conspiratorial, there is no such thing as being too careful when dealing with folks that share beliefs and tactics with groups such as the Proud Boys. This is the ideal time to step up and prove how much we value library staff.

In that same vein, the team bonds within the library can be strengthened by smart handling of the situation. Protecting the staff by not revealing identities is a big part, but other things are also important. Make sure folks know that they can speak their minds during staff discussions, even if they disagree. Let them know that the values that they are constantly being told are important and that they have to embody *are* important because they are indeed the same ones that are guiding the organization's actions.

Staff should feel that the convictions that led them into this profession are universally held at every level. Working to make everyone on staff feel involved, appreciated, and empowered will not only help the organization get through the process smoothly, but also solidify team relations and boost morale.

Another opportunity to pivot this experience into something positive is to go public with the story and let folks know what is happening. This can be accomplished without naming the person or persons that filed the challenge, but if the circumstances were unusual, that information is worth sharing. Let nearby library systems know what is happening, including those in area schools. Sending a warning signal to others will not only help them prepare for what might be in their future but also help build a support network. Contact the press, including any outlets you suspect would be in favor of defending the First Amendment. The public should know what your library's convictions are and that the organization will stand for them. With the country seemingly moving in reverse in matters of acceptance and civil rights, your patrons that would benefit from keeping "controversial" titles on the shelves need to know that libraries have not stopped progressing. Folks that think that libraries can be intimidated and pushed around also need to know that we will not give up without fighting for what is right.

To take further advantage of the situation, really get out and advocate for libraries and freedom of speech. Let people know that a few lines or a few panels do not make art into pornography. Still shots from Disney movies can appear downright filthy when taken out of context, and passages from the Bible can be isolated to make the subject of the text seem like incest or hate speech. Libraries contain something for everyone, but with more genres and titles coming out than ever before, all materials are not for everyone, nor should they have to be. Nearly seventy years later, the sustained need for the ALA's Freedom to Read Statement proves that many things have not changed. While much of that is certainly disappointing, the fact that libraries have stuck to their core values should be broadcast and celebrated. It is essential for libraries to remain available for all, which is possible only if a wide variety of materials are on the shelf. Libraries have to continue to operate with the trust that patrons will be willing to walk away from titles that they do not like.

Conclusion

Overall, going through a material challenge, or multiple challenges, in the modern age can be a harrowing experience. Undoubtedly, it can be stressful, trying, and disheartening. With some hard work and determination, though, the experience can actually strengthen your organization and build support for the library within your community.

References

American Library Association, Association of American Publishers. (2004, June 30). *The freedom to read statement*. https://www.ala.org/advocacy/intfreedom/freedomreadstatement

Chappell, B. (2021, October 28). *A Texas lawmaker is targeting 850 books that he says could make students feel uneasy*. NPR. https://www.npr.org/2021/10/28/1050013664/texas-lawmaker-matt-krause-launches-inquiry-into-850-books

Book Discussed in This Chapter

Kobabe, M. (2020). *Gender queer: A memoir*. Turtleback Books.

PART 3

External Support for Librarians

CHAPTER TEN

Supporting Texas Librarians Facing Materials Challenges

Dorcas Hand

Introduction

I worked for more than forty years in school libraries and cared about students' freedom to read throughout—but it was never all that hard to build a collection that represented many perspectives and reflected my students. As school awareness of the need to diversify the student body and my own awareness of diversifying the library collection progressed over time, I worked to include more titles that portrayed different kinds of families and different cultural perspectives.

During this period, I faced three challenges to books in the collection. One was completely unusual; one an internal challenge; and one for a one-off title by an author of a very popular series. I stood strong through two, defending them successfully; the last was not age appropriate, but I had not read it in advance given the popularity of the rest of the series.

My Place (1994) by Nadia Wheatley was my first challenge. It is a charming picture book that includes colorful illustrations and maps, telling the story of a particular place over two hundred years. Because it was a bit sophisticated in concept despite the picture-book format, I had cataloged it as fiction. Nevertheless, a precocious kindergartener found it and requested to check it out. His father thought it was inappropriate to expose kindergarten students to Rousseau's concept of the "Noble Savage." My principal did not agree; all was resolved quickly.

Philip Pullman's *The Golden Compass* (1995) was a bit trickier. At the time, I worked in a school with religious ties. The head of school felt pressure to remove the book on the day the movie was released; he was convinced the criticism of church hierarchy in the fictional plot would be ill-received in our community. He gave me forty-five minutes of warning before sending an e-mail to all the parents. I responded with the standard wording about following policy, which he had approved—but he felt it was important to act before the church did. I sat quietly through calls from parents and press, referring all of these to his office. Amazingly, the parents were vehement in their support of the library, insisting that the book be returned to the shelf—which it was, by the next morning. It was an intense twenty-four hours, in which my silence spoke louder than any press interview—a statement that is so seldom true. And eventually, the local church leadership made it clear that the book was never at risk.

Lastly, we come to the *Willow Falls* series by Wendy Mass. The series was a hot topic with my fifth-grade girls; they could not get enough of them. I was buying whatever I could find by Mass—including *Heaven Looks a Lot Like the Mall* (2008). This last title has an older main character who has not made great decisions; I remember a theme around weight obsession as one aspect of the story. One family called the school, irate that it would be given to a fifth grader, so I got the book returned and read it. It was not suitable for my library. The school ended in the eighth grade. The book's treatment of anorexia was too glib for the audience, especially the youngest middle schoolers. These parents were right that our students did not need to read about a sixteen-year-old's mistakes in the way this book was written. I pulled the book.

In 2016, I retired and began advocating for school libraries, with no clue of the excitement ahead.

The Next Phase

We all know the earthquake that began to rumble across the library world in the fall of 2021: organized efforts to ban books from libraries. As part of my role in the Texas Library Association (TLA), I work with advocacy and related concerns. The speed with which these challenges were coming catalyzed TLA to find ways to support our members behind the scenes as well as publicly. Book bans continue to come fast and furious. One idea that came up was a helpline that Texas librarians could call for moral support and resources as they face intellectual freedom challenges. I stepped up to co-coordinate this helpline and went to work. The American Library Association Office for Intellectual Freedom (ALA OIF) does amazing work, which we do not want to duplicate or replace, but having a Texas peer librarian to talk to seemed a good idea, especially someone with familiarity with Texas laws and personalities. (Just to be super clear, we do not offer legal advice.)

Why would I do this? I remember feeling very alone when those challenges came to me many years ago. I was, for most of those years, the only librarian on the PS-8 campus—who could I talk to? I have always found membership in both TLA and ALA important for the network of peers to which they connected me. The attitudes coming from a few loud Texans require that librarians have help at the ready, help with more local awareness than ALA would have from Chicago. Plus, I had time to pull together the structure needed and train the volunteers.

The Helpline is open to any librarian; membership in TLA is not required. The link to request support is on the TLA website (https://txla.org/tools-resources/intellectual-freedom/tools-resources/).

The volunteers who answer calls to the hotline come from TLA membership. We initially invited the Intellectual Freedom Committee and the main divisions. Plenty of volunteers stepped up. Intellectual freedom challenges in different library types do look different. Youth challenges are often similar between school and public libraries, but in academic libraries and public libraries, adult services issues are more subtle, and the structure of both the complaints and the governance is different.

Fear can be a motivator of behavior with respect to book challenges. Who wants to confront potential job loss because there are materials in your library that someone deems inappropriate? Is it not easier to just eliminate the problematic titles?

While the answer might seem to be an easy yes, self-censorship is not best for your library patrons or community. And this is ultimately the purpose of the helpline. Many Texas librarians are the only librarians in their community—school or public libraries in rural areas do not have a community of librarians for moral support. And even in larger public library or school systems, some people are more willing to stand up to challenges than others. Moral support is really important. When you do not feel alone, it is easier to stand strong and develop creative ways to do what is right. Direct confrontation is sometimes necessary. The helpline volunteers have begun to create some tip sheets for specific topics that we get repeatedly, like how to handle challenges from within your organization. This format allows a few of us to brainstorm together the best resources and put them into a format that other volunteers can use.

As I dug into this work of planning the TLA Intellectual Freedom Helpline, I discovered Shannon Oltmann's *Practicing Intellectual Freedom in Libraries* (2019), which helped me better understand the breadth and depth of intellectual freedom concerns. Self-censorship is the abrogation of library ethics. Intellectual freedom is a core value of librarianship, that is, intellectual freedom for every library patron regardless of age, background, or topic of interest. But standing alone in the face of the vehemence often presented by challengers, whether your supervisor, a random community member, or a parent of one of your students, is both threatening and discouraging. Librarians have been steeped in the belief that open access to information is forever a good thing, that information helps students and patrons to better understand the world and to form useful opinions that will inform their voting, their community activities, and their work. We look to the ALA Freedom to Read Statement (2006a), the ALA Library Bill of Rights (2006b) and its myriad interpretations, and our ALA Core Values and Code of Ethics (2010) for confirmation of these tenets. We learn them in library school and refer back to them repeatedly over our careers.

The current onslaught of organized challenges brings to mind *1984* (by George Orwell, 1949) and its Big Brother mentality denying individual freedom of thought, and even the 2022 Newbery Medal winner *The Last Cuentista* (by Donna Barbra Higuera, 2021), in which a misguided collective works to deny freedom of thought to guarantee the calm and controlled behavior of all involved as they inhabit new planets after Earth is obliterated. Humans need variety and independence to use our creativity to the benefit of all. Those times and places where thought control has become the rule, enforced by the elites, may succeed for a while, but the controlled population is forever finding small ways to be individual. These titles also bring to mind current news stories set in other nations of our world, nations the United States has prided itself on not resembling.

So, if self-censorship (or any form of censorship) is not the answer, what can the helpline offer, and how could it be organized to help Texas librarians? To begin, I saw two aspects: a structure for the volunteers and callers to work within, and a collection of resources. Once the hotline was up and running, I began to see gaps in the resources that I could research and specific hot topics to support.

Structure

While I began to compile useful resources, we reached out to membership for volunteers. We requested basic contact information, including the kind of library where they work now as well as an outline of their experience in libraries. We also asked if potential volunteers had ever experienced a challenge themselves—saying no did not disqualify them, but we keep that information on file as we decide who gets the next question.

We realized it will be very important throughout our work to use personal e-mail addresses and phones: we ask that all Helpline work be kept off their library's Wi-Fi, devices, and phones. Many librarians are fearful for their jobs, even as they decide to stand for intellectual freedom. When they seek support, they want to be as sure as possible that their conversations remain private. We already see press Freedom of Information Act (FOIA) inquiries on the topic of censorship generally; we want to prevent either our volunteers or our callers from being persecuted. Now we have a robust list of ready and willing folks, which includes six to eight volunteers for each type of library (school, public, and academic). Once I had these names, I spent about thirty minutes with each, both to get a sense of them for matching to callers and to show them the resources I had compiled.

When a request comes into the helpline, we give it a case number to protect confidentiality. Many of the helpline callers are very concerned that no one knows they have asked for help; we remain mindful of that need. After a volunteer speaks with them, we ask the volunteer to complete an internal report: what the question was, what resources were offered, and how they felt the situation was resolved. TLA needs some sense of what the helpline has done, and the helpline needs to know if there are types of resources we would like but do not have. None of this will ever be public.

Resources

I found resources in e-mail, on Facebook and Twitter, and through ALA and TLA websites. Initially, I just grabbed them and put everything in a single Google Doc. I began with the basic intellectual freedom resources listed on every state library organization website and largely based on the ALA OIF offerings. But then I discovered the National Coalition Against Censorship (NCAC), PEN America, and many more organizations offering toolkits on various topics. There were newspaper and journal articles from all over, more practically every day. The National Council of Teachers of English, several state library organizations, and other groups have made statements in support of intellectual freedom. In a very short time, I had twenty pages of resources collected—it was time for my sense of organization to kick in.

In December 2021, this was the topic list:

Bookmarked Table of Contents

- Proactive Tips—Infographics
- Worried about a Possible Challenge
  - All Library Types
  - Schools
  - Public Libraries
  - Academic Libraries
  - Boards of Trustees and Friends Groups
  - CRT Focus
  - History Focus
  - LGBTQ+ Focus
  - Privacy
  - Student Activism
  - Books by Problematic Authors
  - Internal Policy/Collection Changes—School
- ALA OIF Reporting
- Toolkits

Bookmarked Table of Contents (*Cont*)

- Mental Health of Librarians
- Other Resources
- Immediate Response Needed
- Support and Guidance beyond TLA
- Reporting Challenges
- Reference Documents
- Other Organizations to Follow
- Current Articles with Quotes and Support
- Legal Info and Support

In early February 2022, I reorganized this as follows:

Bookmarked Table of Contents

- Proactive Tips and Infographics
- Worried about a Possible Challenge
    - All Library Types
    - School Libraries
    - Public Libraries
    - Academic Libraries
    - Boards of Trustees and Friends Group
- Types of Challenges and Related Topics
    - CRT Focus
    - History Focus
    - LGBTQ+ Focus
    - Privacy
    - Programs
    - Books by "Problematic" Authors and Author Voices
    - Graphic Novels
- Books under Attack
    - Internal Policy/Collection Challenges
    - School—Internal Challenges
    - Silent/Self-Censorship
    - Parents' Rights
- Digital Resources under Attack
- Engaging Stakeholders
    - Engaging Students
    - Engaging Parents
    - Engaging Teachers/Faculty/Admins
    - Engaging the Community
    - Engaging Your Governing Board
- Toolkits
- Mental Health of Librarians
- Other Resources—Texas and Beyond
    - #FReadom
    - ALA/OIF
    - Policy Templates from ALA
    - NCAC
- Reference Documents *(bookmark)*
    - *Collection of Anti-Censorship Statements*
- Other Organizations to Follow
- Legal Support
- Additional Articles with Quotes and Support *(bookmark)*
- Understanding FOIA

It became clearer and clearer how many subtopics were important to separate out—and we still discover specific questions that need better support. This compilation will continue to grow, but it is carefully protected. Every volunteer has full access and can copy/paste whichever few resources are most pertinent to the question at hand when they are answering the helpline. No caller needs the stress of a huge list of resources; they just need immediate recommendations to help them today. Additionally, we do not need to hand our book ban enthusiasts the compilation of our thinking.

As can be seen, the opening topics are more preparatory, offering callers advice to head off potential challenges. By now, as I write in June 2022, we certainly hope that every library and district has taken care of these details, but having the resources for future reference is still important. Every year, new librarians enter jobs that may not have kept good records or filled in these essential policies appropriately—or prepared to stand against governance when needed.

Then we focused on types of challenges both by topic and by origin. The fight about digital resources is only just beginning, but we hope to have thought ahead. In addition, I have pulled together toolkits and statements from all kinds of sources. While all of these focus on intellectual freedom and First Amendment rights, they use different vocabulary—and sometimes those differences are useful locally.

Example Topics

Heading Off a Challenge

The first line of defense against challenges remains preparation—and Texas has too many school librarians and district leaders who had not attended to these details over time. We also have many librarians who are not members of TLA, do not have master of library science degrees, and may not be fully certified. We have district superintendents and school board members unfamiliar with the basic policies who think they can just do as they wish. The rural districts may have only one K–12 school and no district leadership with much library awareness. With that in mind, and recognizing how many resources are available to support stronger policies ahead of actual challenges, I gathered them—everything from the usual ALA links to some infographics I found from Texas and beyond. Sometimes we need to see the same information in a new way.

ALA offers a Selection & Reconsideration Policy Toolkit for Public, School, & Academic Libraries (2016), which gives basic guidance to ensure every library policy is adequate. Additionally, there are articles such as "What's It Like to Be the Target of a Book Banning Effort? School

Librarian Martha Hickson Tells Her Story" (Hickson, 2022), which offers a few new insights into how to write your policy. There are also infographics like the one found in Ryzewski (2021). This may help a different administrator or school board member see that these policies are largely the same in all districts across Texas. The helpline resources have been culled from publicly available sources from across the country, found through articles, e-mails, and conversations with my wide network of peer librarians.

Privacy: Parent E-mail Alerts to Book Circulation

Libraries do their best to protect patrons' privacy—all patrons, including minors—even when it seems easiest to not do that. So, I collected the Privacy Field Guides offered by OIF (ALA OIF, 2014). Each topic has its own nine- to thirteen-page guide; all are totally free to access online.

I saw, as the book challenges of 2021–22 heated up, that some school districts were already automatically notifying parents of books their children were borrowing. These administrators were not steeped in librarian ethics and values and were caught between parents and information. This "movement" snowballed widely, and some library management system vendors began to see how such auto-notification could be enabled. In response, many librarians rose up together in collective concern for their students' privacy. I watched the fierce online debate and the vendor responses until, finally, the vendors backed off (Burbage, 2022; Maughan, 2022).

Public debate on a dicey topic remains the most likely way to make a change. In the process of that widespread action, the helpline did receive a few questions about student privacy.

Internal Challenges

One of the most difficult challenges is the one from your supervisor. I have faced that myself, and it was not fun. In these cases, librarians should rely on the policies already in place, already approved by the governing board. After a number of helpline requests focused here, we wrote a tip sheet that pulls together court cases and general advice. Some librarians noted that they noticed books vanishing overnight, which led to the suggestion that librarians take some screenshots of their catalog to keep off-site for future use as needed, if they are worried that "disappearances" might be imminent. It is also important to remind supervisors and board members that the Supreme Court has consistently supported the freedom to read and has opposed districts that did not follow their own policies.

Mass Challenges: Moms for Liberty Activists and Legislators

We had multiple requests for help when a legislator or community member presented several (seventy-five or more) challenges at once. No matter who presents the list, the source of the list is likely not local but copied from a national group such as Moms for Liberty. The challenger is not always a parent of a current student but possibly an activist working to disrupt normal procedures.

Even knowing this, the response should be the same. Wait for the correct paperwork, the official reconsideration form, and require one form per title. Start at the top of the pile and proceed one at a time to review the titles. Your standard reconsideration procedures are your best defense in these situations. I saw one district mentioned in a newspaper that states publicly that their review committee will review one book at a time, one book per month, not including the summer. They are refusing to compromise the time their educators need to spend by rushing the review process.

On the Horizon: E-books and Digital Resources

To date, most of the press has focused on challenges of print resources, but digital resource challenges are happening too. One Texas public library board canceled their access to OverDrive through a consortium subscription, because they felt it was too easy for children to access books that the board deemed inappropriate for minors.

Additionally, the state-funded TexQuest and TexShare subscription collections of digital resources have undergone particular scrutiny, especially for K–12 access. The Texas State Library and Archives Commission has gone to great lengths to work with vendors and legislators to ensure all the subscriptions align with state law, while maintaining the subscriptions for Texas students. Other states are looking at even more restrictive laws concerning state-supported online access points (Natanson, 2022).

The helpline will be working on additional resources in this area, which is likely to remain a hot topic for some time. The same paranoia about children having access to content described as "pervasively vulgar" or "obscene" has led some fanatics to search the major databases for material that will cause the subscription to be invalidated. For some reason, these people are opposed to the vetted content found on subscription databases, preferring the Wild West atmosphere of the open internet. To date, while legislatures have acted against access to some digital resources, supporters of intellectual freedom have not been able to duplicate the problematic searches.

Foundational Teaching

Engaging Stakeholders to Understand Intellectual Freedom and Support Library Efforts

This topic may not seem like it belongs, but having your community's support when a challenge comes can be huge, even if it is only part of the community. Part of being prepared for a challenge is working to ensure that your community knows what the First Amendment is and why it matters to them.

> Amendment I
>
> Congress shall make no law respecting an establishment of religion, or prohibiting the free exercise thereof; or abridging the freedom of speech, or of the press; or the right of the people peaceably to assemble, and to petition the government for a redress of grievances. (US Constitution, Amendment I)

Librarians know that freedom of speech and the freedom to read are intertwined. If I write my ideas but no one can read them, the ideas are effectively lost to discussion by a wider audience. Libraries facilitate readers getting access to a wide assortment of ideas; as ideas are read and discussed, the "marketplace of ideas" determines their value. Readers of all ages respond to ideas and apply them in life according to their understanding. These creative applications and interpretations fuel further development, whether in economics, space travel, understanding of climate change, or [insert your favorite topic here].

Librarians want to ensure that the marketplace of ideas remains open, and one of the best ways to do that is to teach library stakeholders about the First Amendment. Even K–12 students can learn how important the freedom to read is to their own education, and how at risk this freedom to read is in the current political climate of the twenty-first century.

There are now several examples of high school groups that activated to reinstate titles removed from their school libraries, examples that are very empowering. There are video clips online of students and parents speaking at school and library board meetings to remind the board members that they were elected by people who favor the freedom to read. There are resources to help educate your community and your elected leaders about the importance to them personally, professionally, and in the next election that they understand and support the freedom to read.

Conclusion

The TLA Helpline is here to support Texas librarians who face material challenges in all the various ways those challenges may manifest. Our volunteers stand ready to spend personal time on private Wi-Fi to coach threatened librarians in potential responses. Often, what a person facing difficulties of any kind needs is just someone who understands the problem to listen and suggest new ways to think about it. That is what we do. I am thrilled that I can use my experiences in school libraries to support this work and engage with current librarians to organize the most robust possible collection of resources in support of Texas librarians facing materials challenges.

References

American Library Association. (2006a). *Freedom to read statement.* https://www.ala.org/advocacy/intfreedom/freedomreadstatement

American Library Association. (2006b). *Library Bill of Rights.* https://www.ala.org/advocacy/intfreedom/librarybill

American Library Association. (2010). *B.1.1 Core values of librarianship and B.1.2 Code of professional ethics for librarians.* https://www.ala.org/aboutala/governance/policymanual/updatedpolicymanual/section2/40corevalues#B.1.1

American Library Association. (2016). *Selection & reconsideration policy toolkit for public, school, & academic libraries.* https://www.ala.org/tools/challengesupport/selectionpolicytoolkit

American Library Association Office for Intellectual Freedom. (2014). *Privacy field guides.* https://www.ala.org/advocacy/privacy/fieldguides

Burbage, K. (2022, May 31). *Swift feedback from librarians influences Follett Library Services proposed parental control module.* Intellectual Freedom Blog. https://www.oif.ala.org/oif/swift-feedback-from-librarians-influences-follett-library-services-proposed-parental-control-module/

Hickson, M. (2022, February 3). What's it like to be the target of a book banning effort? School librarian Martha Hickson tells her story. *School Library Journal.* https://www.schoollibraryjournal.com/story/from-the-breaking-point-to-fighting-anew-school-librarian-martha-hickson-shares-her-story-of-battling-book-banning-censorship

Maughan, S. (2022, April 2). Follett reverses course on parental controls for customers facing censorship legislation. *Publishers Weekly.* https://www.publishersweekly.com/pw/by-topic/childrens/childrens-industry-news/article/88929-follett-reverses-course-on-parental-controls-for-customers-facing-censorship-legislation.html

Natanson, H. (2022, May 10). The next book ban: States aim to limit titles students can search for. *The Washington Post.* https://www.washingtonpost.com/education/2022/05/10/school-library-database-book-ban/

Oltmann, S. M. (2019). *Practicing intellectual freedom in libraries.* Libraries Unlimited.

Ryzewski, S. (2021, December 22). Policies prove pivotal as Keller ISD navigates library book content. *Community Impact Newspaper (Keller-Roanoke-Northeast*

Fort Worth). https://communityimpact.com/dallas-fort-worth/keller-roanoke-northeast-fort-worth/education/2021/12/22/policies-prove-pivotal-as-keller-isd-navigates-library-book-content/

Books Discussed in This Chapter

Higuera, D. B. (2021). *The last cuentista*. Levine Querido.
Mass, W. (2008). *Heaven looks a lot like the mall*. Little, Brown.
Mass, W. *Willow falls* series.
Orwell, G. (1949). *1984*. Harcourt Brace.
Pullman, P. (1995). *The golden compass*. Scholastic.
Wheatley, N. (1994). *My place*. Kane Miller.

CHAPTER ELEVEN

Building a Grassroots Movement to Support Intellectual #FReadom

Becky Calzada and Carolyn Foote

Introduction

In September of 2021, Texas state representative Matt Krause sent a letter to school superintendents in the state with an attachment, listing 850 book titles. In the letter, he requested that superintendents verify ownership of these titles in school libraries; in addition, he requested that districts share other titles that could cause shame or guilt based on race or sex, as well as document how all titles were purchased. Ultimately, Representative Krause's "bald political stunt" was called out by Texas house public education chair Harold V. Dutton via Twitter, but the damage was already done (Lopez & Pollock, 2021). Shortly afterward, Texas governor Greg Abbott doubled down, claiming educators had inappropriate books in their libraries.

As Texas librarians, a group of us felt the urgent need for a counternarrative to address the name-calling and misinformation about librarians and libraries. What started as a casual text message conversation between two librarians became a late-night meeting between four colleagues and eventually turned into a nationwide grassroots movement to defend intellectual freedom on behalf of students, librarians, teachers, and authors.

What drew the four of us, who eventually became the "FReadom Fighters," into this fight? We all had a strong commitment to the way librarians served and supported all students on K–12 campuses. As librarians, we knew the hard work that went into providing diverse and inclusive library materials and resources to our students. We knew the many powerful authors whose works were being targeted and the direct impacts of these targets because we knew the students to whom those books mattered. This deep commitment to students was the "why" that motivated all of us to fight for students' rights to access books in their libraries and classrooms.

In the past decade, most school librarians across the country have reaffirmed deep commitments to evaluating their libraries to be sure the diverse collections they were building were serving their students. The publishing industry has also answered the call for diversity of stories and authors, bringing more and more voices into young adult and children's publishing, and librarians have responded by adding those titles to their collections. Most districts still have much work to do in creating more equitable libraries. Unfortunately, the current heated environment has slowed down many districts' progress in refining their library collection.

Overall, school libraries play a unique role in schools, making the tools of literacy accessible to all students from all families in a school district. Libraries provide a welcoming refuge for students who may not be able to explore their own lives and interests in the classroom. Librarians are (or should be) committed to providing a collection where all students can see themselves via the materials purchased for their campus collections. Even in 2023, there are many "book deserts" across the country, a term used to describe poor access to books (Wong, 2016). This is key because not all students have access to a public library or can afford to purchase their own books; disproportionally, students of color are without access to books at a much higher level (Wong, 2016).

We also know censorship can encompass many different acts, categorized by Emily Knox (2019) as the four Rs: redaction, restriction, relocation, and removal. Our first concern was that school districts might engage in some of these restrictive practices as a response to the letter from Representative Krause, especially if they did not have information about best practices for library management.

Consequently, when we heard the Texas governor doubling down and misrepresenting the work of librarians, we felt it essential to speak up. What began as a one-day attention-getting event on social media turned into far more than we imagined. Along the way, we have learned on-the-ground lessons in fighting censorship.

Our Story

How do you begin a grassroots organization? One way is to start with people you already know. The four of us had been working together on presentations for conferences occasionally, and when we heard what the Texas governor said, it prompted a spontaneous brainstorming session. Our first thought was to create a uniform hashtag, as we had noticed there was no consistent one tracking growing censorship; after some discussion, we coined the hashtag #FReadom. Later, in an evening brainstorming session, two of us texted and came up with the idea to conduct a secret takeover of the Texas legislative hashtag (#txlege) to gain attention from Texas legislators and any followers of this specific hashtag. One of the advantages of being active on social media as librarians was that we had existing professional networks. Over the next few days, we quietly reached out to our professional networks, library organizations, and author networks and asked all of them to consider tweeting on November 4 to share how diverse books impacted them. We asked them to share a title or two and how the books they shared made a difference to them. We had no idea what the response on this day would actually be; we knew we had shared our request widely and felt confident everyone we had connected with understood our purpose and goal. So we waited.

To our amazement and surprise, on November 4, over 13,000 tweets celebrating diverse books and authors were shared on Twitter and the hashtag #FReadom trended sixth on Twitter for most of the day. It was then we realized there was a real need to defend diversity in libraries, and we decided we needed to start a Twitter account. One of our members spearheaded designing a website, and we began adding resources to help librarians navigate the many challenges by sharing how-to instructions, news, resources, and more. As the need for advocacy grew, we have created additional resources for community members and students (which can be found at www.freadom.us). We even worked with an Etsy designer to create a T-shirt that followers could purchase as a way to help build a sense of community among librarians fighting censorship, and we donated proceeds to the Texas Library Association (TLA) Intellectual Freedom fund. We hoped wearing the T-shirt would also make librarians feel empowered and part of a larger and connected team.

One of the goals of our work has been to elevate and support librarians. Having a book challenge or multiple book challenges can be very isolating. Often librarians feel they cannot speak about a book challenge in public. Typically, unless there are Freedom of Information requests, the challenges are not revealed publicly. In the current heated and politicized environment, librarians may feel unsafe to speak openly about book challenges. Also, there is always self-examination and the implication that perhaps a book selection was an anomaly or error, when, in fact, many libraries have probably purchased the same title. In this especially difficult climate, the librarian might also be facing harassment on social media or in school board meetings. Consequently, our ultimate goals were to support librarians and students, celebrate authors and their work, and create robust resources to assist. Most of all, we wanted to offer hope and establish a connected network to hold on to during these difficult times.

We also wanted to advocate on behalf of librarians who work tirelessly in a profession we know is critically important to students. As research shows, school libraries are strongly correlated with student achievement, success, and graduation rates (Lance & Kachel, 2022). We know libraries provide a safe place for students. We know school library programs not only open up the world to students but also prepare them with literacy instruction and information literacy lessons. We know the impact the library has on supporting the entire school community. And we know the power of diverse literature to reach students, allowing them to see themselves within the pages or experience the life of someone else.

To engage and unite our new followers, we began our efforts with themed "FReadom Fridays," asking our followers to celebrate reading and diverse books. We highlighted books as gifts, books that moved us, and also included new books. One FReadom Friday included an opportunity for authors to post powerful letters they had received from students. These examples showcase how books are meaningful, via the words of student readers. We also did some monthly advocacy projects, including asking followers to write a letter to their school board or a letter to the local newspaper editor. These actions called attention to intellectual freedom work, and we soon found ourselves responding to requests for interviews about book banning and the precarious situations in which school librarians were finding themselves. Over time, we fielded more and more private inquiries from librarians revealing challenges their districts were facing, and we also began connecting them with resources.

In this current climate, where book challenges are often politically motivated, we have found the landscape evolving, from fighting off individual book challenges, to fighting off group challenges, to trying to resist replacing policies wholesale, to holding back potential state legislation. As those changes have happened, our messaging and support of librarians has continued to evolve.

How Do You Organize a Grassroots Effort?

Based on our experiences, these are some steps that can be followed to develop a grassroots effort.

1. Determine your goals and mission and document them.
2. Find a few like-minded partners.
3. Create a uniquely identifiable name that is not utilized by others and conveys your mission.
4. Decide if your advocacy will happen through a social media channel. Will it be a Facebook group (private or public), or will it be advocacy through Twitter, Instagram, or another social media tool? If so, would a common hashtag

help your advocacy? Consider your audience and where they normally communicate.

5. Create places you can share and store information. For safety, set up a non-work or non-school e-mail and Google folder to store things jointly. Be aware to not use work e-mail for advocacy.
6. Decide on roles as you learn the strengths of your team. This may evolve naturally, or you may want to codify it. It is a cooperative effort, so being able to tag team your partners is helpful.
7. Use your new social media account to tag others in your social network about your launch, or consider an attention-getting launch event to boost your following more quickly. (We learned this by accident.)
8. Figure out the best way for your small team to communicate internally. For us that has changed over time. Texting gets too cumbersome sometimes and we have moved to Slack, tried Google Docs to keep up with daily events, and so on. Be open to evolution over time.
9. Brainstorm some initial goals. These may change, but it gives you guidance for future decisions. Identify what actions you want to take, and how those might impact the conversation.
10. Keep your tone professional and as nonpartisan as possible to build a sense of community in your work.
11. Grow your group by tagging allies on social media, letting folks in organized library organizations know about your effort, connecting to current news events, and speaking up for your mission. The more you grow, the wider impact you can have.
12. People are often ready to be galvanized but are just looking to those who speak up. One advantage of a grassroots group is it shields individuals in the group somewhat and allows the advocacy to come from the group.
13. ANYONE can start a grassroots group. Is there a library cause that you are passionate about? Then that person could be you.

Some Other Things We Learned along the Way

Find Trusted, Like-Minded Partners

We learned by experience, but one of the most important mainstays of our work has been our trusting relationships with each other. Previous to this, we all met at conferences or via social media, bonding about our intellectual freedom work in libraries. We have worked together informally and in formal capacities over time. These relationships have helped us work through challenges and difficulties, and having a basic level of trust with partners who are part of leading a grassroots effort is key. This is where having strong personal learning networks is helpful.

Develop a Goal Statement

One significant step we took to keep our work aligned was to draft goals. Even though we were an informal group at first, these goals helped us pick and choose when we were offered different opportunities or when questions about our reach occurred. We periodically return to those goals and make sure we are aligned with them. We listened to each other as we drafted those goals so that we were all comfortable with them.

Find Each Other's Strengths

Whether you do some sort of formal strengths finder, or it evolves naturally as ours did, look and listen for each other's strengths. Maybe one person is a great web designer or good with social media, maybe someone else is a good communicator and spokesperson, someone else may have the ability to temper others during stressful times—identifying and harnessing those traits helps you work smarter together as you start advocating and doing all the intellectual freedom work.

Keep Your Leadership Team Small

It is easier for a small team to act quickly. It is easier for a small team to make decisions and act on them. It is harder and more taxing when the work gets bigger and bigger. Consider how to keep the framework of quick advocacy working as you grow, or as you need to add new members to the team.

Leverage Social Media

Social media is a powerful organizing tool and a tool that can drive action. Having someone on your team (or several people, as we did) who understand how to leverage social media is crucial to growing your work. You do not have to be everywhere, especially if your team is small. Pick and choose which tools work best for the audience you want to reach. If you are trying to mobilize families, Facebook may work best. If you are trying to mobilize library workers, Twitter or Instagram may be more effective. Each tool allows for different ways to engage and requires different levels of monitoring—something to keep in mind.

Uplift Supportive Partners

You are likely to find other informal organizations doing the work you are. By connecting with them informally, you are able to grow your network, elevate and complement each other's work, and gain allies along the way.

Develop Tools for Others

One of the most valuable pieces of our work was our "how to" page on our website. We realized many people want to help, but do not know what to do or how to help. We created a series of instructions, such as: "How to speak at a school board meeting" and "How to write a letter to the editor," to help followers and communities respond to censorship. We created sample template letters followers can freely use and descriptions of what librarians do. We asked a student to create a page of tips for other students. For anyone seeking to start a local advocacy group, we created a specific set of step-by-step instructions for how to launch one, which are also posted on our "how to" page. These tools have been one of the most utilized portions of our website and help to spread our reach to fight for #FReadom. They can be found here: https://www.freadom.us/how-to-instructions.

Just Do It

There is an immediacy needed for grassroots organizing. Being willing to jump into something quickly is key. If your goals and mission are clear, they can help you determine when to engage. This is also where strengths come into play—when you know who can quickly take the lead on something, it speeds the response. It takes a leap of faith to start a grassroots advocacy group, and it takes courage to jump into the fray. Thoughtful, rapid response is the name of the game.

Take Care of Yourself

Fighting censorship is taxing, emotionally, especially in volatile climates both locally and nationally. Be sure to find ways to step away and take care of yourself; share how you take care of yourself publicly to be a model for others who are following your work. Let your team know when you need a break.

Other Organizations Involved

We have envisioned our role as purely a grassroots, thoughtful, rapid response sort of operation. Many well-established organizations have also been involved in this work, providing support for members and providing public commentary. The American Library Association's Office for Intellectual Freedom is a long-standing group with many resources for librarians needing help or needing to report censorship happening in their district. ALA has also started an advocacy effort called Unite Against Book Bans, working to pull together partners to support an intellectual freedom message.

Some states have created advocacy groups, such as Texas Library Association's Texans Right to Read and Michigan's Right to Read group. PEN America, the National Coalition Against Censorship, the Freedom to Read Foundation, and EveryLibrary are also providing valuable resources and webinars to support librarians and communities in this heated environment. EveryLibrary combined work with Dr. Tasslyn Magnusson to document cases of censorship in a large database stored on their site. The National Council of Teachers of English has provided sample rationales for teaching specific book titles that teachers or librarians can use. There are many other organizations involved in fighting censorship, and we have created a list of supportive materials from many of these organizations on this Wakelet link: https://wakelet.com/wake/ygY18xcyC2BqQwfHoJvr3.

Conclusion

As educators, we recognize these are some of the most difficult times our profession has ever faced. We believe in the power of public education as a great equalizer, and school libraries play an important role in the progress and power of public education. We know books build empathy. They help us to see others and understand a person's lived experiences. Every human being deserves to be seen and valued for their full and authentic self. Every reader has the right to choose what they read or do not want to read.

As professional school librarians, we are charged with providing books and information that cover a broad range of topics and fulfill the interests of *all* our students. We are ready to settle into our collective professional strength and defend the right of *every* student to have access to information that is age relevant and identity affirming.

A grassroots movement like ours is just one of many ways librarians are asserting the importance of our school library profession in defending intellectual freedom. Collectively, organized efforts help lift up voices and can carry more weight, and we appreciate and applaud the diverse ways so many of our colleagues have found to advocate for #FReadom and student access. We know library professionals are dedicated to their professional ethics and are actively resisting efforts requiring them to commit what is basically educational malpractice. The book banners may have some success in some moments, but their efforts are an attack on our democratic values, and ultimately, they will not prevail. Working together in movements that harness the power of our networks gives more opportunity to impact the direction of these events. Every one of us has the opportunity to play a role in defending #FReadom and, most importantly, our democratic values.

References

Knox, E. J. M. (2019). Silencing stories: Challenges to diverse books. *The International Journal of Information, Diversity & Inclusion, 3*(2), 1–16. https://doi.org/10.33137/ijidi.v3i2.325929

Lance, K. C., & Kachel, K. E. (2022). Why school librarians matter: What years of research tell us. *Phi Delta Kappan, 99*(7), 15–20. https://kappanonline.org/lance-kachel-school-librarians-matter-years-research/

Lopez, B., & Pollock, C. (2021). How a YA oral-sex scene touched off Texas' latest culture war. *The Texas Tribune.* https://www.texastribune.org/2021/11/12/gender-queer-texas-books-investigation/

Wong, A. (2016, July 14). Where books are all but nonexistent. *The Atlantic.* https://www.theatlantic.com/education/archive/2016/07/where-books-are-nonexistent/491282/

CHAPTER TWELVE

Answering the Call: ALA GNCRT Responds to Surging Challenges to Comics

Matthew Noe, Amie Wright, and Moni Barrette

Introduction

The year is 2021. Readers can access comics anywhere they have a wireless connection, and manga are among the most popular items in libraries (Noe, 2022). The Comics Code Authority—the once powerful force, fueled by moral panic, that limited comics' potential—is defunct (Nyberg, n.d.). Comics sales are up by more than 50 percent, and the market is flying past the $2 billion mark for the first time in history (Milliot, 2022). This is also the year that a comic, *Gender Queer: A Memoir* (2019) by Maia Kobabe, topped the American Library Association's Office for Intellectual Freedom's (ALA OIF) banned books list with a record 729 documented challenges (ALA, 2022a).

The challenges to *Gender Queer* largely revolve around two issues. The first is that it falls into the broader realm of queer stories, books by and/or about authors who are open about their identity and that encourage the reader to expand their empathy and understanding of the world. These books historically have topped lists of banned or challenged titles, and this continues as we see backlash expand and heighten around books by or about trans and/or nonbinary creators and characters. The second issue is that comics, with their powerful combination of words and images, can be easily manipulated for use out of context. This is particularly true for *Gender Queer*, in which challengers have taken a few panels that depict mild sexual activity and branded the book as "pornographic," leaving out all context (which ultimately makes these moments tender and important). Combine this charge with the continued belief that all comics are for young children—a claim that has never been true—and it becomes easy to see how challengers can hide their desire to remove *all* queer stories from public access behind misinformation about a particular comic.

The growth in these challenges, not only to comics and across all variety of subjects (emphasis has been on titles by or about queer, Black, Indigenous, and people of color [BIPOC]), poses significant challenges to libraries to fulfill our missions (PEN America, 2022). With countless library operating models—from local board control, to state and national funding concerns, to differing library types (school, public, academic, etc.), as well as various kinds of reconsideration or challenge policies—it can be difficult to offer broad assistance in preventing library book removal (MacDonald, 2022). That is the goal, however, of a recently formed committee of the Graphic Novels and Comics Round Table (GNCRT).

Background

The period 2021–22 had more bans and challenges than any other in the past twenty years, and a concerning aspect to these escalating actions is the high level of communication and potential for dialogue among challengers via social media. In an article by *Slate* magazine examining the recent bans and challenges, Emily Knox, author of *Book Banning in 21st-Century America* (2015), explains:

> people who are bringing the challenges are able to speak to each other much more easily. Social media has exacerbated the problem a lot. So *Maus* was just banned in Tennessee. We might hear it gets banned in Oregon tomorrow, which would not have been true before social media. This is a phenomenon that's been around forever, but because people are able to communicate much more easily, it's manifesting differently. (Ismail, 2022)

While Knox's point appropriately acknowledges the high level of connectivity across technological platforms in 2022, it does overlook that this is not the first well-connected, organized, and community-engaged action on banning and challenging materials, especially those perceived to be for youth audiences. In discussing today's current climate of bans and challenges, many have forgotten that the "freedom to read" is not absolute, and that for the better part of several decades, comics and graphic novels were censored, restricted, and, in many countries, banned under the criminal code due to concerns of child well-being. In 1954, the U.S. government—during the height of the polio epidemic, which especially afflicted children—took comics to trial, considering them, in the words of vocal instigator Dr. Fredric Wertham, an urgent "public health problem" (United States, Congress, 1954). The U.S. Senate Subcommittee Hearings on Juvenile Delinquency and Comic Books concluded that there were concerning links between comics, crime, and sexual depravity and that children should be protected from this perceived harm. Following the hearings, the comics industry introduced an updated self-regulatory comics code, altering and censoring content, which impacted comics' content well into the 1970s and was not officially discarded by all comics publishers until 2011 (Comic Book Legal Defense Fund [CBLDF], 2022; Hajdu, 2009; Nyberg, 1998).

Further, while notable individuals such as Dr. Fredric Wertham, author of *Seduction of the Innocent* (1954), tend to be well remembered in history, less discussed is the extensive action undertaken for decades by organizations such as the National Organization for Decent Literature, the Committee for the Evaluation of Comics (from Cincinnati), the Catholic Women's League, and the Citizens' Committee for Better Juvenile Literature (based in Chicago). These organizations had been concerned about child health and reading since the 1930s and were composed of parents and community activists, as well as educators and librarians. Throughout library history, many "best of" reading lists were created specifically to guide children to what were perceived as "better" reading choices—this was also an integral part of anti-comics crusades. In the 1950s, the Chicago Public Library and the Citizens' Committee for Better Juvenile Literature partnered on a special program, "Operation Good Reading," which included storytimes, recommended reading lists, and created summer reading initiatives (Twomey, 1955).

The United States was not alone in these campaigns. Similar legislation or restrictions also existed in the United Kingdom and France, with the UK campaign against "horror comics" bolstered by the support and endorsement of the National Union of Teachers (Barker, 1984) and Belgian comics targeted by bans and challenges in France (Europe Comics, 2021). In Canada, "crime comics"—an umbrella phrase used for any graphic content perceived to incite or glamorize violence, including *Crime Does NOT Pay*, *Dick Tracy*, and even *Superman*—had been part of the Criminal Code "corrupting morals" clause under obscenity since 1949 (Fodden, 2013; McGinnis, 1988). Additionally, well-connected Canadian groups such as the British Columbia Parent Teacher Association (BC PTA) Crime Comics Committee and the Advisory Board on Objectionable Materials (ABOP) in Alberta worked with schools, libraries, parents, and students themselves to problematize comic book reading. Copies of the ABOP's pamphlet *What's Wrong with Comic Books?*

(1956), inspired by sources such as Wertham's work and the U.S. hearings, were distributed by the Canadian Library Association (CLA) to attendees of the 1956 CLA Annual Conference. Additionally, several prominent Canadian librarians served on or worked with the ABOP, including former CLA presidents Bruce Peel and John Dutton, and noted children's librarians Louise Riley from the Calgary Public Library and Jean Thomson from the Toronto Public Library (Wright, 2022, p. 90).

Furthermore, significant levels of connection, dialogue, and mutual support existed between these groups and prominent stakeholders on domestic and transnational levels. Suggested reading lists from the Committee for the Evaluation of Comics were printed in *Parents' Magazine* (Nyberg, 1998, p. 23), and before publishing *Seduction of the Innocent* in 1954, Wertham authored multiple articles on the dangers of comic book reading in prominent periodicals—articles that were reprinted and read by millions internationally. Wertham's "The Comics . . . Very Funny" was initially published in the American edition of *Reader's Digest* (RD) in 1948 and later reprinted into five of the thirteen RD international editions (Fredric Wertham Papers). In Wertham's collection at the Library of Congress, a multitude of correspondence exists from international colleagues from Sweden, Germany, Belgium, France, Canada, and elsewhere. BC PTA Crime Comics Committee chair, Eleanor Gray, was a frequent correspondent of Wertham, sending him clippings of news stories from Canada and other parts of the British Commonwealth (Fredric Wertham Papers). Indeed, chapter 11 of Wertham's *Seduction of the Innocent* is entitled "Murder in Dawson Creek: Comics Abroad" and discusses cases of comic books and juvenile violence in Canada and internationally. These highly networked, organized, well-publicized, and *transnational* comic book bans and challenges of the 1950s were all centered, like today, around concerns of child health, heteronormative ideas of the family, and perceptions of what constitutes "good reading."

The Present

In February 2022, the GNCRT of the ALA officially announced the creation of a new committee: Preparing For and Addressing Challenges to Comics in the Library. This committee, approved by the 2021–22 GNCRT board in December 2021, was created in response to an increasing number of requests from GNCRT membership for assistance with challenges to comics in their libraries. The committee seeks not to duplicate the efforts of existing ALA groups such as the Office for Intellectual Freedom but rather to provide practical, on-the-ground advice and tools for library workers when it comes to comics. It is our contention that comics, due to their visual nature, provide an easy target for challenges and also require unique approaches to arguing in their defense.

The committee, which was initially intended to be a short project but has already been determined to be larger and longer term in scope, is charged with developing resources that can aid library workers in not only handling challenges when they happen but also preparing for them in advance. This preparatory element is vital, as librarians are all too often reactionary thinkers and actors, leaving us vulnerable to the kinds of coordinated efforts to challenge books we are seeing today. In addition, there are few resources available that offer advice on what to do *after* a challenge has concluded. We emphasize this space as well, in recognition that facing these kinds of battles is emotionally draining and can leave people feeling alone and abandoned in the profession—a recipe for burnout and, if unaddressed, abandonment of library work altogether.

Throughout the first half of 2022, the committee took a multipronged approach. They worked to gather information on existing resources for library workers facing challenges or bans, which helped determine any gaps that needed to be filled and what areas were already so well covered there may be no need to revisit them. They delved into the history of comics challenges (see the "Background" section of this chapter) to better understand how we got to this moment and just what role libraries have played in the constant battle against access. And, perhaps most importantly, in April 2022, the committee launched a survey to learn more about three main things: respondent training and background in dealing with challenges; the context around any comics challenges respondents have experienced; and how we can help—what resources, knowledge, talking points, and community support do respondents need to prepare for and address challenges to comics in their libraries (ALA, 2022b). The survey sought responses from educators, library workers, administrators, library students, public libraries, academic libraries, and K–12 school libraries.

By combining the initial survey results (from the period of April 15 to May 31, 2022) with research into existing resources and the history of censorship in libraries, the committee developed and launched the first of many resources to come: the Be Prepared! "What to do when a challenge comes" Checklist! More about the survey's results and methodology can be found by watching the recording of a recent Booklist webinar (2022). Figure 12.1 is the condensed, postcard version of the checklist that GNCRT has now made part of our conference and convention booth handouts. The checklist, which can be found in full on the Preparing For and Addressing Challenges to Comics in the Library Committee page of the ALA GNCRT website, is divided into the phases of facing a challenge: before, during, and after.

While there is insufficient space here to dive deep into every point on the checklist, it is important to highlight a few elements and larger concepts. The "before a challenge" section focuses on being proactive, rather than reactive, to challenges. For some libraries, this represents a dramatic shift in workflow—a surprisingly large number of respondents to our survey indicated that their

Be Prepared! "What to do when a challenge comes" checklist:

BEFORE a challenge:

- ❑ Do you have a SELECTION POLICY? Is it transparent and accessible? Does it include comics?
- ❑ Do you have a separate CHALLENGE POLICY in place? If not, create one
- ❑ IDENTIFY STAKEHOLDERS in your library system--who are the deciders on book bans?
- ❑ COMPARE POLICY MODELS. Are your policies the best they can be?
- ❑ PAY ATTENTION to those books that are being challenged around the nation; build advocacy

DURING a challenge:

- ❑ What are the REVIEWS of the book?
- ❑ For schools, are there CURRICULUM connections?
- ❑ For both school and public libraries, does this comic book FILL A NEED? Is it an award winner?
- ❑ Is your CHALLENGE PROCESS being followed?
- ❑ What COMMUNITY SUPPORTS are available to you?
- ❑ REPORT the challenge to the ALA Office of Intellectual Freedom: https://www.ala.org/tools/challengesupport/report

AFTER a challenge:

- ❑ Win, lose, or draw, make it a point to THANK the people who helped you - you may need them again.
- ❑ UPDATE your policies where needed to strengthen them against future challenges
- ❑ Many challenge policies have a "COOLING OFF" period, where the same book cannot be challenged again for # of years. Is this in place for your library?
- ❑ PREPARE by asking - are there books similar to your challenged comic that may also trigger a challenge?
- ❑ LIVE to library another day. You are not alone.

Toolkit: https://bit.ly/GNCRTchallenge-toolkit

We want to know more!

Take our 5 min SURVEY to tell us about your experiences with challenges

https://bit.ly/GNCRTchallenge-survey

Figure 12.1 Be Prepared! "What to Do When a Challenge Comes" Checklist. (Source: Graphic Novels and Comics Round Table, 2022)

library either has no challenge policy in place or it is so far out of date as to be useless in practice. Libraries *must* be proactive when it comes to collection development and that means creating, using, and regularly updating not only collection development policies but also sub-policies that specifically address challenges. These challenge policies should, at minimum, address "how challenges are handled; how reconsideration requests take place; who is the first point of contact, and what steps are there in the process" (GNCRT, 2022). Times of limited challenge activity are also the perfect opportunity to build and reinforce your network of support so that when challenges do come, you know where you can turn for help.

"During a challenge" is the part of this process that is discussed most often by other resources and is the time where library workers should be reaching out to the ALA Office for Intellectual Freedom to report *all* challenges underway. This reporting helps begin a process of additional support and informs annual statistics on challenges that guide future policy and association resources. During a challenge is also when you want to mobilize that coalition of community partners to come to your aid. This is especially true if you are facing a challenge in a school library, where support from teachers, students, and parent groups can mean the difference in being viewed as a partner in education or as a rabble-rouser.

An important, and often overlooked, aspect of library challenges is what happens after a challenge concludes. This is when you might consider how your policies need to adjust in light of the challenge process and outcome. Perhaps there are books that are similar to those recently challenged that you want to prepare yourself to have to defend in the near future. Most vital, however, is taking the time to breathe, to thank those who helped you throughout the challenge, and to allow yourself grace and a chance to rest. Challenges can be an emotionally draining affair, and in today's climate, they can result in personal attacks (Harris & Alter, 2022). It is our hope that this checklist offers a place to start and plan for library workers, while recognizing it is only a beginning and that there is more work to be done.

The Future

Systemic efforts to ban and challenge library comics collections are on the rise, and GNCRT's Preparing For and Addressing Challenges to Comics in the Library Committee is dedicated to gathering, providing access to, and maintaining proven best practices to support library workers to defend collections. These resources will be continuously expanded and updated, and outcomes will be evaluated and shared. Specific committee initiatives include: utilizing collected survey data to study recurring themes, such as soft censorship, lack of internal policy follow through, absence of updated—or any—collection development policies (especially when comics-specific practices are not addressed or become outdated); developing samples of collection and challenge policies built on examples from survey submissions and the committee's professional expertise; and spreading awareness of these efforts by providing more webinars, resources, and access to tangible support. The committee's survey on experiences with challenges is, at the time of this chapter's publication, expected to remain open so long as the committee continues to operate—which is, currently, indefinitely.

Conclusion

Providing and defending access to resources is a core mission of the library profession. The disconnect between groups seeking to ban books and those looking to preserve free access continues to grow. Library workers must remain up to date to maintain comics-specific defensive strategies. While GNCRT and other groups continue to support library workers' efforts, bandwidth and awareness remain limited. Gatekeeping and stigma toward comics need to be eliminated in the profession, and like-minded organizations must band together to monitor the changing landscape, study outcomes, keep best practices updated, report out regularly, and work against bans and challenges with a strong united front. Together we can work toward common ground to restore and maintain trust in professional comics collection development and library worker expertise in our communities.

References

American Library Association. (2022a). *State of America's libraries special report: Pandemic year two.* https://www.ala.org/news/state-americas-libraries-report-2022

American Library Association. (2022b, April 15). *GNCRT seeks information about censorship of comics in schools and libraries.* https://www.ala.org/news/member-news/2022/04/gncrt-seeks-information-about-censorship-comics-schools-and-libraries

Barker, M. (1984). *A haunt of fears: The strange history of the British horror comics campaign*. Pluto Press.

Booklist. (2022, July 21). *Be prepared! The GNCRT guide to addressing comic book bans, censorship, and challenges.* https://www.booklistonline.com/webinars-archive

Comic Book Legal Defense Fund. (2022). *The comics code.* https://cbldf.org/the-comics-code/

Europe Comics. (2021, February 26). *Censorship in Belgian comics.* https://www.europecomics.com/censorship-belgian-comics-p-1/

Fodden, S. (2013, December 7). Crime comics and the remnants of a moral panic. *Slaw: Canada's Online Legal Magazine.* www.slaw.ca/2013/12/07/crime-comics-and-the-remnants-of-a-moral-panic/

Fredric Wertham Papers, Box 112 (Comic Books Abroad), Manuscript Division, Library of Congress, Washington, DC.

Graphic Novels and Comics Round Table. (2022). *Preparing for and addressing challenges to comics in the library committee.* https://www.ala.org/rt/gncrt/preparing-and-addressing-challenges-comics-library-committee

Hajdu, D. (2009). *The ten-cent plague: The great comic-book scare and how it changed America* (1st Picador ed.). Picador.

Harris, E., & Alter, A. (2022, July 18). With rising book bans, librarians have come under attack. *The New York Times.* https://www.nytimes.com/2022/07/06/books/book-ban-librarians.html

Ismail, A. (2022, January 31). There's a simple reason that demands to "ban" books like *Maus* are soaring: And it's not only coming from the right. *Slate.* https://slate.com/human-interest/2022/01/maus-banned-tennessee-holocaust-graphic-novel.html

MacDonald, H. (2022, June 10). Comics librarians are up for the fight. *Publisher's Weekly.* https://www.publishersweekly.com/pw/by-topic/industry-news/libraries/article/89572-comics-librarians-are-up-for-the-fight.html

McGinnis, J. D. (1988). Bogeymen and the law: Crime comics and pornography. *Ottawa Law Review, 20*(1), 3–23.

Milliot, J. (2022, July 1). Comics/graphic novel sales jumped 62% in 2021. *Publisher's Weekly.* https://www.publishersweekly.com/pw/by-topic/industry-news/financial-reporting/article/89752-comics-graphic-novel-sales-jumped-62-in-2021.html

Noe, M. (2022, July). State of comics librarianship. *Booklist's Guide to Graphic Novels in Libraries, 2022*, 3. https://www.booklistonline.com/State-of-Comics-Librarianship/pid=9764520

Nyberg, A. K. (n.d.). *Comics code history: The seal of approval*. Comic Book Legal Defense Fund. http://cbldf.org/comics-code-history-the-seal-of-approval/

Nyberg, A. K. (1998). *Seal of approval: The history of the comics code*. University Press of Mississippi.

PEN America. (2022). *Banned in the USA: Rising school book bans threaten free expression and students' first amendment rights*. https://pen.org/banned-in-the-usa/

Twomey, J. (1955). The Citizens' Committee and comic-book control: A study of extragovernmental restraint. *Law and Contemporary Problems, 20*(4), 621–629.

United States, Congress, Senate. Juvenile Delinquency (Comic Books): Hearings before the Subcommittee to Investigate Juvenile Delinquency of the Committee on the Judiciary. Government Printing Office, 1954. 83rd Congress, 2nd session.

Wright, A. (2022). Alberta's forgotten censor: The Advisory Board on Objectionable Publications (1954–1976) and the continued campaign against comics post 1954. *Canadian Literature, 249*, 82–100.

Books Discussed in This Chapter

Knox, E. J. M. (2015). *Book banning in 21st-century America*. Rowman & Littlefield.

Kobabe, M. (2019). *Gender queer: A memoir*. Oni Press.

Spiegelman, A. (1996). *The complete Maus*. Pantheon.

Wertham, F. (1954). *Seduction of the innocent: The influence of comic books on today's youth*. Rinehart.

PART 4

How to Face Challenges and Bans

CHAPTER THIRTEEN

Responding to Challenges: In the Moment and Beforehand

Kristin Pekoll and Shannon M. Oltmann

What Is a Challenge?

A challenge is an attempt to remove, restrict, redact, or relocate a resource of any type based on the objections of a person or group. A ban is the removal of materials from a library or public institution based on the objections of a person or group (Garnar & Magi, 2021). Sometimes a ban is the outcome of a reconsideration policy procedure, despite the First Amendment rights of library users, and other times a ban is enacted to avoid controversy or because of unethical disregard for policy.

Books are not the only things challenged in libraries; other resources and materials have been challenged at various times. Challenges and bans are not limited to just libraries but happen in many types of institutions, including schools, museums, and community centers. Public and school libraries are currently the most common targets. Some people find "offensive content" in music, magazines, newspapers, games, exhibits, databases, displays, reading lists, bookmarks, films, and other online resources (Garnar & Magi, 2021).

Challenges do not simply involve a person expressing a point of view; rather, they are an attempt to remove resources from the curriculum or the library, thereby restricting others' ability to access it. Challenges may occur in the form of a written complaint, an official form submitted to a library, a call to action on social media, an e-mail message, a letter to the editor, or as public comments at a board meeting. When judging whether a situation qualifies as a challenge, consider the complainants' motivation or intention. If the intent is to restrict the access of other people, it is a challenge. Most libraries outline how a user can express a challenge using official policy and procedure. This official paperwork, often called a "request for reconsideration," captures the details of a challenge, like the type of resource, the reason for the concern, and the specific request for how a library should deal with the material. While the American Library Association (ALA) recommends that every library have reconsideration procedures to address user concerns, it is not required that the procedure be filed for a challenge to have occurred. Even the best policies cannot completely prevent censorship (ALA Office for Intellectual Freedom [OIF], 2018).

Challenges may lead to censorship or to a change in the status of the resource. Examples of censorship include removing the resource, restricting access by placing the resource behind the circulation desk or in an office, limiting the resource to certain ages/grades, requiring parental permission, hiding the resource, and vandalizing pages by blacking out words or changing images. Removing the challenged item is considered banning.

In the Moment

Each library should establish a process for addressing verbal concerns raised in the library, because informal complaints such as these can happen anytime. When patrons express concern to library staff or educators, these patrons should be referred to the person responsible for responding to concerns (usually supervisors, administrators, or seasoned library workers) (Garnar & Magi, 2021). Not only is it important for directors and leaders to be aware of the situation, but their training can also be a guide for those who may be less familiar with the library's policies and nuances of the community member and landscape.

> *Conversation Tip*: While library workers should not put off a concern, it does not necessarily mean it needs to be dealt with immediately or in that exact moment. "Thank you for sharing your concern. I think it's important that we bring in Luciana. Do you mind if I see when she's next available?"

It is unlikely that the person expressing concerns understands or knows about the concept of intellectual freedom or the core values and purposes of libraries. These can be library-specific terms and concepts, unfamiliar to most patrons. This moment is an opportunity to share the principles of the freedom to read and equitable access for all users and the role of the library in the community. For a person to be receptive to these ideas, they need to believe their opinions and values are also being respected and truly heard. Even if two people disagree, there can still be respect, especially in a professional capacity. This respect will show value for the relationship, which will ultimately make the interaction more successful.

Empathic listening is a structured listening and questioning technique that allows you to develop and enhance relationships with a stronger understanding of what is being conveyed, both intellectually and emotionally. As such, it takes active listening techniques to a new level.

In conversations, especially heated ones, it is important not to start with an immediately defensive posture. Refrain from stiffening the shoulders, crossing the arms, or glaring with hard facial muscles. Instead, try to lean forward, nod thoughtfully, and smile compassionately. Reframe your thoughts to resolution rather than confrontation, listening rather than arguing, and acceptance rather than rejection. Even if a person 100 percent disagrees with the other person they are talking with, there can still be respect and professional courtesy. Acknowledge that every person has the right to question library resources. Having their objections formally considered is part of our obligations to our community (ALA, 2019). Library users' complaints should be taken seriously by library staff. Often, just having someone listen to them sympathetically may resolve the issue.

Remember that parents and guardians should generally guide their children's library usage; this may be an important point to share if the patron is concerned about books or other resources for minors. Sometimes those who are concerned about youth programs or books want to have items removed from the library's collection to "protect all the children." They may make similar arguments in favor of restricting access to or canceling programs or other events. This conversation can be an excellent opportunity to clarify that families can decide what is right for their particular family, and they must extend that same right to other families (Garnar & Magi, 2021). They may not fully understand that their request to remove a library resource is considered censorship or book banning and that they are asking to make a decision on behalf of every other person in the community.

> *Conversation Tip*: If you are familiar with the community enough to mention a mutual acquaintance, you might consider putting a face to other families. "I appreciate that you feel strongly about this book, but as a public (library, school, institution), it's important that we don't make decisions for other families like the Murrays or the Garcias. We all have different beliefs, values, and viewpoints. Would you want them to make decisions for your family based on their viewpoint?"

After an individual patron expresses their personal concern, that may be the end of the conversation. Sometimes a person only wants their viewpoint to be acknowledged, and further action is not needed. In these cases, thank the person for their time and involvement in the library, then report the conversation to the administration (such as the library director) and make notes for future use (Garnar & Magi, 2021).

However, sometimes, the concerned individual will not be satisfied with an informal discussion and will still want the item removed from the library or restricted in some way. At this point, explain the library's formal reconsideration process and the timeline for review. Start with the mission of the public institution. Explain how the mission guides how resources are selected, the criteria used, and the professional experience, education, and training of the library workers who select the items and services. Include a statement about whether the material will continue to be available while under review (best practice is that the item will not be restricted during reconsideration). Many times, individuals want the instant removal of a resource and do not realize how long the process may take, so clarify this as well (Garnar & Magi, 2021).

> *Conversation Tip*: If you can, sit together at a table with the library's mission, the policy about selecting resources, and the reconsideration form. After expanding on the written policy with verbal explanations, explain why the library has a reconsideration process. "We provide a lot of resources for our community so it's understandable that someone may have a concern about one of our resources. Libraries provide a way for you to formally share your request to us and for us to respectfully and deliberately consider it. By filling out this public form, you're asking us to ban this book from everyone in our community. As you can imagine, this is a serious request. So we have a procedure outlined for how to make a decision. This copy of the policy and reconsideration form are yours to take home and read through carefully. If you choose to move forward, return the form to me. I'm happy to answer any questions about the library or help you find resources that meet your and your family's needs."

When discussing the next steps with the concerned individual, give them a copy of the mission statement and collection development policy along with the formal reconsideration form. Explain that no further action will be taken until the form is completed and returned by the individual. Once the form is submitted, it becomes part of the public record, and the formal reconsideration process is initiated (Garnar & Magi, 2021).

At any point, before, during, or after a challenge, library staff and educators can contact ALA's OIF. If you want encouragement, support, and reassurance that you are proceeding appropriately, the OIF can assist with that. The office can also help ensure that your processes conform to best practices in the field. Occasionally, leaders in your community or your institutions may not follow formal policy, and this is another good time to contact OIF for support and guidance. The office can help you explain why a resource should be included in your collection. They can assist with complaints on social media, finding supportive representatives for a public meeting, or responding to media messaging (e.g., if a local reporter contacts you). When your committee completes its reconsideration process, you can contact OIF to discuss the outcome (and hopefully celebrate the retention of the item!). Finally, you can reach out for support if others in your network are tired of intellectual freedom discussions (ALA, 2022).

We Are All People

These conversations and procedures are vital, regardless of who is initiating the concern about a resource. Whether it is a parent, a community member, a principal, an elected official, an activist group, or a board member, the policy and principles are the same. Whether this person's or group's values clash politically, religiously, educationally, morally, or culturally with that of the library or library worker, there can still be commonalities. It can be helpful to bring to mind someone else who also contradicts your values but whom you respect and with whom you share some things in common. For many people, it may be a family member, friend, teacher, or coworker.

Understanding the complexities and backgrounds of people limits the assumptions and stereotypes that can be made mistakenly about people. This can also reduce the negative assumptions about their motivations. Even if the situation does not allow for full understanding, at least recognizing that there may be more to a person than just this one interaction or conversation can go a long way to successful empathetic listening and de-escalating the situation.

Know that behind this person's opinions are experiences that have shaped them and environments they have lived in beyond their control. Know that their emotion and passion is often caused by fear, anxiety, and loss of control. Know that their conviction on a topic does not necessarily equate to their opinion of libraries or the freedom to read and access information. Rarely is the person with a concern about a library resource speaking to library staff solely because they fit into a stereotypical category of a censor. Visualizing the person as a neighbor, a friend, or a family member is an important step in having a successful response that may de-escalate a tempered situation. By recognizing that there is more emotion and history behind the words that are being expressed in the conversation, library staff have the knowledge to reframe the conversation.

Start with a Conversation

When someone comes into the library and they are upset, it makes sense to apologize. It is a common reaction to a fellow human being who is upset.

It would be unusual for users to visit the library in the hopes they will find something that offends them. It is appropriate to start with an apology and regret that they are upset. You are not apologizing for the material, the content, or the viewpoint, but rather that they are having an emotional and negative experience in the library.

Begin by understanding their concern. Try restating the problem in your own words without judgment. The goal is to understand and communicate with the person you are talking to that you are listening to and understanding their concern. If this escalates their emotions, just let them know that you want to make sure you are understanding them and that there is nothing wrong with their concern. Every person has the right to question library resources.

> *Conversation Tip*: Positive facial expressions, body posture, gestures, eye movement, touch, and the use of space can communicate more than words. "To make sure I understand, your teenager was reading a book with profanity that you find offensive, and you don't approve of them using it or want them to be exposed to that. Is that accurate?" Stated on its own, the previous statement could be interpreted many different ways. But physical mannerisms and behaviors can help the statement be interpreted without judgment and with respect.

One tactic to respond to a challenge during the initial conversation is to shift the conversation away from the resource and their personal opinions and values to why they came into the library in the first place. By reemphasizing the reasons they visited the library, you can highlight the library's purpose and relate to them on a personal level. Rather than focusing on the offending item, library staff can treat the situation as a customer service or reference situation and use the opportunity to help the person find the resource or service that would meet their needs in visiting the library.

At this point they have had a chance to articulate their concerns, they have got a sympathetic listening ear, they know that you understand what the issue is; now you go back to the fundamental relationship between a librarian and a patron, helping them find the resource or service they need or want. This can take a negative encounter and shift it to a more positive one.

Obviously not all library users will be satisfied with this response, and they might demand more action. Then the conversation segues to a more formal process for reconsideration. But the power and ability to start with this conversation is possible because we have a policy and process for formally addressing demands to remove materials if the challenge escalates.

Unfortunately, there are times when concerns about a resource are initiated outside of a conversation. It is becoming more common for concerns and challenges to be expressed on social media, in an e-mail, or during a public comment at a board meeting.

It is highly recommended to reset the clock with a conversation if at all possible. Reach out to the person, thank them for expressing their concern, and request an in-person meeting to take it back to that first conversation.

> *Conversation Tip*: Approach the person before they leave the meeting or call them directly after you read their e-mail or see their post on social media. "Thank you for bringing up your concerns at a board meeting." "Thank you for sharing your views on social media." "Can we schedule a time so you and I can have a conversation? I'd really like to hear your concerns."

If the challenge is taking place on social media, try to get the conversation off social media and in person. Social media is almost never a productive venue for a "conversation." Oftentimes, comments are misinterpreted, reactions are not successfully communicated in real time, and emotions fester. If more people join the social media post without fully understanding the situation, it can reflect the mentality of a mob attack. As much as possible, communicate in person. Make the request by phone and not e-mail so that library staff are seen as real people with names and faces with feelings. Being able to hear the kindness, respect, and empathy in a person's voice will go a long way to calming the situation.

Preemptive Response

Every single situation is different, and every single library has a different policy, community, and history. While the reconsideration and selection policies are the backbone that support intellectual freedom in a library, they are not the only way to respond, especially preemptively, to challenges.

By laying a strong foundation of values and purpose, any response to an actual challenge will be ten times stronger because the community will already know what to expect of their local institutions.

To lay a strong foundation, be intentional and vocal about the institution's mission. Be transparent about policies and procedures. Train staff, volunteers, and governing bodies not only on the procedures but also on the underlying values of why the libraries do what they do. ALA's *Libraries: An American Value* states:

> By embracing these principles, libraries in the United States can contribute to a future that values and protects freedom of speech in a world that celebrates both our similarities and our differences, respects individuals and their beliefs, and holds all persons truly equal and free. (ALA, 1999)

If a library is intentional about serving everyone, it will be clear in its actions to celebrate, inform, and recognize multiple races, religions, cultures, families, and holidays. When libraries care about creating an informed democracy in their communities and developing critical thinkers, it will be evident in their comprehensive programs and varied and accurate resources.

By shaping the physical and digital environment, libraries can also shape the expectations of our community. When a library or school boards recite their missions, values, or vision before the start of each public meeting, they are laying a foundation. When policies transparently include professional core documents such as the Library Bill of Rights and the First Amendment, they are laying a foundation. When services, physical spaces, communications, and programs align with and highlight the library's values, they are laying a foundation. All of these actions are ways that a library or public institution can preemptively respond to the overwhelming challenges and bans that are happening today.

Conclusion: You Are Not Alone

Whether a library worker is responding to a challenge in the moment, restarting a conversation, or laying the foundation, there is support. Even if the library staff is well trained, with strong policies and a supportive governing body, it is recommended to call in support. Asking for support or informing stakeholders and colleagues is not the same as going to the press or alerting the public. When caution is needed, use phone calls or in-person conversations, and personal e-mails instead of public e-mails, but still reach out. Professional support networks understand the importance of discretion or the need for confidentiality. Support is a two-way street.

By informing professional support channels (like state and national libraries or educational associations, library workers in other types of institutions, neighboring libraries, or organizations with similar values and mission) about a specific situation, a library is exhibiting transparency in the process and its values. The library is providing support and encouragement for all involved—staff, community, and governing bodies. It is showing fortitude and courage to other libraries and is being an example of intellectual freedom success. In a time when we hear about unethical administrative decisions, the library profession needs to hear about the successes, the libraries that are prepared, and examples of how they have weathered the storm and responded with compassion and resilience. Asking for support is showing others that it is alright to ask for support. Knowing that our neighbor libraries are responding to challenges strengthens the unity of our profession and displays the power of numbers.

Reporting the challenge contributes to the vast knowledge of censorship in America. Each piece of data gleaned from a challenge helps professional organizations and intellectual freedom experts strategically focus their energy on providing resources to protect the right to read. The ALA estimates that 82–97 percent of challenges go unreported. In 2021, 729 challenges were recorded. That means that as many as 24,000 challenges happened in libraries that no one knows about, and 24,000 responses to challenges occurred that could educate and support other libraries. While the data and trends around censorship right now are unprecedented and terrifying, the principles that shape America's libraries are constant and firm. "We celebrate and preserve our democratic society by making available the widest possible range of viewpoints, opinions, and ideas, so that all individuals have the opportunity to become lifelong learners—informed, literate, educated, and culturally enriched" (ALA, 1999).

References

American Library Association. (1999, February). *Libraries: An American value.* https://www.ala.org/advocacy/intfreedom/americanvalue

American Library Association. (2019, January). *Challenged resources: An interpretation of the Library Bill of Rights.* https://www.ala.org/advocacy/intfreedom/librarybill/interpretations/challenged-resources

American Library Association. (2022). *Challenge support.* https://www.ala.org/tools/challengesupport

American Library Association Office for Intellectual Freedom. (2018, January). *Selection & reconsideration policy toolkit for public, school, & academic libraries.* https://www.ala.org/tools/challengesupport/selectionpolicytoolkit

Garnar, M., & Magi, T. (2021). *Intellectual freedom manual.* ALA Editions.

CHAPTER FOURTEEN

When Policy Does Not Stop the Ban: Reflections on Moving Forward

Jenna Kammer and Mernie Maestas

The Role of Policy in School Libraries

In recent years, three types of school library policies have been utilized to support the right to read in schools. Specifically, policies for selection, deselection, and reconsideration are some of the best lines of defense against censorship (Adams, 2021). Should a book be added to the collection and a stakeholder disagrees with its inclusion, a reconsideration policy will explain the procedures for filing a formal complaint about that item. The American Library Association Office for Intellectual Freedom (ALA OIF, 2018) recommends that the reconsideration process allows for the public to challenge a work in the collection, but within a preapproved process that includes communication and de-escalation strategies. At this point, a variety of designated stakeholders from the community form a committee, review the book in comparison with the complaint, and make a recommendation to retain or remove it. A reconsideration process is an important intellectual freedom practice as it is designed to allow the public to have input on the collection and increases the credibility of the library (ALA OIF, 2018).

However, while updated, comprehensive policies are a fundamental part of a strong school library program, they are not legally binding and may have loopholes. Additionally, those outside of the library may not know about the policies, understand how to use them to reconsider a book, or find them adequate. Some school or district administrators may even ignore the policy process to avoid conflict. Recently, several school boards seemed to follow existing policies, yet still ignored the recommendations of the committees in making decisions about which books should be removed from the school library (e.g., see Adams et al., 2015; Aldrich, 2022; Grumke, 2022; Hixenbaugh & Schwartz, 2022; Pelman & Lynch, 2011; Random House, 2022; Wagner, 2022).

While a school library's selection policy is often approved by the school board and resides with other district policies, many lack consistency, may not be publicly available, or are incomplete (Dawkins & Eidson, 2021). In their study of school library selection policies, Dawkins and Eidson (2021) found that 81 percent of districts in their random sample had publicly available selection policies in place. A *School Library Journal* survey also found that 81 percent of libraries in their sample had formal book challenge procedures (SLJ Research, 2016). However, they also reported that the majority of school library selection policies describe criteria for inclusion of works in the collection, which is important, but stop short of defining intellectual freedom and stating the importance of including materials that may be controversial or cover sensitive topics.

One problem within the policies may be the need for them to be developed more fully. Specifically, Dawkins and Eidson (2021) found that of the policies they reviewed, only 44 percent described specific challenge procedures, and many of them lacked the components recommended by the *Selection & Reconsideration Policy Toolkit for Public, School, & Academic Libraries* (ALA OIF, 2018). This toolkit provides a comprehensive list of items to include in a school, public, or academic library selection and reconsideration policy, as well as sample language to use or adapt.

School librarians who have experienced a challenge (within or outside of the reconsideration process) will often describe the emotional toll of the experience (e.g., see Adams et al., 2015). Chavez et al. (2021) also wrote that some Texas librarians were afraid of losing their jobs after a book challenge, or facing criminal charges, once school officials decided to do their own review of the library collection because they felt the library selection process had failed. Another school librarian explained that her experiences with a book challenge were difficult but led her to make improvements such as increased justifications for acquisitions, advocacy for student's First Amendment rights, meeting more student requests, and educating students on the Constitution and the Bill of Rights (Adams et al., 2015).

Ideally, selection and reconsideration policies are publicly available, easily readable, and followed by administrators and the school board should a book challenge arise. In an example of successful application of policy and process, the Ottumwa School District (Iowa) was effective in utilizing their reconsideration process over a challenge of *The Absolutely True Diary of a Part-Time Indian* by Sherman Alexie (2009) (Hawk, 2022). The news story about this challenge explained that a review committee consisting of librarians, teachers, students, community members, parents, and administrators was formed, and each member read the entire book and examined book reviews, while also discussing the points raised by those challenging it. The committee chose to retain the book, and this decision was supported by the school board president. The book remained in the curriculum and school library. The Ottumwa challenge is an example of the successful implementation of policy and procedures.

When Library Policy Is Not Followed

The goal of writing library policies is to establish procedures and processes of which all stakeholders are aware and follow as established rules of order. However, there have been several instances of book challenges where the school board chose not to follow the established and approved library policies. For example, in the Wentzville School District (Missouri), the school board voted to remove Toni Morrison's *The Bluest Eye* (1970) after a committee had determined that keeping the book was in the best interest of students (Grumke, 2022). This case is discussed in detail in this chapter. Similarly, parents from Orange County, Florida (who are also cofounders of the Freedom to Read Project), described how the school board in their school district did not follow established book challenge policies for removing the book *Gender Queer: A Memoir* (2022) by Maia Kobabe from library circulation (Random House, 2022).

Some administrators have removed books from school libraries under political pressure or to avoid conflict. In some cases, books are found to be missing on the shelf (likely because they have been removed without notice), or sometimes administrators ask a librarian to remove a book. In the Granbury Independent School District (Texas), the superintendent removed 130 titles from the libraries in the school district under pressure from conservative parents, while declaring his own review process of library content (Hixenbaugh & Schwarz, 2022). The extent of this problem can be found in PEN America's (2022) Index of School Book Bans, which documented book challenges occurring between July 1, 2021, and March 31, 2022. In this index of 1,587 titles, 381 were banned from libraries while the rest were removed from classrooms and curriculum, while remaining in libraries. Of those 381 titles, however, only 25 were reviewed through a formal challenge, and the remaining 356 removals had been originated by a school administrator (see figure 14.1).

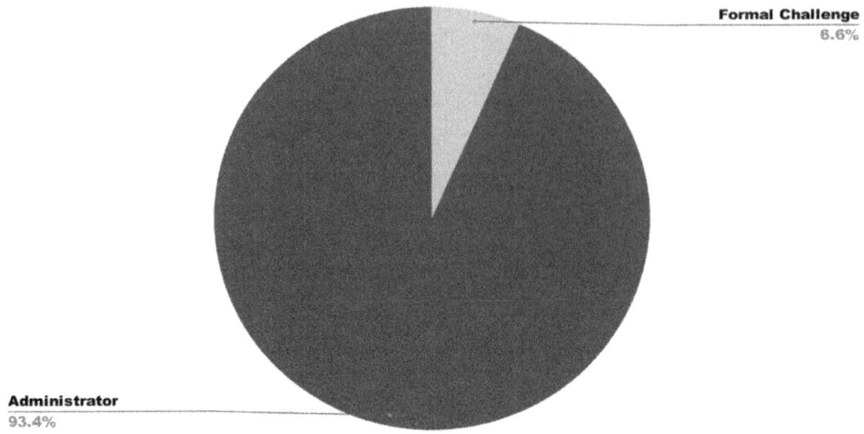

Figure 14.1 The Origin of Challenges in the United States Involving School Libraries within a Nine-Month Span. (Source: PEN America, 2022)

Why Policy Is Not Followed

Failing to follow policies in place for reconsidering books is not new. Pelman and Lynch (2011) described how, in 1976, the Island Trees School District (New York) appointed a committee of parents, administrators, and community members to review a list of contested books in the school library. While the committee chose to retain most of the books under review, the school board removed all of the books and rejected the committee's recommendations. This is the now famous *Board of Education v. Pico* (1982) Supreme Court case, where one student, Steven Pico, contested that the board's decision violated his and his peers' First Amendment rights. The resulting court case ruled in favor of the students' right to receive the information found in the books and the books were returned to the shelves after seven long years (Pelman & Lynch, 2011).

With library selection and reconsideration policies already in place in most school libraries, it is perplexing as to why some school boards ignore policies or choose to remove books outside of policy. One possibility is that school board officials may see their role as protectors of the students, acting in *loco parentis*, which refers to the legal responsibility for an adult to make responsible decisions for children in their care and is particularly relevant for educators working with children in schools (Oltmann, 2019). In this regard, an adult uses their own *discretion* to protect students as they choose (Pelman & Lynch, 2011). Protecting students is often the focus of statements from administrators or board members who have been involved in removing a book. For example, one board member from Dare County Schools (North Carolina) is quoted in the news as saying:

> In a typical review, you know, somebody fills out the paperwork, sends it to the school, the school has a committee or forwards it to the district office to review. This one was a little bit different, just because it had strong sexual content in it that wasn't really needed to be in the public-school setting. (Wagner, 2022, para. 3)

These statements suggest that the board used their own discretion to bypass the formal review process in order to protect students. On the other hand, administrators or school board members who imagine they are removing books to protect students are actually failing to protect the First Amendment rights of students who might benefit from the content.

Failure to follow policy may simply be related to lack of awareness that there is a policy. A typical news story related to book banning will discuss the decision to remove a book, often citing minutes from school board meetings, but will fail to mention how existing library policy was or was not followed to make the decision. Stripling (2015) suggested that school boards should be held accountable for following their own policy, which can be accomplished by establishing connections between school boards, librarians, and community members. These partnerships can lead to positive change and outcomes and help to establish intellectual freedom as a priority.

The assumption in this chapter is that school library policy is good policy, supportive of libraries, librarians, and the student's right to read, explore, and learn from the materials in their library collection. However, new policies that are not created by librarians and library professionals are being developed by school boards or at the legislative level. In a concerning turn of events, new legislation enacted in some states requires school boards to create policies to routinely review books in existing school library collections. In some cases, these new review policies may exist in addition to existing school library policies or may completely disregard policies already in existence. For example, the state of Tennessee has attempted to standardize school library policy by enacting the Age-Appropriate Materials Act of 2022, which requires the school boards of all local education agencies to adopt policies to regularly review the library collection for appropriateness and suitability (Aldrich, 2022), although most school districts in Tennessee already have their own selection and reconsideration policies.

The ALA OIF has explained that policies or procedures that are overly complex are often ignored or bypassed. While we have not noticed this in the selection or reconsideration policies of school libraries, many school boards and administrators are unclear on the policy or are unsatisfied with the process. In their content analysis, Dawkins and Eidson (2021) found that while most selection policies were in the school district's policy manual or on the website, these researchers were still unable to locate over nineteen selection policies of the ninety-nine they sought (approximately 19 percent). If researchers who are actively searching for the policies are unable to find them, it can be assumed that school boards, administrators, and parents are also unable to find them—if they are even aware that such policies exist.

Reflections: Wentzville School District

The Wentzville School District[1] (WSD) has been a fast-growing district in Missouri, moving from one elementary, one middle school, and one high school to its 2022–23 structure of twelve elementary, four middle schools, four high schools, two alternative learning centers, and an early childhood center, in just over thirty years. It has employed full-time, certified librarians in each of its schools for more than fifteen years. The district also employs an individual who acts as the library assistant in each school and learning center, enabling assistance throughout the day for all learners. The school libraries are well-funded and expected to provide materials to support the curriculum and to "reflect the ideals and beliefs of religious, social, political, historical and ethnic groups, and their contributions to American and world cultures" (WSD 6310 Policy, 2008, para. 1). WSD school librarians are tasked by the district to provide intellectual access to age-appropriate resources and materials "free of constraints resulting from artificial barriers" (WSD 6310 Policy, 2008, para. 2) for all students and staff.

To accomplish this, WSD students are taught by their librarian early on how to select books and materials that will meet their personal needs. They are guided in how these materials are organized within the library space and encouraged to use the provided signage so they may become independent users of the library. For personal selections, students are taught to consider such things as topics that interest them, the length of the book, the white space on the page, the size of the font, and illustrations, so that they may select books that will be just right for them. Children are also taught to consider what they are already reading, to balance a longer fiction book with another interest such as cooking, drawing, or a biography. Students beginning in kindergarten make personal choices within the library by utilizing these skills and navigating through thousands of books.

School librarians in the WSD, while serving in *loco parentis*, work with each child to encourage their academic growth, recreational reading, and personal interests. Because these minor children are not accompanied by their parents at the time of selecting their materials, school librarians are tasked with respecting each child's family values and guiding the child's selections to best respect their family's wishes through a collection that is intentionally created for a diverse population. To accomplish this, families are encouraged to communicate with their child's school librarian so that a collaborative, respectful approach can best meet the academic and social learning needs of their individual child. Through relationships and good communication, many potentially difficult situations can be avoided. WSD 6310 Regulation (2008) encourages the use of informal procedures such as parental permission and patron notes to aid school librarians in this task.

Policies, Processes, and Regulations in Place

District policies, processes, and regulations for school libraries are created to communicate the broad expectations surrounding the school libraries to staff, administrators, families, and the school board. In WSD, two active policies, 6310 for school library instructional services and 6241 for challenged material, were established in 2003 and revised in 2008. These policies provide the foundation for selection and deselection of materials and the process with which "honest differences of opinion" (WSD 6241 Regulation, 2008, para. 1) regarding a book or material will be handled.

Documents such as these in school districts, along with the Library Bill of Rights (ALA, 2019), provide the foundation for securing intellectual freedom for students and staff (LaRue, 2018). WSD, like other school districts, relies on the foundations of these policies to ensure the right to read for students. WSD's policy for challenged material goes so far as to state that "the principles of academic freedom and the freedom to read must be defended, rather than the materials" (WSD 6241 Policy, 2008, para. 3).

For nearly fifteen years, these WSD policies, processes, and regulations have served to uphold intellectual freedom and the right to read. Even when tested shortly after the revision in 2008, these policies defended students' rights. A formal challenge was filed regarding an elementary library book about puppies that contained an appropriate use of the term "bitch." The school board reviewed the committee's findings and voted in accord with the committee. The book was retained and returned to the libraries for circulation. This policy was not actively used again until the fall of 2021.

The 2021–22 Book Challenge Onslaught

The fall of 2021 found WSD in the middle of a collective effort among conservative groups to "clean up" school libraries. Members of private Facebook groups throughout the country shared editable documents containing passages from books that they deemed to be inappropriate. Many members of this Facebook group were also members of the national organization No Left Turn in Education, which opposes the teaching of critical race theory and comprehensive sexual education in schools (Grumke, 2021). The challenged books in WSD had lesbian, gay, bisexual, transgender, and queer/questioning (LGBTQ+) authors or content, or content by or about people of color.

Individuals were encouraged to challenge the access of books on this list for all minors, not simply their own children, and nine challenges were filed.

These challenges did not allow for any communication or de-escalation strategies as suggested within policy, because the intent of the challenges was to deny access to all students. There was not an opportunity for the school librarians to act in *loco parentis* or to add notes to students' accounts. In fact, the majority of the nine challenges were filed by a community member whose children attended a private school. Therefore, there was no opportunity for any adult collaboration.

The intent of the challenges was not only to interfere with students' access to information in the school libraries but also to inflame the community and intimidate the school librarians. Open forums during school board meetings were used to read isolated passages from challenged material, enrage community members, and secure necessary votes to remove books before board members even considered the WSD policies. Additionally, police reports were filed on two separate occasions, alleging a school librarian was distributing pornography to students. The police arrived at school to question the school librarian. These tactical moves served to discredit the professionalism and collection standards of the school librarians throughout the district and to divide community members.

Following the required protocol as outlined in school board policy became increasingly difficult. Finding enough staff, community members, or parents (as outlined in the policy) to fill spots on numerous committees was complicated. Since many of these titles were also being challenged in districts across the country, purchasing enough copies for each committee member presented additional delays. Repeated sunshine law[2] requests for district communication about challenged items was not only costly and time consuming but created a communication challenge between administrators, librarians, and other stakeholders throughout the process. Additionally, when committee members' names were acquired through the sunshine law, many individuals withdrew as committee members, as they were publicly scrutinized in these Facebook groups.

Nearly four months after the initial challenge was filed, the first committee met for the book *The Bluest Eye* by Toni Morrison. The discussion surrounding the book was divided, but the members voted to retain the book without restriction. Per policy, the findings of the committee were presented at the next school board meeting. However, before any committee information was openly discussed, several school board members presented a collaborative effort to repress any discussion, and a motion was made and seconded to remove the book from the WSD libraries and all curriculum. Following some candid comments by individual members stating they would never vote to retain any of these books, *The Bluest Eye* was officially banned with a 4–3 vote of the WSD school board members.

Wentzville's book banning became a national news item. The Today Show (Campoamor, 2021) and *Time Magazine* (Waxman, 2022) were just two of the many national news organizations to report the WSD school board decision. Local media maintained ongoing reporting as information regarding the book ban evolved (Grumke, 2021, 2022; Henderson, 2022), and within a short time, new headlines emerged as a lawsuit was filed by the American Civil Liberties Union (ACLU, 2022) on behalf of two minor WSD students for infringement of their First Amendment rights. In response, the WSD school board held a special meeting where they reversed their decision and reinstated *The Bluest Eye* to classrooms and school libraries. This did not end their troubles, however, and the lawsuit remained. Not only had access to *The Bluest Eye* been withheld from students and staff for months but so had all the other titles that had yet to go through the challenge process.

The Impact of Policy Loopholes

The policies of collection development and request for reconsideration at WSD were written broadly to provide foundations for school librarians, staff, administrators, and families, but because they were not written to consider an attack on intellectual freedom, loopholes provided an avenue to escalate this extreme conservative agenda. Because there is no stipulation in the policies as to who can challenge material, members of the community with no children in WSD schools were able to disregard the steps of working with the librarian and instead began these challenges at the district level, escalating the situation at an alarming rate. Additionally, the regulation for the process of a challenged material states that the books will be removed from the shelves pending a committee review and vote of the board. This loophole accompanied by the number of simultaneous challenges allowed these individuals to work the system and eliminate access to many of these titles for most of the school year.

An additional loophole was that of evaluating the book through isolated passages. While the policy itself states that the committee members read the book in its entirety, an open forum in the school board meeting allowed for isolated, out-of-context readings for all in attendance and those viewing the recorded meeting. These passages inflamed the audience and created an immediate question regarding the value of the book and the professionalism of the school librarians. Many community members, staff, and administrators began to express their opinions about these books without having read them.

Another loophole is in relation to the role of the school board. While the policy states that the committee will prepare a written report of its findings and submit these to the superintendent, there is nothing to ensure that the school board members will read or discuss the report as a recommendation. Additionally, the school board member who sits on the committee has an amplified voice during school board meetings, enabling their opinion to be heard outside of the of the committee. Finally, school board members were found to vote on emotion without having read the book or the report. Many board members acted with rashness (as intended by the challengers) because of the out-of-context readings.

While many policy loopholes are detriments to upholding the intellectual freedom of students and staff, one remains a benefit. There is nothing in these policies determining a length of time for a ban or a method for reconsideration. This leaves hope to continue to build a collection that will defend the "principles of academic freedom and the freedom to read" (WSD 6241 Policy, 2008).

Moving Forward: Policy and Beyond

The research for this chapter identified that there are several concerns for librarians to acknowledge as they work to support intellectual freedom in their schools. First, school library policy should be clear, specific, and well written, and include the elements described in the *Selection & Reconsideration Policy Toolkit for Public, School, & Academic Libraries* (ALA OIF, 2018). Second, school boards and administrators should be made aware of and learn about existing policies, so that they can be followed, and then used, should the school district be tasked to develop policy for reviewing library materials. Last, school librarians must consider additional approaches, beyond policy, so that students can understand and demand their own intellectual freedom, instead of relying on adults to protect their intellectual freedom.

Within the WSD, the efforts to defend intellectual freedom and the right to read will continue to be a focus, but with a clearer vision than before. For WSD, revisions to policies will require prudent timing but must be an immediate focus to ensure they are well written with the appropriate elements as outlined in the *Selection & Reconsideration Policy Toolkit for Public, School, & Academic Libraries* (ALA OIF, 2018). Additionally, the content of policies needs to be part of the school librarians' ongoing communication. This will ensure that stakeholders understand that the school librarians are directed by the school board to create a diverse, representative library so that the students may have the opportunity to learn about the world outside of their immediate surroundings. Finally, direct instruction needs to occur with students and staff about the meaning of the First Amendment and the role libraries of all kinds play in providing this right to our citizens. Libraries are places where patrons choose what information to read, and, to fulfill the ethical role of the librarian, the library must utilize resources and space to support diversity and inclusion (ALA, 2017).

While these are the currently available avenues being taken to ensure students' freedom to read, new roadblocks are forthcoming for all Missouri school librarians. Since the challenges at WSD, a new law was enacted that allows for librarians to be criminally prosecuted for knowingly providing access to materials with sexually explicit images (Legiscan, 2022). If found guilty of providing access to books with sexual images (which includes many of the titles being challenged now, particularly related to LGBTQ topics and graphic novels), they could be convicted of a Class A misdemeanor, the most severe of the misdemeanor convictions. This would be punishable by up to a year in jail and a fine up to $2,000 (Missouri Sentencing Advisory Commission, 2016). Implementation of this bill is expected to have an impact on library selection.

Moving toward Intellectual Freedom as a Sustainable Practice

As demonstrated in this chapter, policy can be disregarded, changed, or bypassed. Because of this, school libraries should consider how to empower intellectual freedom within all areas of library operation. Sustainable practice, a term adopted from environmental science, asserts that healthy conditions are established in a specific environment to allow actions to continue without causing undue harm to others. In libraries, efforts to increase sustainability are often driven by crises, which lead to solutions that can improve the future. With the number of book challenges and removals nationwide, it might be said that intellectual freedom for youth in schools is indeed in crisis. Burgess (2021) described "sustainability" as a type of justice work that ensures the future generations will flourish, and we can apply this concept to plans for building future intellectual freedom efforts. As a direct response to the book challenges experienced in 2021–22, developing a culture of intellectual freedom is a necessary practice for school libraries to sustain the freedom to read.

The many examples of school boards that ignored recommendations to retain a book in a school library collection, including the specific examples from WSD, suggest that sustaining intellectual freedom starts with policy but cannot end with it. Policies should be revised to be relevant and current, instructional components of the school library program should be utilized, and professional development for other stakeholders should be provided as basic strategies for sustaining intellectual freedom. We conclude with some additional recommendations that may help school libraries to work toward a sustainable culture of intellectual freedom.

- *Teach children about the right to read*: Pelman and Lynch asked, "How is the freedom of speech taught in schools? Sometimes it is taught when it is violated by the school board and students have to fight to protect their rights" (2011, para. 2). While learning about freedom of speech and First Amendment rights after a book ban is not ideal, it is often these moments of crisis that can propel positive action and changes. Utilizing the celebration of Constitution Day, September 17, is an ideal beginning-of-the-year strategy to teach students about their First Amendment rights.

- *Allow children to become part of the governing process*: Though rarely included in many library selection policies and processes, providing opportunities for children to participate in a process that directly impacts them is one strategy for teaching children about their rights, while also incorporating youth voices into the governing process (Koren, 2020). A librarian might consider student involvement in policy, library governance, programming, services, selection, weeding, or the design of the library.
- *Train school board members and administrators about intellectual freedom*: Children have a right to be taught, informed, and led by educators who understand their rights. As one of the only educators in the school specifically trained in intellectual freedom, the school librarian can educate school board members, administrators, and other teachers regarding the importance that unrestricted access plays in developing intellectual curiosity, personal interests, and identity for children (Koren, 2011). Librarians can also include links to the ALA Library Bill of Rights (ALA, 2019) or snippets from existing policy in communication with stakeholders.
- *Include materials on children's rights in the library*: Koren (2011) suggested that one of the most direct ways for librarians to teach children about human rights is to provide developmentally appropriate reading materials about human rights. In addition to Banned Books Week, librarians can select stories with characters who fought for their rights and succeeded by continually seeking information. For example, *A Computer Called Katherine: How Katherine Johnson Helped Put America on the Moon* (2019) by Suzanne Slade tells the journey of this Black female mathematician, her efforts to work for NASA during the time of segregation, and her crucial contributions toward the success of the Apollo missions.
- *Revise and improve existing library policy*: Librarians can review existing policy to consider how to apply intellectual freedom definitions, support for intellectual freedom, and rights-based language. This includes (but is not limited to) a definition of intellectual freedom, a description of who can submit a reconsideration request (such as parents and those within the school district), specification for the review process (including requiring all committee members to read the entire book), reference to supporting documents such as the ALA Library Bill of Rights (ALA, 2019) and the Freedom to Read Statement (ALA, 2004), and rights-based language that explains the value of choice and unrestricted access as necessary for the development of children in school. In addition, the process can include a public review of the final committee recommendation in school board meetings.

Conclusion

As we conclude this chapter, many questions remain unanswered. How will new policies at the state and district levels impact school libraries? How will school librarians change their practices due to these policies and experiences? How can librarians, administrators, and school boards work together to support a child's right to read? How can school librarians empower students to understand and utilize their rights to read? The future of the school library as a space for curiosity, exploration, inclusion, learning, and intellectual freedom relies on how these questions are answered.

Notes

1. Information from the Wentzville School District comes from the personal experiences of one of the authors who began teaching in the WSD in 1986 and has served on four challenge committees, including the one about puppies and *The Bluest Eye* by Toni Morrison.

2. Missouri's Sunshine Law, https://ago.mo.gov/missouri-law/sunshine-law, ensures transparency of public governmental bodies by requiring, upon request, the provision of documents related to any committees or other public forum business.

References

Adams, H. (2021). The materials selection policy: Defense against censorship. In A. Dawkins (Ed.), *Intellectual freedom issues in school libraries* (pp. 53–54). ABC-CLIO.

Adams, H., Leu, D., & Venuto, D. A. (2015). Standing by their principles: Two librarians who faced challenges. *Knowledge Quest, 44*(1), 42–47.

Aldrich, M. (2022). Age appropriate school library bill heads to Tennessee governor's desk. *The Tennessean.* https://www.tennessean.com/story/news/education/2022/03/15/tennessee-age-appropriate-school-library-bill-heads-gov-bill-lee-desk/7049218001/

American Civil Liberties Union. (2022, May). *C.K.-W. V Wentzville R-IV School District.* https://www.aclu.org/cases/ck-w-v-wentzville-r-iv-school-district-0

American Library Association. (2004). *Freedom to read statement.* https://www.ala.org/advocacy/intfreedom/freedomreadstatement

American Library Association. (2017). *Professional ethics.* http://www.ala.org/tools/ethics

American Library Association. (2019). *Library Bill of Rights.* https://www.ala.org/advocacy/intfreedom/librarybill

American Library Association Office for Intellectual Freedom. (2018). *Selection & reconsideration policy toolkit for public, school, & academic libraries.* http://www.ala.org/tools/challengesupport/selectionpolicytoolkit

Board of Education v. Pico. (1982). 457 U.S. 853.

Burgess, J. (2021). Towards an ethics of unity: An ecological approach to overcoming dispossession in academic libraries. *Canadian Journal of Academic Librarianship/Revue canadienne de bibliothéconomie universitaire, 7*, 1–15.

Campoamor, D. (2021). Missouri school district bans Toni Morrison's "The Bluest Eye." *Today*. https://www.today.com/parents/teens/missouri-school-district-bans-toni-morrisons-bluest-eye-rcna13967

Chavez, N., McMorris-Santoro, E., & Dolan, L. (2021, December). *Some school librarians fed up with book bans are organizing and fighting back*. CNN. https://www.cnn.com/2021/12/21/us/texas-school-librarians-book-challenges/index.html

Dawkins, A. M., & Eidson, E. C. (2021). A content analysis of district school library selection policies in the United States. *School Library Research, 24*, 1–27.

Grumke, K. (2021). *Schools across St. Louis face more attempts to remove books from library shelves*. STL PR NPR. https://news.stlpublicradio.org/education/2021-11-18/schools-across-st-louis-face-more-attempts-to-remove-books-from-library-shelves

Grumke, K. (2022). *St. Louis group launch banned book program to distribute challenged books*. STL PR NPR. https://news.stlpublicradio.org/education/2022-01-28/local-organizations-launch-banned-book-program-to-distribute-challenged-books

Hawk, E. (2022). Reconsideration committee, school board vote to keep controversial book in curriculum. *Ottumwa Courier*. https://www.ottumwacourier.com/news/local_news/reconsideration-committee-school-board-vote-to-keep-controversial-book-in-curriculum/article_cdd8a654-ec1f-11ec-8e1e-9bf86f5c69ff.html

Henderson, J. (2022, January). Librarians, others stand against Wentzville's book ban. *St. Louis Post-Dispatch*. https://www.stltoday.com/entertainment/books-and-literature/librarians-others-stand-against-wentzville-s-book-ban/article_5679df49-c7dd-54d0-8258-fc94f5d0078b.html

Hixenbaugh, M., & Schwartz, J. (2022). *Texas superintendent tells librarians to pull books on sexuality, transgender people*. ProPublica/Texas Tribune. https://www.nbcnews.com/news/us-news/texas-superintendent-librarians-books-sexuality-transgender-rcna20992

Koren, M. (2011). School libraries and human rights. In L. Marquardt & D. Oberg (Eds.), *Global perspectives on school libraries: Projects and practices* (pp. 153–158). Walter de Gruyter.

Koren, M. (2020). Library governance in view of the rights of the child: The sustainable development goals as catalyst. In E. Abbott-Halpin & C. Rankin (Eds.), *Public library governance* (pp. 187–236). De Gruyter.

LaRue, J. (2018). Intellectual freedom. In S. Hirsch (Ed.), *Information services today: An introduction* (2nd ed., pp. 434–449). Rowman & Littlefield.

LegiScan. (2022). *Bill text: MO SB775/2022/Regular Session/Enrolled*. https://legiscan.com/MO/text/SB775/id/2585012/Missouri-2022-SB775-Enrolled.pdf

Missouri Sentencing Advisory Commission. (2016). https://www.courts.mo.gov/hosted/JUDEDintra/MOSAC/Criminal_System.html

Oltmann, S. M. (2019). *Practicing intellectual freedom in libraries*. Libraries Unlimited.

Pelman, A., & Lynch, B. (2011). The school library versus the school board: An exploration of the book banning trend of the 1980s. *The Journal of Research on Libraries and Young Adults, 1*(2). https://www.yalsa.ala.org/jrlya/2011/02/the-school-library-versus-the-school-board-an-exploration-of-the-book-banning-trend-of-the-1980s/

PEN America. (2022). *Index of school book bans* [data set]. PEN America. https://docs.google.com/spreadsheets/d/1hTs_PB7KuTMBtNMESFEGuK-0abzhNxVv4tgpI5-iKe8/edit#gid=1380530296

Random House. (2022). *Banned books: When books are threatened where do we turn* [video]. YouTube. https://youtu.be/CvobjBtGyIE

SLJ Research. (2016). Controversial books survey. *School Library Journal*. https://s3.amazonaws.com/WebVault/SLJ/SLJ_ControversialBooksSurveyReport_2016.pdf

Stripling, B. K. (2015). Creating a culture of intellectual freedom through leadership and advocacy. *Knowledge Quest, 44*(1), 14–19.

Wagner, M. (2022, March). *How one book disappeared from Dare school libraries.* The Outer Banks Voice. https://www.outerbanksvoice.com/2022/06/10/how-one-book-disappeared-from-dare-county-school-libraries/

Waxman, O. B. (2022, January). Why Toni Morrison's books are so often the target of book bans. *Time.* https://time.com/6143127/toni-morrison-book-bans/

WSD 6241 Policy. (2008, December). *Challenged materials.* Wentzville R-IV School District.

WSD 6241 Regulation. (2008, December). *Challenged materials.* Wentzville R-IV School District.

WSD 6310 Policy. (2008, December). *School libraries.* Wentzville R-IV School District.

WSD 6310 Regulation. (2008, December). *School libraries.* Wentzville R-IV School District.

Books Discussed in This Chapter

Alexie, S. (2009). *The absolutely true diary of a part-time Indian.* Little, Brown.

Kobabe, M. (2022). *Gender queer: A memoir.* Oni Press.

Morrison, T. (1970). *The bluest eye.* Vintage International, Vintage Books, a Division of Penguin Random House.

Slade, S. (2019). *A computer called Katherine: How Katherine Johnson helped put America on the moon.* Little, Brown.

CHAPTER FIFTEEN

Whom Do We Serve? A Youth Librarianship Perspective

Cindy C. Welch

Introduction

In 2022, there was new legislation under consideration in at least eight states across the country, seeking to limit the availability of various content in K–12 libraries. Some proposals were more successful than others at being written into law, and, in every case, it was a shocking and revealing process. For those closest to the fray, it was intimidating, scary, disheartening, and other energy-sapping adjectives that make us wary of doing our jobs. How do we combat the fear and hesitation that these legislative initiatives created? How do we find the courage and will to continue to supply the information needed by our youth, at the point of need, regardless of politics, social norms, or personal beliefs? We must reflect on how we personally relate to the foundational tenets of our field. We must examine what we know and think we know about our youth-specific service areas. We must think carefully about how we characterize our audiences, in all their many aspects. Most importantly, we must determine who it is that we truly serve.

Foundations and Aspirations of Our Field

Discussion of any aspect of intellectual freedom and freedom of access, particularly for youth materials, can be difficult. Our societal perceptions of youth and their needs evolve, sometimes slowly and not always in a progressive way, and the whole of it is complicated by the many roles and perspectives we may take along the way: former youth ourselves, mentors/coaches, teachers, parents, librarians, and so on. In addition, it is always necessary to acknowledge—and sometimes negotiate—our own morals, sensitivities, and beliefs as we strive to provide quality resources and service for others. Yes, we are people, too, and are entitled to our own set of beliefs and values. Our profession, library/information work, however, demands that we aspire to high standards, perhaps requiring us to set aside our feelings, to provide the best level of service.

Thus, part of the process of our work involves an examination of our relationship to the foundational and aspirational documents that define our profession. To be very clear, personal beliefs and values are valid and important, and yet, they cannot be permitted to override our professional promises to our communities, as embodied in the American Library Association (ALA) Library Bill of Rights, the Freedom to Read Statement, and the ALA Code of Ethics (mentioned later in this chapter). The first step in best practice, then, must be reading and rereading these documents to see what can be immediately embraced and what might be personally problematic about applying the principles to our work with youth.

The Library Bill of Rights, like our U.S. Bill of Rights, is accompanied by "Interpretations" that help us keep this document current and relevant in changing times. Several of these interpretations address youth specifically. "Access to Library Resources and Services for Minors," for example, notes that "library resources and services should not be abridged based on chronological age, apparent maturity, educational level, literacy skills, legal status, or through restrictive scheduling and use policies" (ALA, 2019b, para. 3). Another interpretation, "Access to Resources and Services in the School Library," focuses more closely on practice for school librarians, noting that best practice avoids

> imposing age, grade-level, or reading-level restrictions on the use of resources; limiting the use of interlibrary loan and access to electronic information; charging fees for information in specific formats; requiring permission from parents or teachers; establishing restricted shelves or closed collections; and labeling. (ALA, 2014, para. 6)

It also states that school librarians "resist efforts by individuals or groups to define what is appropriate for all students or teachers to read, view, hear, or access regardless of technology, formats or method of delivery" (ALA, 2014, para. 5). "Minors and Online Activity" reminds us that

> prohibiting minors from using social media or participating in online communities prevents youth from engaging in opportunities to learn and develop skills needed for responsible speech online, civil engagement, and

> personal-privacy protection. Instead, libraries and library workers should educate youth about online activities that are appropriate for their maturity level without blocking access for others. (ALA, 2019a, para. 7)

Another interpretation, "Internet Filtering," specifically addresses the Children's Internet Protection Act and its requirement that school and public libraries filter to receive funding. The interpretation offers analysis of the shortcomings of filtering, concluding that "in many cases students are prevented from creating and sharing their documents, videos, graphics, music and other original content with classmates or the wider world; thus valuable learning opportunities are lost" (ALA, 2015, para. 7). These are among the interpretations that most specifically apply to or name youth in their language; other interpretations, not named here, encompass youth as part of the larger public served and can be accessed on the ALA website.

In addition to these general documents, ALA divisions also have best practices, standards of conduct, and the like, which seek to guide us in professional practice. The American Association of School Librarian's (AASL) National School Library Standards spotlights intellectual freedom as one of six "common beliefs" that undergird the profession, identifying it as "every learner's right" (AASL, 2018, p. 13). The Association for Library Service for Children's (ALSC) Competencies for Librarians Serving Children in Libraries advocates for the "best possible access to materials and resources for all children and their caregivers" (ALSC, 2020, Reference and User Services Section, #1) and for "overcoming systems of oppression, discrimination, exclusion, and ethnocentrism" (ALSC Education Committee, 2020, Outreach and Advocacy Section, #4). The Young Adult Library Services Association's (YALSA) Teen Services Competencies for Library Staff encourages cultural competence, responsiveness, and protected equity of access, among other things. Teens need us to support their development of "self-concept, identity, coping mechanisms" (YALSA, 2017, Interaction with Teens Section) and to "ensure access to a wide variety of library resources, services, and activities for and with all teens, especially those facing challenges to access" (YALSA, 2017, Equity of Access Section). YALSA goes further with its own Core Professional Values for the Teen Services Professional that name inclusion, integrity, and social responsibility, among others (YALSA, 2015).

It is important to remember that these living documents were not composed by a building or an institution; they were created, argued over, resisted, and refreshed by us—librarians and library workers—amid the day-to-day struggles of doing what is best for our communities and users.

Why do these documents matter? Because our profession is not devoid of bias, hate, or even exclusionary practices, past or present. Children's and teen librarians have been, past and present, condescending about services to diverse populations and very prescriptive about what youth "should" be reading, and yet during—and sometimes because of—these very moments in time, our peers created and revised these aspirational documents to guide us in our practice. We can do better; we should do better. Awareness and affirmation of our national organization and foundational documents grounds us in the bigger world and illuminates the true nature of what we aspire to do—no matter the level at which we function or the nature of our jobs.

We must also examine our personal thoughts about censorship, especially as they intersect with doing our jobs. What if I simply move a book to a "restricted" area? What if I keep it in my office? What if I just do not tell anyone it is here? What if I put an age or reading level label on it? What if it is "offensive" to contemporary audiences? Is that censorship? Yes, yes, it is. Any time, in any circumstance, in which we choose to *limit or restrict* access *on behalf of others*, without their knowledge or input, is censorship.

Demographics and Data-Driven Decision-Making

As we reaffirm our understanding of the nature of our work and the documents that motivate us as we serve our communities, we begin thinking about those communities. How do we know who is in our service area? How do we decide our customer base? Most often, it is a matter of observation, of watching who comes in our doors, who completes our library card applications, and who engages with us on social media or our website. We may note changes in our neighborhoods as we drive to or from work daily or scan local media for information about changes in demographics or community interests. If our library plans a costly financial change of any kind, our leadership can consult census data, using tools that increasingly allow us to drill down to granular levels, to build data profiles that allow us to look at data by state, county, zip codes, even congressional districts, and provide basic information about income, education, employment, age, and so on. In addition, the U.S. Bureau of Labor Statistics, the Statistical Abstract (of the Census), and even the White House Briefing Room package data that may be useful in determining services, programming, and resources for all ages, including youth. There is a tendency with these tools, though, to lump youth together, often in one category, birth through age seventeen, so use these tools advisedly. Local information may also be available from chambers of commerce, better business bureaus, local real estate organizations, and other civic groups. School districts can be timely sources of information about youth in our communities, to complement what we see from other government sources.

In addition to this "traditional" way of thinking about data, it is necessary to build support for all youth within a particular service area. As we think about who we serve, and why, there are other very important data points to bring forward for professional and community consideration. For example, considering the current challenges involving gender expression and gender identity, data on bullying and harassment, and even suicide, are pertinent to any community conversation. Sources like the Youth Risk Behavior Surveillance System Youth Online, sponsored by the Centers for Disease Control and Prevention, can provide state-level data on being bullied, carrying a weapon, dating violence, and attempted suicide. The Trevor Project's national survey on lesbian, gay, bisexual, transgender, and queer/questioning (LGBTQ+) mental health also provides powerful statistics that underscore the need to support and affirm all youth. The Williams Institute, a think tank located at the University of California, Los Angeles School of Law, reports information about quality of life for LGBTQ+ people and has a section devoted to youth.

Immigrant youth and youth of color also experience challenges and may have unique information needs. The Southern Poverty Law Center maintains a list of hate crimes and groups across the United States, and it is eye-opening to realize where these groups are headquartered and/or functioning. The information can be sorted or filtered by state, ideology, focus, and so on. The American Immigration Council, on the other hand, provides more positive-forward data in the "Economics of Immigration" section of their website, where the emphasis is on the positive impact immigrants have and are having on many aspects of American life. Moving beyond census data helps expand the definition of "community" and provides additional justification for materials in youth collections.

There are other think tanks, nonprofits, and research institutions working on youth issues, and using data from them creates a fuller picture of the life and the needs of modern youth, as well as the responsibilities of supporting youth in our service areas. Thinking broadly about "youth," in all its messy glory, will help individual community librarians brainstorm these additional data point sources. Do not hesitate to use them.

Why do we want to bring in these other factors, when the picture they paint is not always a pretty one? Children, tweens, and teens are endangered and die or are killed every day. If there is a way to help prevent that, is that not something we want to do? Again, whom do we serve? The adults in the room who have already run this gauntlet, or the youth who are just trying to navigate their lives in an increasingly alarming world? Reminding censors of the sometimes-brutal realities youth face may help them better understand the need for a wide range of content on our shelves and in our databases.

The Fear Factor and the Ethics of Our Work

In the preceding sections, we have thought about how we position ourselves in relation to our chosen profession's aspirational goals, and we have looked at a few new ways to think about characteristics of our service areas, but this can be very scary—and very lonely—work. It is worth taking a moment to acknowledge that yes, what we do is revolutionary in the best sense, and yes, bad things can happen to good people. In workshops, when asked about their fears and reservations for rocking the boat, so to speak, these are participants' common responses to the question, "What scares you about doing this job?"

- Someone will find out I have this [insert material type here], and I will have to defend it.
- I don't like to confront; I don't like to argue.
- Parents will complain to the [fill in administrative entity here], and I will be in trouble.
- I will get fired, and I have no recourse.
- I have no support from [fill in place of employment].
- Even if I fight, I'll lose anyway.
- Honestly, it's offensive to me, too; I don't really want to fight for it.

What else concerns us about doing this work? Why does it matter what concerns us? One of the most insidious forms of censorship is self-censorship, when we are in the selector's seat, considering materials to add to our collections, and we make choices that limit rather than expand access. This is another one of our little professional secrets, that most of us at one time or other have self-censored during collections work. It is difficult to be brave when there is no guarantee of support or a positive outcome. We think through this aspect of the work so that if/when it happens, we can be somewhat prepared. Censorship in any form is still censorship, and our job, in as far as we can do it, is to avoid even the appearance of censorship. It is important to note that there is a difference—regardless of what others outside of our profession might say—between professional judgment (selection) and censorship. As Lester Asheim famously said,

> Selection seeks to protect the right of the reader to read; censorship seeks to protect—not the right—but the reader himself from the fancied effects of his reading. The selector has faith in the intelligence of the reader; the censor has faith only in his own. (1953, p. 67)

We look for reasons to choose an item (a positive response) rather than reasons not to choose it (a negative response). In addition, thinking back to the previous section, youth need us to be brave alongside them. They need to see themselves on the shelves and need to have access to all kinds of information as they try to discern their worlds. They need allies; they need us in our bravest persona.

As we consider our personal reactions to the danger and potential conflicts of this work, it may be useful to think about the role of ethics in decision-making. In *Foundations of Library and Information Science*, Dr. Richard Rubin noted four factors that impact how we respond ethically to any situation. In any ethical or moral dilemma, we (consciously or unconsciously) consider:

- Social utility—what will best serve my library's mission and goals for our community?
- Survival—how will this affect me personally?
- Social responsibility—what will best serve the community and its expectations of the library?
- Respect for the individual—does this choice support or act against an individual's decision-making ability (2016, pp. 546–549)?

Our ALA peers also addressed ethics in the *Code of Ethics*, stating:

> We do not advance private interests at the expense of library users, colleagues, or our employing institutions. We distinguish between our personal convictions and professional duties and do not allow our personal beliefs to interfere with fair representation of the aims of our institutions or the provision of access to their information resources. (ALA, 2021, principles 6 and 7)

Bringing ethical considerations forward in our professional reflection process may help strengthen our resolve about avoiding self-censorship. Again, this is a personal reflection and reaction, although opportunities to share these types of reflections with our professional peers, in supportive discussions, can provide the additional strength needed to stand firm in the face of oppositional noise.

Another part of self-awareness that may impact our decision-making has to do with our own thoughts on the topic, treatment, or presentation of the material. Being aware of our own sensitivities and biases can help us avoid making judgments based on personal assessments rather than professional ones. For example, if someone is sensitive to profanity, how might that impact their decision about a teen book with the "f-word" or other colorful wording? Similarly, someone with an aversion to or an actual experience with violence may have a difficult time assessing a text that addresses that topic or includes it in an overt way. Self-awareness cannot be overrated in work like this.

Conclusion: Whom Do We Serve?

We have examined and (hopefully) affirmed our professional beliefs, acknowledging that they may be different from our personal beliefs; we have thought deeply and consciously about the good, bad, and ugly of growing up in America right now; and we have considered how our own sensitivities and experiences may impact our collections processes. This is all good work. However, nothing takes the place of well-constructed, thoughtful, compassionate policies. There is no substitute for doing the things we know need to be done ahead of time, to be ready if any of our community seeks a greater understanding of why we made the choices we did. There are countless articles, books, and websites about doing this well. Briefly, we should:

- review our library policies and make sure we have both collection (includes selection, gifts, weeding, maintenance, scope, etc.) and selection (more specific than collection) policies;
- make sure we have a clear and (again) compassionate reconsideration process in place and easily accessible to everyone—including every person who works in our library;
- do staff and board training at least annually, including role-playing, to give everyone the chance to practice with the documents, to think through and even voice their own concerns, and then to be ready to react kindly rather than defensively, to refocus the conversation from what *should not* be on our shelves to what we should add;
- do the selection work thoroughly and thoughtfully, including professional reviews and customer/personal reviews, and use a wide range of sources that help us find more than just mainstream thinking about new materials;
- cultivate allies in leadership positions in our community and do the same with local media. If they understand what we are about, they realize we are all on the same side and can be powerful voices for elevating the library story; and
- have faith in our profession and our process, talk about it, and report any incidents to ALA and other interested parties.

The Office for Intellectual Freedom at ALA is not the only organization interested in our experiences. The American Civil Liberties Union has an office in every state and is available to talk about individual communities and situations. Good information about challenges is also available online from the National Coalition Against Censorship toolkit, and the Comic Book Legal Defense Fund includes a wealth of resources specific to comics and manga on their site.

At the end of the day, we return to the question posed in the title; whom do we serve? As library workers, we may be tempted to answer by saying, "everyone." That is true to some extent because we seek to address the needs of all the people in our community. However, when it comes to sensitive information, youth have the most to lose. I suggest to you that the "who" in this question must be the youth themselves rather than any adult raising their voice against access. We know our youth, and we know their needs. As adults, we may seek to block out our own path to adulthood and that may lead to a desire to protect others. Some adults may be led by misinformation or disinformation or lose sight of the importance of supporting youth in favor of pursuing their own political image. The question comes down to who needs us most. Youth-serving or youth services or school librarians: we all serve youth. Show up, in your bravest professional persona, and keep the focus where it belongs, on making sure any youth in crisis or in celebration can find and get to what they need, without judgment, from us.

References

American Association for School Librarians. (2018). *National school library standards for learners, school librarians, and school libraries.* American Library Association.

American Library Association. (2014, July 1). *Access to resources and services in the school library: An interpretation of the Library Bill of Rights.* https://www.ala.org/advocacy/intfreedom/librarybill/interpretations/accessresources

American Library Association. (2015, June 30). *Internet filtering: An interpretation of the Library Bill of Rights.* https://www.ala.org/advocacy/intfreedom/librarybill/interpretations/internet-filtering

American Library Association. (2019a, June 24). *Minors and online activity: An interpretation of the Library Bill of Rights.* https://www.ala.org/advocacy/intfreedom/librarybill/interpretations/minorsonlineactivity

American Library Association. (2019b, June 25). *Access to library resources and services for minors: An interpretation of the Library Bill of Rights.* https://www.ala.org/advocacy/intfreedom/librarybill/interpretations/minors

American Library Association. (2021, June 29). *Professional ethics.* https://www.ala.org/tools/ethics

Asheim, L. (1953). Not censorship but selection. *Wilson Library Bulletin, 28,* 63–67.

Association for Library Service to Children. (2020). *Competencies for librarians serving children in libraries.* https://www.ala.org/alsc/edcareeers/alsccorecomps

Rubin, R. (2016). The values and ethics of library and information science. In *Foundations of library and information science* (4th ed., pp. 533–579). American Library Association.

Young Adult Library Services Association. (2015, June 27). *Core professional values for the teen services profession.* https://www.ala.org/yalsa/core-professional-values-teen-services-profession

Young Adult Library Services Association. (2017). *Teen services competencies for library staff.* https://www.ala.org/yalsa/sites/ala.org.yalsa/files/content/YALSA_TeenCompetencies_web_Final.pdf

CHAPTER SIXTEEN

Parent Education for Anti-censorship: A School Librarian's Guide

Rhona Campbell

Introduction

In 2020, 39 percent of book challenges were initiated by parents, and 44 percent of these were in school libraries, according to the American Library Association (ALA, 2020). Some of these parents were social conservatives acting on behalf of political and/or religious groups trying to effect value-based changes in their communities. Others, however, were merely scared parents. They were not equipped to respond to their children encountering certain content and reacted in the only way that seemed available. This chapter focuses on these types of parents, and on what school librarians can do to front-load them with information about what to do when their children encounter difficult or painful content, languages, or ideas in books . . . because those encounters are inevitable. Why? Because books contain perspectives, ideas, concepts, and thoughts, and it is impossible to know precisely which of these will be challenging, and to whom.

In an ideal world, parents will find their school librarian to be a compassionate, knowledgeable, relatable, and approachable partner in their child's education. School librarians should work to set up this dynamic through any forum possible: a library session at Back to School Night, a talk at a Parent-Teacher Association (PTA) meeting, making a video or letter to send home with children, and so on. The key is that the librarian comes across as someone who knows the literature in their domain, cares about each individual child, is empathetic, and is driven by the desire to educate—*not* indoctrinate. Timing and regular scheduling of these forums matters. If done early in the school year, every year, it will help embed these important ideas into your community.

The first step is to adopt an empathetic mindset. Parenting is hard! With some exceptions, most parents fiercely love their children. They want only the very best for them. They want everyone else to genuinely know and appreciate their kids. They never, ever want anything awful to happen to their offspring. In short, they are fearful, hopeful, and utterly invested in that child who walks into your library. All most parents want to do is protect their beloved children.

Parental Concerns

Consider the types of things that parents have frequently challenged in books: sexual explicitness; lesbian, gay, bisexual, transgender, queer/questioning, intersex, and/or asexual (LGBTQIA+) representation; perceived profanity; offensive racial representation; anti-police rhetoric; political viewpoints; "woke" ideology; and concepts related to critical race theory (CRT), among others (ALA, 2020). Behind all these complaints is the desire to protect or prevent children from being exposed to ideas that might frighten the parents themselves. Sometimes they worry their child "is not ready" to encounter a particular thought or idea. It might confuse them, destroy their innocence, or force confrontations with unpleasant truths about their place in the world. All these fears are rooted in the idea that "protecting" children means keeping difficult content at arm's length.

Parental worries fall into two main categories. One category is the fear of their child being indoctrinated to antithetical values, such as when homophobic parents challenge Raina Telgemeier's *Drama* (2012) for presenting likeable gay characters. Normalization of offensive humor or behaviors falls into this category as well, such as with objections to Dav Pilkey's *Captain Underpants* series. A second category is worry about children experiencing secondary trauma, such as when a family that has experienced violence wants to keep the casual violence of Suzanne Collins's *The Hunger Games* (2008) far away from their child who is processing a personally traumatic lived reality. Many parents conflate the two categories, thinking that it is genuinely traumatic to be exposed to thoughts, values, or ideas opposed to their own, instead of merely emotionally and mentally taxing. I prefer to think of these as two separate categories, because they must be dealt with differently from a child's perspective.

First, let us look at the fear of books introducing, or "indoctrinating," children to antithetical ideas. Start by putting aside how you, the librarian, may feel about the wrongness of certain worldviews. This is not where you reproach homophobes, no matter how good it might feel! Rather, this is the place to present the question: Does keeping certain information or ideas away from children prevent them from learning that it is out there? The answer to this is: no, it does not. (More on the nuances of this argument later.)

A second question: Do children benefit when they are exposed to ideas, concepts, and worldviews that differ from their own? On two levels, the answer is a resounding "yes." The first is on a child's individual level. This is, in fact, what education is all about. Children develop their character and their values from learning about the world. The have been many research studies over the past twenty years that show a definitive correlation between reading about others and having more empathy and compassion (Keen, 2022). We also know that empathy helps people understand others' motivations and that it is a vital part of cooperative and pro-social behavior (De Vignemont & Singer, 2006).

If you are indeed dealing with white supremacist, homophobic, and/or transphobic parents, this is where things get tricky. Given the list of topics that are highly challenged, it is easy to see there is a preponderance of fear about content featuring LGBTQIA+ people and "woke" ideology, or worldviews promoting recognition of the struggles and biases primarily challenging people of color. The aforementioned parental concern is precisely that their children *will* learn to empathize with people whom the parents themselves fear. Reading about a Black child who experiences harm at the hands of white police is interpreted as "anti-white," and "indoctrination of distrust in the police," as in the challenges to Angie Thomas's *The Hate U Give* (2017) (Gomez, 2018). Sympathetic trans characters (e.g., *I am Jazz* [2014] by Jessica Herthel and Jazz Jennings, or *Melissa* [2014; formerly titled *George*] by Alex Gino) normalize the validity of trans identity. These are not parents for whom the empathy argument will resonate.

This leads us to the second point: that it is good for our society, in general, for people to be exposed to differing views, ideas, concepts, and worldviews. This is the concept that is expounded upon in ALA's Freedom to Read Statement, which states:

> The freedom to read is essential to our democracy . . . free communication is essential to the preservation of a free society and a creative culture. . . . Totalitarian systems attempt to maintain themselves in power by the ruthless suppression of any concept that challenges the established orthodoxy.

> The power of a democratic system to adapt to change is vastly strengthened by the freedom of its citizens to choose widely from among conflicting opinions offered freely to them. To stifle every nonconformist idea at birth would mark the end of the democratic process. Furthermore, only through the constant activity of weighing and selecting can the democratic mind attain the strength demanded by times like these. We need to know not only what we believe but why we believe it. . . . Parents and teachers have a responsibility to prepare the young to meet the diversity of experiences in life to which they will be exposed, as they have a responsibility to help them learn to think critically for themselves. (ALA, 2004)

(Whew! That's heady stuff!)

Diverse Books

Let us take a closer look at racial and ethnic diversity in literature and its benefits for individual children and for our democracy. For children whose identities have been historically underrepresented in media, including books, the recent increase in stories featuring those identities is powerful. All children should feel included and important and connect with literature more closely because it holds up a "mirror" to themselves. As Rudine Sims Bishop (1990) famously wrote: "Literature transforms human experience and reflects it back to us, and in that reflection we can see our own lives and experience as part of the larger human experience. Reading, then, becomes a means of self-affirmation." Author Walter Dean Myers (2014) wrote about this on a more personal level:

> As I discovered who I was, a black teenager in a white-dominated world, I saw that these [white] characters, these lives, were not mine. I didn't want to become the "black" representative, or some shining example of diversity. What I wanted, needed really, was to become an integral and valued part of the mosaic that I saw around me.

But books are not only mirrors. They are also "sliding glass doors. . . . Readers have only to walk through in imagination to become part of whatever world has been created or recreated by the author" (Bishop, 1990). Whether the parents in your community like it or not, our communities are becoming more ethnically, culturally, and racially diverse, and the highest percentage of people of color is found among our youngest citizens (Frey, 2021). Clashes across ethnic and racial differences have increased, as has far-right white supremacist extremism. People in our communities need to learn to understand and accept each other, if for no other reason than to simply be able to coexist peacefully. This argument may not hold a lot of sway with the most bigoted among your parent community, but mention race-based violence specifically against children and it might gain some traction. For example, did you know that data from the late 1990s shows that 23 percent of hate crimes were against children? Among those, 38 percent were anti-Black, 13 percent were anti-Hispanic, and 22 percent were anti-white. Moreover, 64 percent of perpetrators were themselves children (Crimes against Children Research Center [CCRC], 2022).

"Readiness"

Back to the question about "protecting" children from challenging ideas. What about the argument that children "are not ready" for certain concepts? Many parents want to control when and where their child encounters certain ideas, so they can be there to provide their own values and explanations at the stage or age at which they feel the idea is most appropriate and/or beneficial for their child to learn. In my own work, I have encountered this attitude particularly with the parents of children in second through fifth grade. But here is the reality: parents may be able to control a certain amount of a child's exposure to things outside their immediate family's purview, but it is not possible to control everything. Books are only one of many ways children encounter new content. Social media, the internet, television, road signs, playground talk, overheard discussions on the street . . . part of growing up is pulling away from parents to learn things on one's own. It is hard for parents, but it is a necessary step toward autonomy for children, and it is vital to their development. (For more on this, see the work of child psychologist Erik Erickson or the popular parenting book *The Blessing of a Skinned Knee* [2008] by Wendy Mogel.)

To make parents feel a little better about this, there is another perspective, too: no, parents may not be able to counter a child's first interaction with an anathema idea. But do they have a good relationship with their child, in which the child will come to them when something is confusing or scary? Remind parents that those "scary" books provide an opening for discussion with their child. If parents frequently ask about what their child is reading, and if parents have an idea of what kind of books their kids check out from their school library, they will be better equipped to know where their child's thinking is headed. To put this bluntly: when a child checks out Robie H. Harris's *It's Perfectly Normal: A Book about Changing Bodies, Growing Up, Sex, and Sexual Health* (1994), chances are good that child is already interested in or curious about sex. Telling them they are not "ready" to learn about it only deepens their curiosity, pushes them to seek information from others, and takes the parent out of the discussion. (More about what goes through children's heads during check-out time later!)

Let us return to *The Hunger Games* example. Some of the parents listening to you have worries that are not philosophical or value-based: their child has real mental health concerns, and certain language/concepts/content can *actually* be harmful to them. Take the time to address this. Name your understanding that for some select children, certain words or scenes can trigger existing mental health conditions such as posttraumatic stress disorder (PTSD), memory loss, dissociation, and more (Van der Kolk, 1998). Reassure families that you are not going to supplant the mental health professional in that child's life, thinking you can provide bibliotherapy to a child. (Bibliotherapy is a practice wherein mental health professionals use literature with patients as a window to help them understand that they are not alone in their experiences, or to encounter situations in a carefully controlled safe space to help with processing.) Ask parents who have concerns of these specific types to alert you to those situations, so you—and your school's mental health providers—can be a partner for those particularly fragile children.

One gray area in this regard is when generational trauma is involved: a child whose whole family went through harrowing circumstances crossing into the United States from Mexico, for example, may find themself experiencing panic when encountering a book passage that mirrors the experiences they have heard from loved ones. Or take the "n-word": many Black and/or African American people in our country have visceral reactions to this epithet. ALA's list of reasons for book challenges includes a number of these concerns. This is where your familiarity with the literature is paramount. Remind parents that while it is unreasonable to assume you have read and are familiar with every single instance where these types of language or situations appear within the pages of the thousands of books on your shelves, you do have a general awareness of certain books that contain these types of things, particularly for more popular titles. Assure your families that you are doing your utmost to know their students, your school demographics, what is being read, and what is being said about these books among the students.

Regarding those who worry that reading about horrific experiences in books will traumatize their children, it should be noted that psychologists have recently begun to study more about what they call "indirect trauma." While no one has yet studied the effects of reading specifically, research about media exposure to traumatic events shows that while viewers may exhibit signs of stress (particularly if it is repetitive exposure), it is generally agreed that these symptoms are short-lived and do not fit clinical criteria for traumatic stress (May & Wisco, 2016). One study about horror films found that prolonged post-viewing stress reactions only were significant for people who came into the film with heightened anxiety levels (Carleton et al., 2010). So, while it is conceivable that an already anxious reader might experience emotional or mental stress from reading disturbing passages, it is unlikely to cause serious or long-term problems.

In sum: Parents cannot prevent kids from encountering ideas. They can follow their child's lead to understand their thinking. They can use books as springboards for discussions about values and ideas with their children. Reading diversely is a good thing. You have now shown yourself as a caring educational professional who is doing your best to stay on top of when and where certain triggers lie in the collection, and as willing to work in conjunction with teachers and counselors for their child's best library experience.

A Child's Perspective

There are still a few more points that parents need to know, and these have to do with understanding the general viewpoint of a child's experience in the library. What is going through a child's head when they are selecting books from the school library? Why do they pick up a book in the first place? Why do they check out one book and not another? How might they respond when a parent reacts negatively toward one of their choices?

Browsing time at school libraries can vary significantly due to the space, shelf organization, number of students browsing at a time, student age, librarian-to-student ratio, checkout limitations, and so on. Give parents a snapshot of what it looks like in your space. Parents often assume that their child spends browsing time in deep thought selecting exactly what they want to read from the shelves, and that the books they bring home reflect their child's genuine reading desires. We librarians, of course, work hard to try to make that true, but it does not hurt to point out the reality to parents. Here are some things that students might be thinking when they are set free to browse the collection:

- I really liked the book by X author. I wonder if they wrote any others.
- Right now, I'm interested in Y. What books are here about it?
- My teacher wants me to read books that are Z, so I will be dutiful and look for them . . . whether or not they really interest me.
- My librarian is so cool/awful, I want to impress/disgust them with my reading choices.
- What will my peers think about the books I look at?
- If I check out X, people will see that I'm carrying around something funny/popular/hard/long/risqué and think differently about me.
- Will I seem cool/intellectual/popular if I choose the same books as So&So?
- If I choose to read X, maybe I'll have something to talk about with So&So.
- Reading is hard for me. I'd rather goof off with friends than use this time to look at books, but since I have to, I'll try to find the ones that will make my peers react the loudest.
- I just want to claim the coveted beanbag/corner/cozy spot, so I'll grab the first book I see.

- This book has appealing pictures/art.
- Wow, that's got a cool cover!

In other words, as sad as it is to admit, parents should never assume that the book their child is bringing home is being read—and/or fully comprehended—by their child. This perspective makes a huge difference when it comes to what a parent–child interaction might look like when a parent finds something problematic in their child's backpack. Staying calm and asking nonjudgmental questions about why they chose that particular book usually elicits some interesting discussions and insights into the child's thinking. (Although, depending upon the child's maturity, vocabulary, and level of self-awareness, the discussion might require a huge amount of active listening. This might be a place to suggest another parenting classic: Adele Faber and Elaine Mazlish's *How to Talk So Kids Will Listen & Listen So Kids Will Talk* [2012].)

Consider, for a minute, the likely outcome of the opposite scenario, in which the parent freaks out about a book in their child's possession. The child may experience feelings of guilt or shame. They may feel defensive, because they are in a period of psychological growth seeking to distance themselves from their parents. They may be hurt because their choice has been invalidated by someone they love. They may develop negative judgments about their peers, which may lead to social or emotional harm. They may buy into their parents' anti-teacher or anti-librarian rhetoric and find themselves in conflict with these caring adults in their lives. And more likely than not, they will feel more invested than ever before in that particular book that caused Mom to go so crazy! (This is not just a kid's reaction. Guess what effect book bans have on sales of those titles?)

Teachers and librarians work with students to improve reading skills such as decoding, comprehension, vocabulary, and fluency, but children will nonetheless apply to their reading many of the same habits they apply to their lives. This is especially true with free voluntary reading. They may skip the boring parts and go straight to the parts that are interesting. They may not take the time to fully consider or comprehend something that is weird, creepy, confusing, or gross to them. (I once asked an enthusiastic reader how she felt about the death of a character in *Harry Potter and the Goblet of Fire* [2000], by J. K. Rowling. She looked shocked and asked, "He died?" To her, the book was simply a trip to a magical castle.) Their life experiences may not enable them to see the same thing in a passage that an adult will, because they simply have no frame of reference with which to understand certain things. This does not mean that the teacher or librarian is not doing their job, by the way. Giving free choice to students is an important part of their development as independent readers, and there are benefits to reading even the things that are beyond a child's skills: vocabulary and syntax, developing a reading habit, seeing new perspectives, and so on.

Book Banning: The Opposite of Parental Choice

There is one final piece that is vital for parents to understand about censorship, and that is the nature of book banning itself: specifically, removing a book from a collection does not simply remove it from one's own child. Rather, the act of censorship removes the option of accessing that content from every single user of that collection. An interpretation of the American Library Association Bill of Rights states:

> Libraries and their governing bodies shall ensure that . . . parents and guardians have the right and the responsibility to determine their children's—and only their children's—access to library resources. Parents and guardians who do not want their children to have access to specific library services, materials, or facilities should so advise their own children. (ALA, 2006)

Parents need to recognize that they are among a school community that includes many different families who may have different values. Some of these community members may be more powerful than others, but that does not justify imposing the values of one family over all others, which is what book banning really is. Everyone in the school community cares about children and wants the best educational experience possible for each of those precious souls in the school's care. You, their librarian, do, and so do all the other adults in that room. Yes, you are going to disagree sometimes as to what the specifics might mean. That is okay, because you are all in this together, and the children are at the heart of everything.

Conclusion

As a school librarian, you will be most effective if you can demonstrate to your parent body that you are open-minded, empathetic, knowledgeable about child development and literature, and you know and care deeply about their students. If you approach your community with an intentionally thoughtful stance from the start of each school year, you may be able to prevent the heartaches that book challenges could otherwise cause for you, your administration, your communities, your parents, and for the students themselves.

References

American Library Association. (2004). *The freedom to read statement.* https://www.ala.org/advocacy/intfreedom/freedomreadstatement

American Library Association. (2006, July 26). *Access to library resources and services for minors: An interpretation of the Library Bill of Rights.* http://www.ala.org/advocacy/intfreedom/librarybill/interpretations/minors

American Library Association. (2020). Censorship by the numbers infographic. *Banned Books Week*. https://www.ala.org/advocacy/bbooks/bannedbooksweek/ideasandresources/freedownloads

Bishop, R. S. (1990). Windows, mirrors, and sliding glass doors. *Perspectives*, 6(3), ix–xi.

Carleton, R. N., Sikorski, J., & Asmundson, G. J. (2010). Terrifying movie stimuli: A new design for investigating precursors for posttraumatic stress. *Psychological Trauma: Theory, Research, Practice, and Policy*, 2(3), 206.

Crimes against Children Research Center. (2022). *Hate crimes against juveniles reported to police*. University of New Hampshire. https://www.unh.edu/ccrc/resource/hate-crimes-against-juveniles-reported-police

De Vignemont, F., & Singer, T. (2006). The empathic brain: How, when and why? *Trends in Cognitive Sciences, 10*(10), 435–441.

Frey, W. (2021, August 13). *New 2020 census results show increased diversity countering decade-long declines in America's white and youth populations*. Brookings. https://www.brookings.edu/research/new-2020-census-results-show-increased-diversity-countering-decade-long-declines-in-americas-white-and-youth-populations/

Gomez, S. (2018, September 6). Banned spotlight: *The hate u give*. *Banned Books Week*. https://bannedbooksweek.org/banned-spotlight-the-hate-u-give/

Keen, S. (2022). *Empathy and reading: Affect, impact, and the co-creating reader*. Routledge.

May, C., & Wisco, B. E. (2016). Defining trauma: How level of exposure and proximity affect risk for posttraumatic stress disorder. *Psychological Trauma, 8*(2), 233–240.

Myers, W. D. (2014, March 16). Where are the people of color in children's books? [Op-ed]. *New York Times*.

Van der Kolk, B. A. (1998). Trauma and memory. *Psychiatry and Clinical Neurosciences, 52*(S1), S52–S64. https://doi.org/10.1046/j.1440-1819.1998.0520s5S97

Books Discussed in This Chapter

Collins, S. (2008). *The hunger games*. Scholastic.

Faber, A., & Mazlish, E. (2012). *How to talk so kids will listen & listen so kids will talk*. Scribner.

Gino, A. (2015). *Melissa* [previously published as *George*]. Scholastic.

Harris, R. H. (1994). *It's perfectly normal: A book about changing bodies, growing up, sex, and sexual health*. Candlewick.

Herthel, J., & Jennings, J. (2014). *I am Jazz*. Dial Books for Young Readers.

Mogel, W. (2008). *The blessing of a skinned knee*. Scribner.

Pilkey, D. (1997). *The adventures of Captain Underpants*. Scholastic.

Rowling, J. K. (2000). *Harry Potter and the goblet of fire*. Arthur A. Levine.

Telgemeier, R. (2012). *Drama*. Graphix.

Thomas, A. (2017). *The hate u give*. Balzer + Bray.

PART 5

Advice from Librarians

CHAPTER SEVENTEEN

Challenges That Provide Insight into a Librarian's Code of Ethics and a Systemic Threat to National Democracy

Dee Ann Venuto

Introduction

Historically, censorship is a threat to democracy, and intellectual freedom challenges are never easy. Writing this chapter, I relived and rehashed my formal challenges and opened the box of primary documents I have saved. A fabulous network administrator suggested I make print copies of everything, since information on the internet is impermanent, as librarians know and teach. It has been cathartic yet once again upsetting to remember the details of that time and process the thirteen years of connections to recent history. For me and others, the challenges were one of life's losses of innocence, but the experience strengthened me as a professional and a person.

I learned that when one elects to publicly share an opinion on a controversial topic, it brings consequences, but that taught me to be a better teacher with the knowledge I gained. I became aware of professional material such as "Just the facts about sexual orientation and youth: A guide for educators," which provided advice for addressing the topics of diversity and inclusivity (Just the Facts Coalition, 2008). This document included the responsibilities of educators to lesbian, gay, bisexual, transgender, and/or queer/questioning (LGBTQ) individuals, a relatively unspoken topic prior to President Obama's election. I recognized that removing books meant to guide and support adolescents is an act that undermines their intelligence and a school's obligation to its diverse value system.

In the past, I was told not to discuss my experiences by administrators; however, there is a time when educating colleagues and an obligation to humankind must prevail. Admittedly, tenure is an asset and factor in my decision to continue the discussion, as it provides security that allows educators the ability to freely discuss controversial ideas. To be clear, there were plenty of committee and conference opportunities, letters, awards, e-mails, and comments of support that continue to brighten my days (I even met Judy Blume, and she told me she loved me!). I became connected with dedicated individuals such as Helen Adams and Hilda Weisberg and experts at the American Library Association (ALA), who supported, educated, and provided me with opportunities. Nonetheless, this was a daunting, formative experience.

From my perspective, there are degrees to the severity of challenges to library materials, and among the worst cases are those that provide a most unpleasant view of society or a glimpse of a frightening future. Being a librarian is seen by many as an easy, peaceful, perhaps unnecessary job, and in theory our code of ethics seems simple to support. However, these principles—specifically intellectual freedom and equitable access—can be tricky, requiring soul-searching and self-examination to uphold in practice, particularly amid public book banning. Similarly, I believe it is difficult to employ the standards of our professional ethics in isolation; these concepts intertwine, especially in the face of a challenge that is political, social, racial, and religious in its nature.

The Hate Fueling Challenges

In 2010, our school board was approached by the county chapter of 9/12, a national organization influenced by Glenn Beck, then a commentator on Fox News. Multiple members of the county group, claiming to be concerned parents and community members, presented the board with research on President Obama's alleged homosexual agenda. They brought information from Jim Hoft's website regarding the "pornographic" books on the Gay Lesbian Straight Education Network's (GLSEN) recommended reading list for LGBTQ individuals. The group wanted three titles from GLSEN's list removed from our collection. In question were the anthologies *Full Spectrum* (2006), edited by David Levithan and Billy Merrell; *Love & Sex* (2003), edited by Michael Cart; and *Revolutionary Voices* (2000), edited by Amy Sonnie, which was eventually banned at my school and the county public library. An editorial writer accompanied the group to the board meeting and wrote about his support for the 9/12 group in the county newspaper the following day (Mullane, 2010). I believe this initial press coverage was beneficial since most schools in our area had little experience in handling challenges. I am not sure I would have had the same level of support if the shocking events at the meeting had not been reported publicly. I had procedures for reconsidering materials in my office, but these were not officially approved board policy. At this time, I became aware that the same group of individuals, who denied affiliation with the 9/12 group, had already protested materials on climate change in the science curriculum and a political cartoon used in an English classroom.

Being a librarian and thus a researcher, I began to deepen my understanding of the challenge by exploring the 9/12 group. I remember clearly seeing the group's correspondence and plans on the social media site "Meet Up," where privacy settings had been ignored and I could read freely. When I saw the members' visceral hate and propensity toward violence, I literally sobbed. I was privy to people commenting about "radical homos" and "smelly Muslims who are . . . not talking right . . . I will grab a baseball bat . . . and rip them . . . a new a-hole," claiming educators were "indoctrinating students with a liberal agenda," voicing a desire to shoot individuals or "take them behind the woodshed," all in a joking yet accepting manner. Group members were writing statements such as "do not try to plant seeds in the mind of our children that this [homosexuality] is just A-OKAY. This is not normal." The individuals wanted to place symbols in local business windows to indicate who agreed with them; they spewed hate and dehumanized Blacks, poor people, gays, and immigrants. They chided members to "mark your calendar for walk naked in America day, to encourage . . . Muslims to commit suicide." The group members argued that the "American government appreciates your efforts to root out terrorists." Their correspondence normalized a hierarchy of human value, with themselves at the top. After twenty years of educating a diverse group of students, I had naively thought that people like this did not exist or at least were not abundant or so transparent with their hatred. I expected and taught civility, and these people did not exhibit those traits, which was truly eye opening. The knowledge of this group's beliefs and their hatred, racism, and homophobia brought me to tears.

I continued to read the abundant correspondence and plans of the 9/12 members. The group was influenced by Fox News, but more specifically the Gateway Pundit, Jim Hoft, whose First Things website proclaimed a mission to "strengthen the role of religion in support of a free and just social order." He wrote that his "purpose is to advance a religiously informed public policy for the ordering of society." The proclamations of Eugene Delgaudio were also commonplace on the 9/12 Meet Up group. Self-proclaimed as "the public advocate" of the United States, he offers "opposition to those who actively support same sex marriage and the furtherance of Gay Rights" as well as "the passage of hate crime and thought control legislation that creates inequality in our state and federal systems." These 9/12 members, with the assistance of the internet, were organizing challenges across the county and, I surmised, the country. Many of these were thwarted, but not without books disappearing from some library shelves and protests in multiple areas about the books recommended by GLSEN.

Group posts suggested that members run for school boards and elected positions or "blitz" school boards and senators' offices with a presentation on the so-called radical homophobic agenda of Obama's czars. Members shared ideas about speaking to doctors and shop owners, and including youth in the group, asking them, "What are you going to do about these evil liberals who have infected our schools and government . . . [you should] support the constitution and remove all domestic enemies." They demanded their rights to "run the schools," since their tax dollars pay educators' salaries. These actions suggested a large, organized network of political action, but of course, these are the tactics that effective movements often employ.

Keep in mind these challenges take months to resolve. As the days unfolded, my tremendously supportive superintendent and I met for hours upon hours to discuss a plan of action. Almost daily, I shared the intricacies of this event with my closest confidantes and colleagues. Those in my inner circle acknowledged the legitimacy of my concerns and to this day continue to do so. Our community worked with authors and state and national associations as well as the ALA. The dedicated individuals at the Office for Intellectual Freedom (OIF) served as advisors and therapists who confirmed their knowledge of the organized efforts to suppress LGBTQ literature. They had already issued warnings of censorship, clearly grasping the scenario. As Martin Garnar (2009) of the OIF blog stated,

> Though . . . GLSEN's critics claim to be upholding American morals and values by condemning the GLSEN book list, they are actually undermining the values of tolerance, free inquiry, and self-determination that inform and sustain our democratic way of life. Stigmatizing particular ideas and engaging in unfounded personal attacks in an effort to censor and suppress opposing opinions and ideas is the antithesis of intellectual freedom.

My second bout of hysteria occurred when my mom and I acknowledged the far-reaching implications of this particular book challenge and how its initiators were a threat to our democracy. I remember pacing the floor on the phone, my heart racing, and us both literally crying.

This scenario repeated itself during a conversation with the director of the National Coalition Against Censorship (NCAC), who confirmed my worst fears by agreeing with me after the rear window of my car was smashed in the night outside my home. I had been attacked in writing publicly by others through comments on news articles and correspondence and by Safe Libraries, who "believes politicians and citizens should control libraries, not the ALA." To my employer, the 9/12 members sent e-mails accusing me of sexualizing children and being a pariah, questioning the work I was doing with ALA and the press. To his credit, my superintendent told them I had First Amendment rights, which included responding to professional organizations. In that call with NCAC, I declined a safe house from a national organization. Instead, I prepared for the days ahead and took the advice of talented, dedicated professionals, gathering talking points and coping skills for stress, sleepless nights, and feelings of isolation and paranoia.

Responding to Challenges

Given the delicate nature of this challenge, my superintendent and I agreed to approach the decision with the steps of inquiry or research, the same process I teach my students. We posed the challenge hearing as a series of questions and provided evidence—twenty-four resources on the bibliography—to help the review committee make an educated decision about the three titles in question. Questions we discussed at the hearing included: Why are the books being challenged? Do the books hold value? Do students have rights to LGBTQ information? What is the procedure for removal of library books? Was the group's behavior on the Meet Up site hate speech? Are social media companies responsible for behavior on their sites? What is considered pornography/obscenity? How do we evaluate information for validity and reliability?

Side note here to a librarian's role. We teach guidelines for evaluating information, such as a checklist for accuracy. There are systematic questions one can ask about a source to determine its quality. Cornell University recommends a guide to "Critically Analyzing Information Sources," which includes learning about the author, publication type, and the purpose of the content, for instance. People should be aware of the Media Bias Chart and examine the spectrum of news sources. Librarians vet and study information and are qualified to teach these skills. Since the challenge, I have been very clear in our curriculum that we need to know these skills because some information and some people have the intent to mislead.

In the end, the committee voted to keep two of the three titles in the library collection. On my way to work after the one book was removed, I listened to Lily Allen's "Fuck You," an apropos theme song for the challenge, and knew I did right by the students I served by not quietly allowing their identities to be repressed. The 9/12 group was again unsuccessful when challenging *Dreaming in Cuban* (1993) by Cristina Garcia, a sophisticated book, simultaneously being challenged in Arizona and found on the suggested reading list of the Core Curriculum. This time, we had a new superintendent who claimed to be an American Exceptionalist, but he abided by process and procedure, although he did warn the committee via e-mail that the board did not have to agree with our decision. With experience from our prior challenge, we assembled a committee that unanimously agreed to keep the book, and the board simply agreed with the outcome of our vote.

Our librarian code charges us with respecting the dignity and rights of every person, not allowing personal beliefs to interfere with advancing social and racial justice. Yes, I defended the books in our collection because it was my duty as a librarian, and I would do so for any item. Truth be told, I was also fueled by an obligation to justice and fear for the lack of respect for human rights and the potential threat to our freedoms that was voiced by the 297 "patriot foot soldiers" in the county 9/12 group. The group eventually informed the school's administration they had folded into the Tea Party movement.

Post-Challenge Reflections on School Librarianship

Internally, I struggled with all this information. I wanted all people to have the right to stand up for their beliefs—that is, intellectual freedom—but at what cost to society? I was left wondering what I could do to inform people of the importance of libraries in a free society and the plans of an ugly segment of our culture. I contemplated running for office or forming an organization. I felt powerless to prevent what was unfolding before my eyes. My decision has been to take opportunities to educate and serve others by speaking and writing through organizations, universities, conferences, committees, and award ceremonies. Nancy Kranich, a longtime proponent of intellectual freedom content in library and information science programs, provided guidance and asked me to speak at Rutgers University several times. We were together during my lecture to students when we heard of Rutgers student Tyler Clementi's suicide, a result of being harassed regarding his homosexuality. We acknowledged the significance of this event, which solidified my resolve to support social justice. It was also at Rutgers, during a colloquium, that a man shouted at me after my presentation ended with my noting that homophobia is a form of discrimination and censorship, and perpetuators of false information are a threat to our democracy. I do not remember his exact words, but he was irate. Others said I was biased about libraries. I would argue that sometimes there is no bias, there is simply the truth. Libraries are, in fact, unique educational institutions that maintain values to serve all—and this is a good societal aim. Librarians open information for examination, which should be especially valued at a time when so many are controlling the information that people can access, preventing full exposure to ideas and connections.

In my professional experience, the goal of schools and libraries is to educate and help, with kindness, servitude, cultural humility, and sensitivity. My work at a large public high school with a diverse population provides an opportunity to gain a perspective on humanity. Teenagers and staff are a diverse group with the potential to teach many lessons, if you remain open-minded and accepting of change, acknowledging each other's strengths, weaknesses, and the shared learning that can occur. What happens and is observed in our libraries and schools is a mirror of society. The practice of teaching lessons, one that requires constant revision and thought, can hold a powerful influence.

I guide the culture of our library according to my profession's code of ethics. I model for my clientele the greatness of the library institution. Through our library orientation, students and staff learn how librarians strive to protect their privacy and freedom to access information. They learn the purpose and uniqueness of a library, "the most open of open universities, where one can enter at any age," a quote attributed to Michael E. Gorman, former Librarian of Congress. I teach the process of research and how this can be applied to burning questions as you age and grow. Our population is made aware of academic library sources. In return, I receive school accolades such as staff mom, most helpful, and unsung hero. Most recently, a student told me I should get a tattoo of a symbol that means "leader for the people." Students acknowledge "the library is a peaceful sanctuary" where they "expand knowledge . . . discover parts of themselves," and conduct "personal inquiries." Though trying and frustrating at times, educating the youth in a well-supported library is rewarding because people appreciate the service and knowledge.

Teaching and helping individuals understand the value of libraries have provided solace and are small efforts that make a difference to our community. In upholding the purpose of libraries, and the values of democracy, I am proud to be a part of efforts by countless numbers who educate people about disinformation, devaluation, and dehumanization. I feel validated (but somewhat frightened) when I read about other individuals standing on the right side of justice, as opposed to extremists who claim to stand for our country's freedoms while in fact limiting them. The examples are abundant.

Connections between the Challenges and the Current State of Our Culture

The *New York Times*, reporting on the insurrection at the Capitol on January 6, explained, "Leading the movement is an organization called Women for America First whose founder emerged from the Tea Party . . . [and] has helped create a coalition involving sitting members of Congress." The violent speech, which resonated on the 9/12 social media site, was parroted by members of the January 6 riot, where individuals tweeted, "We Want Blood" and "Bring Plenty of Rope."

Ibram X. Kendi, in *Stamped from the Beginning* (2017), makes the connection, writing:

> All those geneticists, Klansmen, anonymous Internet racists, and of course members of the Tea Party . . . formed on February 19, 2009—and other segregationists were organizing like there was no tomorrow after the election of Obama. The notion of a postracial America quickly became the new dividing line between racists and antiracists. (2017, p. 498)

Most recently, in 2021, Barton Gellman confirmed the Gateway Pundit's influence, also a factor in our challenges, on the conservative right in the *Atlantic* article "Trump's Next Coup Has Already Begun." In writing this chapter, I discovered the Gateway Pundit is now blocked on Twitter (for how long is undetermined). Of course, the debate over social media's responsibility to society is commonly discussed and hotly contested. However, the normalization of hate speech is now widespread.

These concepts are commonplace conversations in schools and society, and so many of the details of our challenge resonate nationally, as we are witness to hundreds of school districts removing books from school shelves because politicians agree with censors and perpetrators of fake news. The current controversies over textbook approval in Florida, Texas, and California, in particular, reflect a similar ideology and systematic organization to that of the 9/12 members in their opposition to critical race theory and social-emotional learning concepts. Most recently in Tennessee, laws governing school board elections have changed, making these contests partisan in nature. "Missouri, Arizona, Florida and South Carolina are among the states where lawmakers toyed less successfully with similar legislation this year . . . and the idea is likely to keep popping up" (Cottle, 2022, p. SR7). These efforts and the increasing number of school library book challenges, some led by Tea Party politicians, are clearly attempts to control schools and limit access to information, using much of the same rhetoric I experienced.

I am encouraged knowing the great minds and journalists of our time are writing to protect democracy. When we live in an era when Madeleine Albright writes a book entitled *Fascism* (2018) and Dan Rather attempts to heal our nation with *What Unites Us* (2017), we should heed their advice. Similar to other writers who are enraged and seek to enlighten, this "everyman" librarian concludes that the seeds of the particular challenges I experienced in 2010 and 2013 were a precursor to the horror to come, where individuals claiming to represent truth and freedom are in actuality actively limiting freedom and influencing control over our schools, libraries, and government.

There is a gem of a graphic novel published in 2021, *On Tyranny* (by Timothy Snyder), that outlines the characteristics of dictatorship to help people recognize the impending signs of disaster. The author offers hope with specific actions to protect humankind from repeating its history of inhumanity. He encourages us to take responsibility for the face of the world. Learn from peers in other countries. Make small talk and eye contact to break down social barriers. There are concepts I can adopt with ease, while others I want to employ, but cannot. He writes:

> The symbols of today enable the reality of tomorrow. Notice the swastikas and the other signs of hate. Do not look away, and do not get used to them. Remove them yourself and set an example for others to do so. (Snyder, 2021, p. 24)

Today, symbols of an exclusionary mindset like the Confederate and Live Free or Die flags are abundant in many neighborhoods across the United States. As my friend states, "Everything is contaminated—the signs are everywhere," reminding us of our potential future. However, I do not see myself physically removing these items that cause a guttural reaction of disgust.

One of the author's points goes bone deep, one I feel librarians can identify with and support:

> Defend institutions. They help us to preserve decency. They need our help as well. Don't speak of "our institutions" unless you make them yours by acting on their behalf. Institutions do not protect themselves. They fall one after the other unless each is defended from the beginning. (Snyder, 2021, p. 13)

As librarians, we have a fabulous, noble institution to defend. Our code of ethics, amended in 2021, states, "We significantly influence or control . . . information. In a political system grounded in an informed citizenry, we are members of a profession explicitly committed to intellectual freedom and the freedom of access to information" (ALA, 2021). In short, information is our essence, and how we organize and retrieve it is very important and telling.

Adhering to equity of access and service, it is said the best librarians keep their personal philosophies out of the equation when serving patrons, and I would like to think I have lived up to these ethics and that the students who follow the ideas of right-leaning citizens, who could find themselves part of an act like the January 6 insurrection, feel their dignity is preserved and they are equally served. However, there was a point when the reality of the dangers of tyranny and the harrowing experience of these two challenges compelled me to have a voice that would offend some I serve.

Conclusion

Upon reflection on these professional obligations and worries, I fear more people who believe they should control the content and perhaps financing of local libraries will gain power. I fear public and school librarians are removing content across our country without committee review to protect their jobs and funding of the institution—or perhaps they too believe materials should be removed? This comes to my mind as no surprise, when I recall that I thought about contacting the director of the local public library during my challenge; I later learned they met with the 9/12 group and removed *Revolutionary Voices* without a committee review or vote.

I question the discussion of our ethics in certain library programs. Given the increase in challenges across the nation originating from political and social motivations, we can hope librarians are becoming better educated and being taught skills to interpret our ethics, what they are and are not. I would think with the rise in challenges and recognition of our role to protect democracy, the public, our administrators, and society should be better educated as to the role our institutions provide as educational and lifelong learning institutes for all the people.

Intellectual freedom is the cornerstone of our profession and our democracy, and a librarian makes a commitment to society to ensure the library and its power are not undervalued or endangered but protected. Librarians all over the country are struggling with challenges and their obligations to our profession while keeping their sanity and employment, with supervisors and governing bodies who have little understanding or value of librarianship. I truly hope our institutions of education will survive the upcoming years, since many children go to school with no libraries or where books are censored. I maintain school libraries are the training ground for informing people about what a library is and means; therefore, they are very meaningful to one's education. Both public schools and libraries in America are unique in their goals to provide a learning opportunity for all people and are certainly worth defending, as is our democracy.

References

American Library Association. (2021). *Professional ethics*. https://www.ala.org/tools/ethics

Cottle, M. (2022, April 24). School board wars are getting worse. *New York Times*, sec. SR, 7.

Garnar, M. (2009, December 11). *Statement by IFC chair Martin Garnar on attacks against GLSEN, Kevin Jennings*. Office of Intellectual Freedom Blog. http://www.oif.ala.org/oif/?p=769

Gellman, B. (2021, December 6). Trump's next coup has already begun. *The Atlantic*. https://www.theatlantic.com/magazine/archive/2022/

Just the Facts Coalition. (2008). *Just the facts about sexual orientation and youth: A primer for principals, educators, and school personnel*. American Psychological Association. https://www.apa.org/pi/lgbt/resources/just-the-facts.pdf

Mullane, J. D. (2010, March 3). Gay essays under fire at RV. *Burlington County Times*.

Books Discussed in This Chapter

Albright, M. (2018). *Fascism: A warning*. HarperCollins Publishers.

Cart, M. (Ed.). (2003). *Love and sex: Ten stories of truth*. S&S Books.

Garcia, C. (1993). *Dreaming in Cuban*. Random House.

Kendi, I. X. (2017). *Stamped from the beginning: The definitive history of racist ideas in America*. Bold Type Books.

Levithan, D., & Merrell, B. (Eds.). (2006). *Full spectrum: A new generation of writing about gay, lesbian, bisexual, transgender, questioning, and other identities*. Ember.

Rather, D. (2017). *What unites us: Reflections on patriotism*. Algonquin Books.

Snyder, T. (2021). *On tyranny graphic edition: Twenty lessons from the twentieth century*. Ten Speed Press.

Sonnie, A. (Ed.). (2000). *Revolutionary voices: A multicultural queer youth anthology*. Alyson.

CHAPTER EIGHTEEN

Book Banning in the United States? Why, It's Perfectly Normal!

Kerrie Lattari

Introduction

Banned Books Week is held each September in celebration of the right to read; during this week, library professionals around the country share stories, advice, awareness, and support regarding the ongoing fight for intellectual freedom. Over the past several years, during my now eight-year tenure as the library media specialist at York Middle School (YMS), I, along with my assistant, Lee, have partnered with our eighth-grade English language arts (ELA) teachers to dive into this topic with our students.

Each September, over one class period with each class section, we talk about what book challenges and book banning entails, look at the Top 10 Most Challenged Books list from the previous year provided by American Library Association (ALA), and share recent headlines from our nation's news outlets. We ask students to consider why various titles may have faced challenges throughout the years and what their opinions are on this issue. The surprise and indignation echo many times over as these teens discover that books such as the *Harry Potter* series (by J. K. Rowling), *The Hunger*

Games series (by Suzanne Collins), and *The Hate U Give* (by Angie Thomas; 2017), books that the majority of them have read and loved, have been and continue to be challenged and pulled from library shelves under the guise of "protection." We introduce them to our district's Instructional and Library Materials Selection Policy and explain the ways in which it supports their reading freedom. We assure them that we will always fight to keep the books on our shelves, should a challenge arise. And without fail, in every class, every year, students ask us: "Has there ever been a book challenge here?" And every year, we have always been able to answer: "Luckily, no."

But that is no longer the case.

When we arrived for our preservice days in August to begin our 2021–22 school year, it was already looking to be just as exhausting, if not more so, than its 2020–21 hybrid predecessor. The small, but extremely vocal, group of far-right community members who frequently critique the district's work had been in full force all summer long, flooding social media and the inboxes of our school committee members with demands that students not be required to mask upon their return to school. Coupled with their simultaneous anti-equity, diversity, and inclusion and anti-critical race theory campaigns, we knew we were in for a conflict-filled fall semester. These culture wars were popping up throughout the country, so it was hardly a surprise that we were facing them locally. But I also had my eye on another crisis rapidly unfolding in communities throughout the United States: book banning. While there was currently no indication that those fighting us on so many other fronts were ready to engage in that battle, I figured it was only a matter of time. I met with our department and building administrators to share my concern for potential challenges and to ensure that they were knowledgeable about our selection and reconsideration policies. At my suggestion, our principal addressed this information with my colleagues at our first staff meeting of the year. We were primed for what seemed like an eventuality.

It's Perfectly Contentious

By the end of October, a Freedom of Access Act/Freedom of Information Act request came to our superintendent, asking for a complete list of all of the titles within our district library collections. The 35,000-item report was submitted, and it was only a couple of weeks later that York resident Patsy Howell Huntsman met with my building principal regarding the book *It's Perfectly Normal* (2004) by Robie H. Harris and Michael Emberley and its inclusion in our middle school library collection. Despite these meetings, Ms. Huntsman submitted the district's reconsideration of materials form on November 11, 2021, which stated her request to have *It's Perfectly Normal* removed from the library.

On the form, Ms. Huntsman wrote that she became aware of this book from a Facebook post. Her concerns about the book included: whether the section "Straight and Gay" is appropriate for grades five to eight, graphic nude cartoons displaying anatomy, the pages on masturbation, which "essentially comprise a How-To manual . . ." information on oral sex, a cartoon image of a boy putting on a condom, and information about abortion. She wrote, "The decision whether to expose young children to this detailed subject matter and explicit graphics should be left to parents, not school administrators or government agencies," and stressed that this book is available to ten-year-olds. Ms. Huntsman also mentioned that the state of Maine requires an emphasis on abstinence and that schools are not required to include instruction on sexual orientation or gender identity.

Immediately upon receiving word that an official request for reconsideration had been filed, I began reaching out for help. My first step was to inform the ALA Office for Intellectual Freedom about the challenge. I also contacted the Intellectual Freedom Chair of our state American Association of School Librarians (AASL) affiliate to let her know about the situation. I e-mailed the youth services librarians at the local public library who also brought their director into the conversation, who ended up being an immense support during this fight. Next, I reached out to several students' families who I knew to be allies of the library and with whom I had a good relationship. I explained the situation, the process we would be facing, and asked, if they were comfortable with it, that they contact the superintendent and school committee to voice their opposition to banning the book and share their support for us and our students. I received replies within minutes from parents who had that very book in their homes, who were outraged that this was happening, and who offered to not only write e-mails to the school committee but also spread the word to other like-minded individuals, and even start a petition if needed.

In the days that followed, I began flipping through a new acquisition that had just come in, *You Can't Say That!* (2021), by Leonard S. Marcus, only to discover that one of the interviews was with Robie H. Harris and her experiences with *It's Perfectly Normal*. Harris said that when her book is challenged, the publisher will often write letters of support for the library in need. Armed with this knowledge, I found the contact information for the book's publisher and sent an e-mail explaining my plight. In just over an hour, the executive marketing manager responded and provided me with a letter of support crafted by the original editor of the book, Amy Ehrlich. My last outreach toward the end of November was to the Maine American Civil Liberties Union (ACLU). By January, they had produced a letter of support that was sent directly to the superintendent.

After sitting with this situation for several days, Lee suggested that she post on her personal Facebook page so that others in the York community would know what was happening. I agreed that the exposure was important, and as soon as she posted the comments started pouring in from people asking how they could help and promising their full support. Her post was shared fourteen times. Our story was spreading, and we were bolstered by the knowledge that so many people were behind us.

Ahead of the next school committee meeting scheduled for December 1, 2021, the superintendent had been informed that those in opposition to keeping the book were going to turn out in large numbers at the meeting, carrying signs with "graphic images." District library staff and several of our colleagues attended the meeting, anticipating an onslaught of misguided and outrageous accusations to be directed at us. But what we found instead was an amazing show of support from the York community. Despite the vitriol they continued to spew on social media, our opposition never showed up. Those who spoke at the podium in our favor included the public library director, several parents (some of whom are librarians in other towns), community members, and the leader of the town's Unitarian Universalist church (who mentioned that she suggests *It's Perfectly Normal* as a resource to parents). Even one of my fifth-grade students spoke about how she should have the right to choose the books she wants to read and that only her parents should be the ones to approve them. It was early in the challenge process, but we left that meeting feeling pretty good about our chances of success.

As per policy, the first step in addressing the request for reconsideration was to form a review committee and submit a report to the superintendent with the recommendation to either retain the book or not. Our committee consisted of myself, my building principal, a seventh-grade ELA teacher, the seventh-/eighth-grade wellness teacher, and the librarian from the lower elementary school. Our report discussed the awards and accolades bestowed upon the book, the numerous positive reviews within selection aids, adherence to other selection criteria, my qualifications and expertise, the appropriateness of the age span, the rights of our students, and the ways in which the book supports our sexual abuse prevention efforts. We submitted our report to the superintendent on December 3, 2021, with the recommendation that the book remain on the library shelves. By December 6, the superintendent informed the review committee and Ms. Huntsman that his decision was to not remove the book and that she could appeal the decision to the school committee. And, of course, she did just that.

It's Perfectly Appealing

During the January 19, 2022, school committee meeting, my principal presented our review committee's reasoning for reaching the recommendation that we provided to the superintendent. Ms. Huntsman then presented the rationale for her appeal of the decision to the school committee. Committee members asked clarifying questions to each of them and concluded the meeting by announcing that the school committee would discuss, vote, and render a final decision at the next meeting. During the public comment section, a couple of community members against keeping the book spoke out, and several allies from the December meeting spoke again, including our fifth-grade student who matter-of-factly stated, “We have a pretty good system for books at YMS and I don’t think we need to mess that up.”

The school committee did their due diligence. Several members met with us to ask us questions about book selection and how we help guide students to their book choices, and one member even came in to view the library and the location of the book on the shelf to have a better idea of how students might access the library and its materials. We as a library department also crafted a statement supporting our students’ right to read and submitted it to the committee and the superintendent ahead of the next meeting.

At the appeal meeting on February 2, 2022, each school committee member shared their process of how they came to a decision about whether or not to keep *It’s Perfectly Normal* in our collection. They shared that they all read the book cover to cover and, while they acknowledged the subject matter is uncomfortable and that parents want to make the decision of when to introduce those topics to their children, the book is a great resource for when that time comes. Several times during the meeting, it was brought up that there are already safeguards in place for parents to restrict their own children from books they deem inappropriate, as was the message that individuals cannot decide for others what their children can access. The school committee chair spoke about the unnecessary fear and inflammatory language surrounding this book and stated his confidence in us as professional librarians.

One committee member spoke for eight minutes, delivering many compelling arguments for keeping the book on the shelf. She noted that most students will be going through puberty during middle school and that not every student has someone they can turn to with their related questions. She acknowledged that the illustrations are a little startling at first glance, but that the diversity of these perfectly normal bodies was important. Her visit to the middle school library was discussed, and she explained how there are no places for children to hide away and access the book secretly, as was a concern from some of our opposition. She said that the book was most likely to be found and checked out by students who are actively seeking answers to their questions because of its unremarkable placement in our nonfiction section. She described the variety of topics covered in the book, including the chapter on healthy relationships and how to recognize if, and what to do if, you are being sexually abused. It was also mentioned that while the book is not part of the curriculum, it does fall in line with the Maine statute about K–12 human development and sexuality.

After several more minutes of discussion, the school committee voted unanimously to uphold the superintendent’s decision to retain *It’s Perfectly Normal* in the middle school library.

It's Perfectly Helpful

Not every librarian is going to have such a positive outcome. But to help increase the odds of successfully battling book censorship attempts in your district, I offer the following advice.

Preparation

You absolutely must be aware of what is occurring around you—locally, statewide, and nationally. The emotional work required to be present and up to date with all of the issues and political battles our nation is facing can be draining. There is only so much a person can take, especially reading post after post that accuses you of being a "groomer" or claims you are providing pornography to students. It can be tempting to stay closed off to protect your mind and your heart. But if you do not know what you are going up against, it will be difficult to be ready to face it. The idea is to be proactive as opposed to reactive. Having created and facilitated a few years of Banned Books Week presentations, I had a solid understanding of how book challenges had increasingly been popping up around the country and what the targets were. The topic stayed in the forefront of my mind before there was even a whiff of a challenge coming my way. This put me in a better position to hit the ground running when it happened.

So, stay current. Read news articles from local publications as well as national news outlets such as the *Washington Post,* the *New York Times*, National Public Radio, and Reuters. Keep up with ALA, AASL, your local AASL affiliate, and the ACLU. Follow social media accounts for librarians, educators, and others focused on books or publishing content. And do not forget to see what the opposition is saying directly. Organizations such as Moms for Liberty, the Goldwater Institute, and the Family Policy Alliance coordinate their efforts and have plenty of resources for their audience to access. Know their talking points, their vocabulary, and the books that are frequently being targeted, and read through their materials. This is what you will read in the e-mails your schools receive and what you will hear when community members speak at public meetings. It is what you will see regurgitated in the comments section of nearly any social media post concerned with this or any education-related topic. Just remember to take the comments with a grain of salt, and *do not engage*. Gather what you have learned to have your defense at the ready, and hope you do not have to use it.

Policy

Do not underestimate the power of a comprehensive library materials selection policy. Our school committee leaned heavily on our policy to make their final decision to keep *It's Perfectly Normal* on the shelf. They consistently referred back to the part of the policy that laid out their task, which was to

> review the book objectively and in its full content; evaluate it in terms of the needs and interest of students, school, curriculum and community; consider it in the light of differing opinions; and review it in light of the criteria for initial selection and purpose as provided herein.

Be sure your policy contains a statement asserting that access to challenged material will not be restricted during the reconsideration process and include a provision for the acceptance of donated materials, so that donations are subjected to the same selection criteria as materials you purchase, and therefore will be accepted or rejected in the same manner. One of the most important parts of our policy, in my opinion, is the statement on parental authority:

> The Committee recognizes that the final authority as to what materials an individual student will be exposed rests with that student's parents or guardians. However, at no time will the wishes of one child's parents to restrict reading or viewing of a particular item infringe on other parents' rights to permit their children to read or view the same material.

Our district policies are on a three-year review cycle, so the opportunity to adjust our policy has come up twice since I started working in York. Several years ago, I added a paragraph that states that our libraries are guided by the principles set forth in the ALA Library Bill of Rights, its interpretive statements, and the Students' Right to Read statement of the National Council of Teachers of English. Review your policies frequently and keep notes on changes you want to make so you are ready the next time the opportunity arises.

Visibility

I cannot emphasize enough how crucial it is that you take your challenge public. E-mail known allies. Contact the media. Our challenge was picked up by the local newspaper without my having to inform them, simply because they frequently write about the happenings of the district. But other newspapers around the state began picking it up as did the local news stations. Post about your situation on social media. You may gain additional resources and support you did not have previously, but more importantly, the book challenge will be out in the open. The number of comments on Lee's Facebook post that thanked her for letting them know this was happening in their own community were numerous. Often, situations like these happen behind closed doors, with most people not finding out about them until it is too late. Not only does the general populace deserve to know what is occurring but openness provides opportunities for people who want to help. When you harness the power of social media, your story can go beyond the confines of your town or state. As I briefly mentioned above: do not engage with negative comments. No matter how enraging the remarks are, it is not worth it to get into a back and forth with an immovable brick wall. It will only serve to derail your focus and leave you feeling angry or defeated. And even in the face of all of that negativity, do not give up. It is *critical* that you share your story, often and widely. A few other Maine librarians reached out to me in the months following our success with the appeal, asking for advice as they too faced a book challenge, one even over the same title. They were familiar with my challenge because news of it had crossed their path, so they had another person to turn to, to help them navigate the muddy waters of fighting for intellectual freedom. So do not be shy. Raise your voice. For you, for the library community at large, and perhaps, most importantly, for your students.

Conclusion: Afterward

In the months that followed our victory, a few people used the public comment section of school committee meetings, and their favorite Facebook groups, to complain about the book *Gender Queer* (by Maia Kobabe; 2019) being available at the high school library, along with a few other titles that were accessible through the CloudLibrary, though no formal challenge has been brought forth. Also, Ms. Huntsman took it upon herself to begin donating children's Bibles to our school libraries (which are being held to the scrutiny of our selection criteria, of course). I have yet to receive mine.

The foray into summer break and a multitude of larger nationwide issues seem to have taken the attention away from us for the time being. I have a feeling, though, that this battle is not over. I feel more ready than ever to take on whatever is headed our way this coming school year. And I am more excited than ever to give our Banned Books presentation in September. Because this year, when our students ask, "Has a challenge ever happened here?" we can say "Yes, and we won."

Books Discussed in This Chapter

Collins, S. (2014). *The hunger games trilogy*. Scholastic.
Harris, R. H., & Emberley, M. (2004). *It's perfectly normal: Changing bodies, growing up, sex, gender, and sexual health*. Candlewick Press.
Kobabe, M. (2019). *Gender queer: A memoir*. Oni Press.
Marcus, L. S. (2021). *You can't say that! Writers for young people talk about censorship, free expression, and the stories they have to tell*. Candlewick Press.
Rowling, J. K. (1999). *Harry Potter* series. Scholastic.
Thomas, A. (2017). *The hate u give*. Walker Books.

CHAPTER NINETEEN

Hindsight Is 2021: Help from the Book Battle Frontlines

Martha Hickson

Introduction

After months of pandemic-prompted online instruction, the 2021–22 school year looked promising for North Hunterdon High School. Like most schools around the country, our 1,500-student school in northwest New Jersey had weathered the interruptions caused by COVID-19. By September 2021, in-person instruction had returned, and freshman library orientations were under way.

Around noon on September 28, my principal walked through the door to let me know he had heard there would be a complaint about *Gender Queer: A Memoir* (2019) by Maia Kobabe at that evening's board of education meeting. A memoir presented in graphic novel form, *Gender Queer* recalls the author's childhood, adolescence, and young adulthood as an asexual, nonbinary person. The book had arrived in the library in 2019 but had never circulated.

I printed the book's reviews, including a starred review from *School Library Journal*, which recommended the book for grades nine and up (Frencham, 2019, p. 61). I also pointed out its distinction as a winner of the 2020 Alex Award, presented by the American Library Association (ALA) to "adult books with special appeal to teen readers" (*Young Adult Library Services Association*,

2020). In addition, I handed him printed copies of the district's library book selection policy, materials reconsideration policy, and materials reconsideration request form, reminding him that board meeting protests are not the means by which objections to materials should be raised.

He agreed, being well aware of the process, due to a prior challenge in which he and I had been involved. In 2019, he and the superintendent demanded that I remove Alison Bechdel's *Fun Home* (2007), another memoir in graphic novel form about the LGBTQIA+ (lesbian, gay, bisexual, transgender, queer/questioning, intersex, and/or asexual) experience. Deeming the book pornographic on the basis of a single image, the superintendent claimed that "the district could be accused of debauching the morals of minors if we were to allow free access to this material" (Price, 2021, p. 84). Ultimately, after several months of public pressure, the book was retained, and the policies were upheld.

Tuning in to Trouble

Assuming that my principal had the *Gender Queer* situation well in hand, I continued my school day. Curious about the complaint, though, that night I tuned in to the live stream of the board meeting. As public comments commenced, a parent approached the microphone. She complained about two books: *Gender Queer*, which remained undisturbed on the library shelf; and *Lawn Boy* (2018) by Jonathan Evison, a coming-of-age novel about a young man's pursuit of the American dream, which her son had checked out the previous day. She said:

> Explain to me how this perversion enriches or benefits the young minds of our students or anyone for that matter. On the contrary, this amounts to an effort to groom our kids to make them more willing to participate in the heinous acts described in these books. (North Hunterdon-Voorhees Regional High School District, 2021)

But she did not stop there. She continued her attack by labeling the "persons responsible for putting this pornography in our school" as "sex offenders" engaged in "promoting child porn and pedophilia" (North Hunterdon-Voorhees Regional High School District, 2021).

When her three minutes expired, another community member continued, decrying Banned Books Week and listing a series of titles that he found objectionable, nearly all addressing LGBTQIA+ themes, including *Two Boys Kissing* by David Levithan (2013), *Beyond Magenta: Transgender Teens Speak Out* by Susan Kuklin (2014), *Being Jazz: My Life as a Transgender Teen* by Jazz Jennings (2016), and *Parrotfish* by Ellen Wittlinger (2007).

Throughout these tirades, the board sat motionless. Their response? Silence, as is their custom during public comments, although board bylaws permit the presiding officer to suspend defamatory speech (North Hunterdon-Voorhees Regional High School District, 2016).

I, on the other hand, watched in stunned disbelief, my pulse racing, stomach churning, and eyes welling with tears. This would not be good.

From time to time over the previous sixteen years, parents had complained about books—including *Looking for Alaska* by John Green (2005), *Me Talk Pretty One Day* by David Sedaris (2000), and *Where the Heart Is* by Billie Letts (1995)—but in each of those cases, the complaint had originated with a call or e-mail to the principal or classroom teacher. We had a conversation with the parent, shared information about the literary value of the work, and assured the parent that other independent reading options were available. Problems solved; challenges averted. Aside from the administrators' *Fun Home* attempt in 2019, never had a book complaint completely skirted district policies or risen to this level of hostility. Clearly something was up.

A quick online search revealed that the same talking points and ambush tactics employed at our board meeting had been used days before to attack *Gender Queer* and *Lawn Boy* in Texas and Virginia, making North Hunterdon among the earliest targets in a series of book challenges that resulted in record numbers of censorship attempts over the coming months (DeGuzman, 2021; Natanson, 2021).

Although the protestors involved in these challenges claimed to be speaking for the community, their talking points were consistent with those used by such far-right organizations as Moms for Liberty, No Left Turn in Education, the Heritage Foundation (funded by the Koch Brothers), and its former visiting fellow, Christopher Rufo (Dailey, 2022).

By enlisting local radicals to invade board of education meetings, these national players are using "astroturfing," a technique designed to create the illusion of a grassroots movement, which, in reality, serves and is controlled by corporate or political interests. The goal: undermine public education (Weingarten & Edelman, 2022). It all adds up to a phenomenon that the authors' advocacy group PEN America calls the "Ed Scare," which threatens free expression in the classroom and seeks to "limit the ideas and perspectives students can discuss and understand" (Walker, 2022).

Reporting the Challenge

Thanks to my 2019 brush with censorship in the *Fun Home* case, I knew what to do and started working even while the board meeting continued. Smartphone in hand, I reported the complaints to the ALA Office for Intellectual Freedom, the National Coalition Against Censorship, the National

Figure 19.1 Library Users Moved This Book about Gender Identity from the 305 Section on the Shelf to the 155 Section and Turned It Backwards So That Other Readers Would Be Unable to Find It.

Council of Teachers of English, and the Comic Book Legal Defense Fund. And I texted my union president.

After a sleepless night, I dedicated the next day to broadening my network of support. I e-mailed the New Jersey Library Association (NJLA), the New Jersey Association of School Librarians (NJASL), and my county library association. Knowing how persuasive community members had been during the 2019 case, I reactivated the North Hunterdon-Voorhees Intellectual Freedom Fighters (NH-V IFF), an ad hoc group that had formed to defend *Fun Home* but that had been laying low since then. Because almost all of the books bashed at the board meeting addressed LGBTQIA+ themes, I reached out to the district's two gender and sexuality alliances (GSAs) so that their members would be aware of the attacks.

By early October, the situation was heating up. Parents had submitted formal reconsideration requests for five books: *Gender Queer*, *Lawn Boy*, *Fun Home*, *All Boys Aren't Blue* (2020) by George M. Johnson, and *This Book Is Gay* (2021) by Juno Dawson. Their objections echoed those that had been repeated around the country: sex, language, and religion.

Some library visitors engaged in ongoing nuisance vandalism in the library by repeatedly hiding books (figure 19.1). In every case, the affected books addressed themes related to the LGBTQIA+ experience or gender identity.

The work atmosphere grew hostile, too. Administrators were actively accusatory and antagonistic. Two days after the board meeting, the acting superintendent exclaimed in front of a coworker and students in the library,

"You sure stirred up trouble." Later that day, my supervisor demanded to know, "How could a school like ours have books with language like that?" In response to my request for information about the status of the challenges, the same supervisor said, "We have no obligation to communicate with you." And when, three days after the board meeting, having had no contact since the lunchtime warning about *Gender Queer*, I asked the principal whether the district would issue a statement of support for me, he replied, "Why would we do that? People can say whatever they want."

Parents sent hate mail, in which they labeled me sick, disturbed, and disgusting. The protestors even attempted to file obscenity charges with the local law enforcement. Fortunately, those agencies understood that no crime had been committed. But criminal complaints against school libraries have been filed in Texas and Florida, and those states along with Iowa have passed bills prohibiting the "teaching or discussing of what they call 'divisive concepts'" (Gunn, 2022, para. 2). Such broad, vague legislation places teachers and librarians at risk for prosecution.

The Reconsideration Committee Convenes

In the meantime, the principal assembled a reconsideration committee to evaluate the challenged books. The principal requested my participation, but because I was a target of the challenge along with the books, the union advised me not to join. Committee members included the principal, an assistant principal (my supervisor), a former classroom English teacher, a board member, a youth services librarian from the county library, and the parent president of the school's booster club. Although the board policy specified that the committee should include a layperson with expertise in the subject area of the books—LGBTQIA+ issues—no such expert was appointed to the committees.

Although I did not sit in on the committee's meetings, for each of the challenged titles I supplied reviews, awards, "best of" lists, and descriptions of prior challenges and outcomes to help inform the committee's deliberations.

The Pressure Takes Its Toll

On the morning of October 20, at the request of the principal, I was drafting a response to a parent complaint. Another incoming e-mail interrupted my work; the district business office had forwarded an Open Public Records Act request demanding purchasing records for all of the challenged books. Some of the books had been in the collection for years, so I set aside the parent complaint and began digging through files. While I was elbow deep in the file cabinet, three GSA members walked into my office. They explained that the club wanted to defend the books and asked me to help them by compiling a list of titles that included non-LGBTQIA+ sexual content.

An image of the library engulfed in flames popped into my head. I explained to the kids that fulfilling their request would only add more fuel to the fire that the book banners were attempting to ignite.

After the students left, panic symptoms overwhelmed me: racing heart, perspiration, nausea, anxiety, and trouble speaking. I walked to the nurse's office, which I had visited several times in the previous two weeks, to once again ask for a blood pressure check. Although my blood pressure is typically in a normal range, the nurse found a dangerously high reading and urged me to see my personal physician. By then, I was sobbing and unable to catch my breath. A union representative called my husband, who picked me up and took me home.

The next day, I visited my doctor. Concerned about my emotional state, elevated blood pressure, abdominal pain, sleeplessness, lack of appetite, weight loss, and digestive distress, she wrote a letter to the district to temporarily remove me from the workplace, prescribed medication for anxiety, referred me to a therapist, and urged me to rest.

The Community Fights Back

The next board meeting was held on October 26. Following the torrent of e-mails, letters, and phone calls that had flooded the district office, the board moved the session from its usual fifty-seat meeting room to the school's theater, where roughly four hundred community members packed in to express their views. A small band of book banners displayed signs with religious themes, but their numbers were dwarfed by the throng that supported intellectual freedom.

When the public comments began, dozens lined up for their three minutes at the microphone, the majority speaking in support of the right to read. Among the most powerful voices were those of students, who, despite audible jeers from the book banners, described the value of seeing themselves represented in the library. With poise, professionalism, and speeches that were heartfelt and personal, the students were models for public discourse, displaying a level of maturity and civility that put the protestors to shame.

A Verdict in Virginia

Although our local situation dominated my thoughts, I continued to keep an eye on book challenges throughout the nation. In mid-November, Fairfax County Public Schools, Virginia's largest school system, reached a decision on its own challenges to *Lawn Boy* and *Gender Queer*, which had preceded ours by about one week. According to the American Community Survey, both Hunterdon County (#13) and Fairfax County (#5) are among the country's wealthiest communities (Johnson, 2022, pp. 4, 12). Median household incomes in both counties exceed $117,000 annually, per capita annual income is at least $58,000, and more than half of those age twenty-five and older hold a bachelor's degree or higher (US Census Bureau, 2020).

Fairfax had decided to keep both books, finding them "valuable in their potential to reach marginalized youth who may struggle to find relatable literary characters that reflect their personal journeys" (Fairfax County Public Schools, 2021). I sent the Fairfax reconsideration report and related press coverage to our principal, in the hope that the decision from a similar community would provide a model for the reconsideration committee.

A decision was still pending by the time of the November 23 board meeting, so the NH-V IFF planned to continue making public statements. When the would-be book banners refused to don masks at the meeting, the board moved into executive session and kept the crowd, which included my 85-year-old father, cooling its heels for two and a half hours. Despite that long wait two nights before Thanksgiving, community members stayed put. During public comments, supporters of intellectual freedom outnumbered book banners once again. I added those committed First Amendment defenders to my gratitude list on Thanksgiving Day.

Back to Work

My doctor authorized my return to work on December 1. Later that week, I attended the annual NJASL conference, where I was inspired by colleagues sharing their work. One of the sessions I attended was led by John Chrastka, executive director of EveryLibrary, a national political action committee for libraries. Although John's presentation focused on advocating for library budgets, his strategic savvy and no-nonsense style suggested that he might have ideas and tools for combating censorship. I approached John after the session, we traded contact information, and for the next eight weeks he guided the NH-V IFF in communicating strategically with the community and the board.

With the holidays approaching, the board canceled its December meeting, but I did not want to let nearly two months pass before the board heard from the community again. So, NH-V IFF launched a "Season's Readings" greeting card campaign. We posted printable cards on our website for supporters to mail to board members. The message: Give students the gift of intellectual freedom (figure 19.2). I sent my own holiday card to the board telling them, "All I want for Christmas is my reputation," a reminder that the false accusations against me had yet to be refuted.

Figure 19.2 Community Members Sent Greeting Cards to Board Members When the December Meeting Was Canceled. (Source: NH-V Intellectual Freedom Fighters, 2019)

Recommendations Revealed

When the agenda for the January 25 meeting was published online late on the afternoon of January 21, it included a link to the reconsideration committee's report. That was the first indication that the committee had adjourned and our first glimpse of its work. The committee approved retaining four of the books. But in eight sentences comprising 134 words, the committee recommended that the board remove *This Book Is Gay* from the district's libraries, describing it as missing appropriate citations, containing slang and "explicit descriptions of sexual behaviors," and "irresponsible in the way it presents information" (North Hunterdon-Voorhees Regional High School District, 2022d). The agenda included a resolution for the board to ban the book on January 25 (North Hunterdon-Voorhees Regional High School District, 2022c).

We had only four days left to save *This Book Is Gay*, but I had a last-minute brainwave. Printed on the cover of *This Book Is Gay* is a name known to anyone familiar with youth literature: David Levithan, an award-winning author of books for young adults, who had written the book's introduction. Although I did not know David personally, I was confident that someone in my professional network might have a way to get in touch with him. On Saturday morning, I sent a message to the NJASL listserv, and librarian pals from across New Jersey started working their magic. Within two hours, David and I were trading e-mails. He agreed to write a message to the board, asking only that a student deliver it on his behalf, as he knew the board was more likely to pay attention to a student than to an author.

While waiting for David's statement to arrive, I lined up a roster of speakers. Because the meeting would be held via Zoom due to COVID-19 restrictions, geography was not a barrier, so our speakers included a student stand-in for David, GSA kids, parents, community members, librarians, and out-of-state alumni.

The NH-V IFF alerted its e-mail list and published an online scorecard to help viewers of the meeting track which board members supported intellectual freedom and which voted to ban books (figure 19.3). That scorecard could also serve as a handy voting guide when board members' terms expired, thereby also exerting subtle pressure on the board.

The Board Votes

On the night of the board meeting, I sat in front of the television to watch the live stream, just as I had four months earlier. Although I knew that the NH-V IFF had used every arrow in its quiver to defend the First Amendment, it seemed doubtful that the board would disregard the recommendations of its committee and vote down its own resolution.

With no place to escape, my anxiety spiked during the two hours of routine board business that preceded public comments. But my hope soared when the first public speaker flashed on the screen—Albin, a student I had not seen or heard from since they graduated in 2016, but who had been on my mind throughout the fight. Albin, always a gifted student and eloquent speaker, explained, "You won't find my name on any of the yearbooks because I am a trans person who changed their name." Albin recalled that,

BOE Scorecard

The next BOE election starts Jan. 25, 2022! Track the roll call vote on the book banning resolutions.

Remember which BOE members abandoned intellectual freedom by voting to ban books, and vote to **ban them** the next time they appear on the ballot.

Yes votes in columns 1, 2, 4, and 5 *retain the book and support intellectual freedom, as does a* **No vote in column 3.**	15.1.1 Lawn Boy 012522-11		15.1.2 Gender Queer 012522-10		15.1.3 This Book Is Gay 012522-9		15.1.4 All Boys Aren't Blue 012522-8		15.1.5 Fun Home 012522-7	
A Yes vote in column 3 endorses book banning... *in 2022 ... in the United States of America.*	Yes Retain	No Ban	Yes Retain	No Ban	Yes Ban	No Retain	Yes Retain	No Ban	Yes Retain	No Ban
Bonomi *Califon Boro, Tewksbury Twp*	X		X			X	X		X	
Chapman *Clinton Twp, Lebanon Boro*	X		X			X	X		X	
Crisologo *Clinton Town, Franklin, Glen Gardner*	—		—			—	—		—	
Farbanish *Union Twp*	X		X			X	X		X	
Hintz *High Bridge Boro, Lebanon Twp*	—			X		—	—		—	
Hoffmann *High Bridge Boro, Lebanon Twp*	X		X			X	X		X	
Kirchberger *Clinton Twp, Lebanon Boro*	X		X			X	X		X	
Melick *Califon Boro, Tewksbury Twp*	X		X		X		X		X	
Solino *Bethlehem Twp, Hampton Boro*	—		—			—	—		—	
Spanton *Clinton Twp, Lebanon Boro*	X		X			X	X		X	
Straight *Clinton Twp, Lebanon Boro*	X		X		X		X		X	
iotto *Clinton Town, Franklin, Glen Gardner*	X		X			X	X		X	

Figure 19.3 A Completed Scorecard from the Pivotal January 25 Board Meeting. (NH-V Intellectual Freedom Fighters, 2022)

while a student, they were supported in a campaign for prom king. "What happened to my school?" they asked (North Hunterdon-Voorhees Regional High School District, 2022e).

Current student and GSA member Mitchell poignantly told the board about the bullying and death threats he received after circulating a petition to oppose book banning. He then went on to dismantle the reconsideration committee's claims:

> Another point brought up by the board in the decision [about] *This Book Is Gay* is because it contained content that wasn't covered in the school's sex ed program and the book contained outdated information. I believe that the board should know that the book covers more than the school's [sex ed] program because the program is based off the NJ legal code that is older than the actual book itself. . . . If they think that book is outdated, then we need to change the whole curriculum as well. (North Hunterdon-Voorhees Regional High School District, 2022e)

Later, Joe, a 2012 graduate and now a suicide researcher at Harvard, spoke about the difficult home life experienced by some LGBTQIA+ youth:

> Remember that these 13- through 16-year-olds rely on their parents, who may be very unaccepting. I was kicked out when I came out. The reality is that possession of [*This Book Is Gay*] at home is not without real danger. As a result, the safest place for our students to access this knowledge is at school, in the library. (North Hunterdon-Voorhees Regional High School District, 2022e)

Following public comment, the board began a fractious voting session, during which three members repeatedly abstained, citing the poorly prepared report from the reconsideration committee. In the end, the board rejected the committee's recommendation to ban *This Book Is Gay* by a vote of 7–2 (with 3 abstentions), retaining it along with the other four titles.

In casting his vote to retain *This Book Is Gay*, board member Robert Kirchberger said:

> I think the bar for removing books from any library should be very high. . . . Both from the report that was given from the committee and from my own personal reading of this book, I think it falls woefully short of that high bar for removal . . . it's not even close. (North Hunterdon-Voorhees Regional High School District, 2022e)

At home, I embraced my husband and wept with relief as the accumulated stress of four months washed over me. But that relief did not last long. Work remained.

Defenders of Intellectual Freedom Respond

Throughout the challenge process, the NH-V IFF had observed procedural and policy lapses, which we compiled in "This Book Must Stay," a seventeen-page report to the board, in which we outlined numerous red flags, provided a line-by-line rebuttal to the committee's report on *This Book Is Gay*, and offered corrective measures to improve future reconsiderations. Our recommendations included establishing policy-based quality rubrics for committee reports, improving the timeliness of the reconsideration process, requiring administrator communication with librarians throughout the reconsideration process, providing a written rationale for each member's appointment to the reconsideration committee, and prohibiting subsequent reconsideration requests for previously adjudicated titles for a period of five years (Intellectual FReadom Coalition, 2022, pp. 16–17).

The board, too, had unfinished business. It had exonerated the books on January 25, but one accusation remained on the table: the defamatory claims against me. For the next four weeks, the NH-V IFF conducted a letter-writing campaign to the board, urging it to refute the baseless charges that had gone unanswered and uninvestigated since September.

In response to those messages, at the February 22 meeting, board president Jessica Viotto read a statement in which she declared:

> The challenges that were brought forward and resolved should not have been personal. There were members of North Hunterdon's staff that were singled out inappropriately. Ms. Martha Hickson, our librarian, has been publicly accused of crimes and of performing her duties with malicious motives. All of which are unfounded. (North Hunterdon-Voorhees Regional High School District, 2022f)

Epilogue

In the aftermath of the book challenges, the board directed school administrators to design a format so that future reconsideration reports would contain greater substance and comply with district policies. Administrators, who only months earlier had treated me with scorn, delegated their assignment to me. I developed a rubric, based on district materials selection criteria, and a report template that guides the reconsideration committee in identifying the merits and drawbacks of the book, supporting its recommendations with evidence, adhering to district goals and state instructional statutes, writing a rationale for its recommendation, and citing the sources consulted (North Hunterdon-Voorhees Regional High School District, 2022a).

In analyzing the reconsideration process, I calculated that investigating and resolving each book challenge had cost the district roughly $1,600 in materials and productivity, for a total of nearly $8,000 for the five challenges (Hickson, 2022, p. 13). For the complainants, on the other hand, the challenges cost nothing but time, and not much of it. Our materials challenge request form, which is based on a widely used sample form provided by the ALA, requires little effort to complete. Complainants can launch a challenge simply by stating their name and affiliation, how they learned about the book, whether they had read the entire book, their objection to the book, their recommendation for a replacement to the book, and the action requested (ALA, 2018).

The minimal effort required to launch a book challenge and the widespread use of the ALA template may have contributed to the record-setting 729 censorship attempts against 1,597 titles that the ALA recorded in 2021 (ALA, 2022). In fact, one household in McKinney, Texas, using a form essentially identical to the ALA template, submitted 282 reconsideration requests in a single day, each with the same complaint: "Contains 1 or more of the following: Marxism, incest, sexual [*sic*] explicit material—in written form and/or visual pictures, pornography, CRT, immoral activities, rebellious against parents, and the material contradicts the ISD's student handbook" (Serrano, 2022). Those forms were not legitimate complaints; they were junk mail.

To discourage such frivolous input, encourage more thoughtful submissions, and set a higher bar for launching a challenge, I proposed a more rigorous reconsideration form, which asks complainants to consult professional review sources and frame their complaints within the context of district selection criteria, district goals, and state instructional statutes (North Hunterdon-Voorhees Regional High School District, 2022b).

As of this writing in November 2022, the district has not taken action on the materials I proposed or the process improvements recommended by the NH-V Intellectual Freedom Fighters. Yet the protestors persist in disrupting board meetings. Without referring to any particular titles, the book banners continue to claim that the library supplies pornography for the purpose of grooming students for sex trafficking. The district's inaction combined with the protestors' obstinance creates the risk of "deja vu all over again," repeating the reconsideration process with the same inadequate tools and processes.

The targets of censorship will likely expand beyond the library, as the protestors' complaints have grown to include opposing New Jersey's instructional standards for comprehensive sex education; mischaracterizing the district's diversity, equity, and inclusion initiatives as instruments of critical race theory; and claiming that the district's curriculum is racist against white men.

In July 2022, three of the protestors who called for books to be banned became candidates for board seats, and one of the board members who voted to ban *This Book Is Gay* is seeking reelection on the November ballot (Makin, 2022). The outcome is in the hands and hearts of the voters.

Already established, though, is the positive impact that the fight against book challenges made on the students who defended the right to read. On June 2, 2022, the NJLA named the district's two GSAs—Prism and Spectrum—as the recipients of the 2022 NJLA Intellectual Freedom Award. Three GSA leaders—Mitchell Dacosta, Alex Ford, and Max Moore—traveled with their parents to Atlantic City to accept the award (figure 19.4). Watching those students take the stage to receive a standing ovation from a ballroom packed with cheering librarians was by far the proudest moment of my career.

Not only did that ceremony close the curtain on the most challenging episode of my professional life, but it also shone a spotlight on the next generation of First Amendment warriors, who will carry on the fight long after I am gone. For a school librarian, there is no better hindsight than a squad of empowered, engaged readers taking center stage, equipped to learn and lead for a lifetime.

Hints from Hindsight

Educational reformer John Dewey (1933) famously said, "We do not learn from experience . . . we learn from reflecting on experience." Having

Figure 19.4 The Next Generation of First Amendment Warriors—Mitchell, Max, and Alex—Celebrate Their 2022 New Jersey Library Association Intellectual Freedom Award with Librarian Martha Hickson.

survived book-banning attempts in 2019 and 2022, I am often asked for advice by colleagues facing their own challenges. Reflecting on those censorship experiences has resulted in this list of tips. For a discussion of each tip, visit tinyurl.com/mh-supplement.

1. Know your policies and keep them current.
2. Follow the news about censorship.
3. Report challenges as soon as possible.
4. Seek and accept help.
5. Know your "why" by documenting your professional obligation to fight censorship.
6. Keep contemporaneous notes.
7. Flex your research muscles.
8. Focus on the merits of the challenged title(s); avoid "what-aboutism."
9. Take care of yourself.
10. Let readers be leaders in defending the right to read.
11. Connect the dots to help administrators see larger patterns of censorship.
12. Never stop networking.
13. Keep the lines of communication open and use a variety of methods.
14. After the decision, analyze the process and the product to identify improvement opportunities.

References

American Library Association. (2018). *Sample school library request for reconsideration of material form.* https://www.ala.org/tools/sites/ala.org.tools/files/content/sampleschool_0.pdf

American Library Association. (2022). *State of America's libraries report 2022.* https://www.ala.org/news/state-americas-libraries-report-2022

Dailey, J. H. (2022, March 10). *The stakeholders of status quo.* Intellectual Freedom Blog. https://www.oif.ala.org/oif/the-stakeholders-of-status-quo/

DeGuzman, C. (2021, September 29). Parents complain about books. *Austin American-Statesman*, B3. https://infoweb.newsbank.com/apps/news/document-view?p=AWNB&docref=news/18550F0C16A92D90

Dewey, J. (1933). *How we think: A restatement of the relation of reflective thinking to the educative process.* Henry Regnery.

Fairfax County Public Schools. (2021, November 23). *FCPS reinstates two books, reaffirming commitment to supporting diversity in literature.* https://www.fcps.edu/news/fcps-reinstates-two-books-reaffirming-commitment-supporting-diversity-literature

Frencham, J. (2019, July). Gender queer: A memoir. *School Library Journal, 65*(6), 60–61.

Gunn, M. (2022). Recent surge in banned books targets titles with focus on race, sexuality. *Newsweek, 178*(11). https://www.newsweek.com/2022/04/29/recent-surge-banned-books-targets-titles-focus-race-sexuality-1696575.html

Hickson, M. (2022, April 2). *Katy, bar the door: Protecting reading rights in the era of book banning.* Canva. https://www.canva.com/design/DAE6gx11MF4/IOoZrNigGdxux2f51L4lSA/view

Intellectual FReadom Coalition of the NH-V Intellectual Freedom Fighters. (2022). *This book must stay: Response to the North Hunterdon-Voorhees reconsideration of "This book is gay."* https://drive.google.com/file/d/1dMN9LV_Y91gmL5z-Ssb8RUDVPbjMgGWu/view

Johnson, S. R. (2022, July 11). The 15 richest counties in the U.S. *U.S. News and World Report.* https://www.usnews.com/news/healthiest-communities/slideshows/richest-counties-in-america

Makin, C. (2022, August 16). *Here's what's attracting so many to run for school boards in Central Jersey.* MyCentralJersey. https://www.mycentraljersey.com/story/news/education/2022/08/16/nj-school-board-elections-2022-central-jersey-candidates/65391975007/

Natanson, H. (2021, September 28). Fairfax school system pulls two books from libraries after complaints about sexual content. *The Washington Post.* https://www.washingtonpost.com/local/education/fairfax-schools-remove-books-lgbtq/2021/09/28/a3bae2fc-1fc3-11ec-9309-b743b79abc59_story.html

North Hunterdon-Voorhees Regional High School District. (2016, May 10). *0167 public participation in board meetings.* https://boardpolicyonline.com/?b=north_hunterdon_voorhees&s=372857

North Hunterdon-Voorhees Regional High School District. (2021, September 28). *NHV BOE meeting* [Video]. YouTube. https://youtu.be/Avz44fJQGrE?t=3627

North Hunterdon-Voorhees Regional High School District. (2022a). *Report of the reconsideration committee.* https://docs.google.com/document/d/18_wbvwevES3DFkLwRbOXQeUiUqjWMWsm8erbpE86Bpo/edit?usp=sharing

North Hunterdon-Voorhees Regional High School District. (2022b). *Request for library materials reconsideration.* https://drive.google.com/file/d/1-2hV9LSuZvZ0gH0-dGrRKi4iPDMzQHPi/view

North Hunterdon-Voorhees Regional High School District. (2022c, January 25). *Board of Education: Agenda, regular meeting.* https://docs.google.com/document/d/1DzVkFDtVUV-7zm8QhHu6uG6VKfkQPE7PcwRkrNjKyfk/edit?usp=sharing

North Hunterdon-Voorhees Regional High School District. (2022d, January 25). *Notes for board from book committee.* https://drive.google.com/file/d/18TmnQ3XRL0Hl6sFstrWBlgMQcivAofdg/view

North Hunterdon-Voorhees Regional High School District. (2022e, January 25). *NHV BOE meeting* [Video]. YouTube. https://youtu.be/wsyLKWYS6ao?t=7298

North Hunterdon-Voorhees Regional High School District. (2022f, February 22). *Board of Education: Minutes, regular meeting.* https://docs.google.com/document/d/1hgikuC1aN-2yfEtJ9YJZOdGlXVZ0P_9ifvoDqtT5jkg/edit?usp=sharing

Price, R. S. (2021). Navigating a doctrinal grey area: Free speech, the right to read, and schools. *First Amendment Studies, 55*(2), 79–101.

Serrano, A. (2022, March 10). Author shocked by book censors. *Houston Chronicle.* https://infoweb.newsbank.com/apps/news/document-view?p=AWNB&docref=news/188AC02170ACE830

US Census Bureau. (2020). *Quick facts: Fairfax County, Virginia; Hunterdon County, New Jersey; United States.* https://www.census.gov/quickfacts/fact/table/fairfaxcountyvirginia,hunterdoncountynewjersey,US/INC110220

Walker, T. (2022, July 28). *Educators fight back against gag orders, book bans and intimidation.* National Education Association. https://www.nea.org/advocating-for-change/new-from-nea/educators-fight-back-against-gag-orders-book-bans-and-intimidation

Weingarten, R., & Edelman, J. (2022, April 29). Extremists are using lies to undermine America's public schools: We need to take a stand. *Time.* https://time.com/6172216/public-schools-extremists/

Young Adult Library Services Association announces 2020 Alex Awards. (2020, January 28). Targeted News Service.

Books Discussed in This Chapter

Bechdel, A. (2007). *Fun home: A family tragicomic.* Mariner.

Dawson, J. (2021). *This book is gay* (rev. ed.). Sourcebooks Fire.

Evison, J. (2018). *Lawn boy.* Algonquin Books of Chapel Hill.

Green, J. (2005). *Looking for Alaska.* Dutton Juvenile.

Jennings, J. (2016). *Being Jazz: My life as a transgender teen.* Crown.

Johnson, M. G. (2020). *All boys aren't blue.* Farrar, Straus and Giroux.

Kobabe, M. (2019). *Gender queer: A memoir.* Lion Forge.

Kuklin, S. (2014). *Beyond magenta: Transgender teens speak out.* Candlewick Press.

Letts, B. (1995). *Where the heart is.* Hachette.

Levithan, D. (2013). *Two boys kissing.* Alfred A. Knopf.

Sedaris, D. (2000). *Me talk pretty one day.* Hachette.

Wittlinger, E. (2007). *Parrotfish.* Simon & Schuster.

CHAPTER TWENTY

Saving Library Books for Kids: A Year Combating Censorship

Tonya Ryals

Censorship at the Craighead County Jonesboro Public Library

In the spring of 2019, I became the assistant director of the Craighead County Jonesboro Public Library (CCJPL). To say I was excited was an understatement. In Northeast Arkansas, this was *the* library, even if you lived in another county. It is an architectural statement piece and has hosted great events. I have fond memories of attending their teen author events during my teen years. Aside from the library being a community icon, I was excited to work with the staff, as I enjoyed meeting them during the interview. I had great respect for the director, David Eckert, as a colleague. I knew that I would learn a lot, taking a great next step in my career.

Around July, our then-teen librarian mentioned that she had tentatively selected an author for our annual October teen author event. This was a day-long event with two events for students and one for the public. One of the author's books was a Stonewall Book Award winner and had placed in the Arkansas Teen Author award. The catch? The author, Meredith Russo, is transgender. The librarian always sought approval from management before booking the author for this event. After reviewing, we determined that this would be a good event and the ball started rolling, the contract was signed, books were purchased, and the school librarians were contacted about students attending.

As the date approached, all seemed fine. Once our newsletter came out, the public became aware that Ms. Russo is transgender. The disinformation factory then churned and claimed that this event would indoctrinate children, the target audience was preschoolers, this was a drag queen story time, and on and on. Rumors swirled. We received calls from people well outside of our county. It was discussed at our regular board meeting, and the board determined that the library would honor our contract and proceed with the event. We opted to host one evening event for the general public. The event went great, we had a good turnout, and there were no major issues that day.

Why do I bring this up? It seems to have been a straightforward issue that was resolved fairly quickly. There were no official challenges. I do not recall reporting an unofficial challenge to the American Library Association (ALA). I bring this up because I believe this was a catalyst for another series of challenges beginning in 2021. I believe that local officials and some community members were disgruntled that a transgender author would be given a platform to talk about their book—particularly when their book is on a typical teenager's reading level, dealing with teen themes, and discussing occurrences that fairly meet the lived experiences of some teens.

The 2021 Censorship

The CCJPL is somewhat unique. It was formed by a city and a county library joining together. Somewhere along the way, their board became such that three trustees were appointed by the city and four by the county. I do not know why that split exists; from a population standpoint, it does not make sense. Between 2020 and early 2021, the county judge had the opportunity to nominate two trustees. His first selection was a personal friend. His second was suggested by said friend.

From 2020 to 2021, things continued in a typical, albeit COVID-impacted manner. We were excited to work on an addition and renovation to the children's library. Due to supply chain issues, we had to move the children's library into our largest meeting space. A problem, certainly, but manageable. This move occurred in June 2021. At the start of June, the staff put up a Pride display, as they had for many years without major incident. The display spread across the children's library. During the move, we discussed taking it down but, ultimately, we decided to leave it up for the remainder of the month.

With the collection in a smaller space, the Pride display became more obvious. Near the end of the month, the spouse of one of the newer trustees wrote a letter to the editor of the local newspaper lambasting the library for having the Pride display. We were also notified of a post made to a fringe political group's social media page on the topic. Not wanting the board to be blindsided and not, at that point, realizing that at least one trustee likely was already aware of the matter, we e-mailed the board to let them know about the display, should they hear about it.

Typically, the board does not meet during June or July to accommodate summer programming. By August, public awareness of the alleged controversy became well-publicized in the newspaper (often through letters to the editor) and through social media posts. Many members of the public contacted the library and board to give their thoughts on the matter. I tracked feedback and found that the favorable feedback outweighed the negative. All feedback went to the board. It was incredibly disheartening to see the community divide and to hear rhetoric centering on erasure and disparagement, particularly in accessible locations. Comments were made online, in news media, and at public meetings. Anyone could find commentary defaming the lesbian, gay, bisexual, and transgender (LGBT) community. It was saddening to know that young people, especially those in the LGBT community, would hear those horrible things, know that this was said by their neighbors, and potentially take those statements to heart.

Many things happened between this point and my resignation in mid-February 2022. Like many libraries, we received formal requests for reconsideration. Ours came in November 2021 and included eight books and one poster. None of us had ever had formal reconsideration requests before, but we utilized our policies to respond. We formed a committee to read the materials and make recommendations. Our committee was formed thoughtfully and included those in various departments, with different backgrounds, and of different ethnicities. There were a variety of ages, family status, and religious views. The group included people with different lived experiences who could speak to the role of how different topics might be approached by their communities. I am incredibly proud of the group and found that they did a marvelous job of thoughtfully reading the material and having deep discussions. No one took the job lightly.

Reconsideration Policy

Our policy stipulated that the staff committee prepare a recommendation. If the patron did not agree with the recommendation, they could appeal it to the board. At that point, the trustees would read the book and materials gathered for the original committee, discuss it, and make a final recommendation. The additional materials included the library mission statement, ALA's Library Bill of Rights, the library's collection development policy, and critical reviews. The committee members could also read peer reviews and other items they thought pertinent, such as interviews with the author.

In general, this structure was helpful. Adding in a time frame would have been helpful, although I struggled with the practical aspects of this. I have since read other policies with a ten-day turnaround. As we had to purchase copies, read them and the additional items, spend time meeting together, prepare the report, and all review the report for final approval, I do not think ten days is realistic. Notably, this happened during a global supply chain crisis, and shipping times were delayed beyond the norm. Additionally, we received all eight requests within the space of about a week or two. While a time frame would have been beneficial so the patrons knew what to expect, it would have been important to have flexibility to accommodate these extremes; ultimately, not being able to keep to that time limit may have been more frustrating for them. Looking back, I would have revised the policy to include a recommendation provided within six months. It is lengthy but gives ample time and an end date. We were fortunate in that the books were not incredibly lengthy. Reviewing a lengthy book could further affect the feasibility of a ten-day turnaround.

Another element I valued was our capacity to maintain the anonymity of committee members. All members were on staff and not known to the public. Given the commentary spread online, I did not want their names available. At least one member was unwilling to join unless their name was kept confidential. Some libraries specify that the committee includes staff, trustees, and members of the community. I can appreciate this; it allows buy-in from the public, ensures a broad view is provided, and transparently shows the interests of the public are represented. My concern with this is twofold. First, we would have lost anonymity. Second, while their views are valuable, nonlibrary staff do not have the same level of training on the role of the library. Most libraries with this in their policy are smaller ones who do not have sufficient staff to form a committee. In these instances, where else will you gather committee members? It is a challenge to balance; each library should consider what is best for their community.

It is also important to note one additional concern relating to selecting committee members, whether they are staff or not. We tend to select people who resemble us. This is particularly well known and documented relating to hiring practices (Kline et al., 2021) and should be a point of interest for every librarian (Strand, 2019). To that end, committee appointees should be thoughtfully selected to include a wide variety of voices. Every committee member should have an opportunity to voice their thoughts and have the right to be listened to by the entire group. As mentioned, our committee was very thoughtful, and I never had an issue with a member dismissing the views of others. Notably, we changed one another's minds on certain titles through thoughtful deliberations. We dissented on certain titles, but I always felt confident that everyone felt free to discuss their views and engage in conversation.

It is important to ensure that Black, Indigenous, and people of color (BIPOC) and lesbian, gay, bisexual, transgender, queer/questioning, intersex, and asexual (LGBTQIA+) voices be included within these reconsideration committees. Unquestionably, we should ensure BIPOC and LGBTQIA+ voices are invited, included, and heard in *all* library spaces, particularly when decisions are being made. This is not because the current wave of challenges centers on topics of race, gender identity, and sexuality. This is a matter of ensuring these voices, who have often been underrepresented, are included in decision-making. The best practice is to always include BIPOC and LGBTQIA+ voices in any discussion, not simply because their community as a topic is present in the discussion.

Within this, almost in the background, is the ALA. I reported challenges to them. I asked for their guidance on what to include in the recommendation report. I also read things non-librarians posted online about the ALA. It was not uncommon to see some, including a former trustee, say that the ALA is a leftist, socialist organization that tells us (librarians) what to buy and gives us reports to issue when we receive a reconsideration request.

There is a misunderstanding from the public about what the ALA does and how it impacts our professional roles and institutions. Even those who seem unwilling to talk with librarians and, instead, gather their information online will not visit the ALA's website to learn about them. It is often not beneficial to reference information as coming from the ALA. Those who are ready to dismiss the ALA for whatever reason will not be inclined to change their mind when presented with the Library Bill of Rights or Freedom to Read Statement.

Consider instead leaning on local resources. Your state library, state library association, and regional associations could lend you credence. ALA divisions can also be helpful as they are more removed. For example, we received a letter signed by the Public Library Association, United, and leadership for both our state library association and our state library advocacy association. This letter provided information about censorship, including legal considerations. It was great to have support and reinforcement to what David and myself were saying in a clear, direct way. This letter framed the big picture of the matter without using the ALA as a direct source. In general, I believe this letter helped local officials gain perspective on the legal and human ramifications of intrusive censorship efforts.

For our organization, more local officials were involved than may be the case in other libraries. As a joint city-county entity, officials from both were involved in the operations via their board appointments. As is true for all political appointments, there is a fine balance between a trustee's role and their role as an appointee by a particular mayor or judge. For public libraries, this can have a chilling impact. An appointee who opts to react upon political motivations taints their service; no longer are they a representative of their community working to better the library. Rather, they are a political factor steering the library toward one aim or another. The cure for this lies at the root: the appointing power. Provided with the insight into the harm a politically driven appointee could cause, those with appointing power should be less likely to seek out and appoint those with a partisan bent. Some appointing powers may see a trustee as a means to their own political advantage. Additionally, libraries with elected trustees may find that some trustees are running on a political platform and openly advertise their political aims. This leads to a three-part advocacy question: how can we educate our local officials, whether they appoint or not; how do we build trustee awareness beyond a political scope; and how do we advocate on both governance and intellectual freedom?

Advocacy

It is not groundbreaking to say that local officials can have an impact on the library or that you should advocate for your library to those officials. What I would urge librarians to do, though, is to seek that relationship early and expand it beyond the library. Let your officials get to know you and make sure they know your library. Be mindful of the official's responsibilities. Undoubtedly, you will not see eye to eye with your officials on all topics. You may be very fortunate and agree on many things; regardless, it is important to seek common ground. Find the things your officials are doing that you can support. Of course, this can be a big task. There are elected officials that I would be hard-pressed to support. However, you could offer the library as a meeting space for a town hall or remind them people register to vote at the library. You may not be able to find vast swathes of common ground with everyone, but the goal is to make those people the exception.

Arrange periodic meetings with your local leaders, whether they are elected, appointed, or community leaders. Seek them out and let them know what the library provides and ask what they would like to see from the library. You can even offer things to them, such as holding a town hall, being part of a rotating display of "local celebrity book picks," or identifying how the library helps meet their goals, such as lowering unemployment through public computer use for job applications. Follow up with them and let them know that you have been able to implement some of their ideas. In doing this, you are creating a better relationship, establishing trust, and paving the way for better communication in the event of an issue. Being able to have an open, honest conversation with an official and knowing that the conversation has equal amounts of positive respect and trust from both parties could be impactful in the event of a material challenge. Lacking communicative capacity hinders the library and, consequently, our residents. In my experience, this was particularly visible as the elected officials also held the responsibility of nominating trustees to our board.

With diligent effort, a strong relationship with officials can be formed. This is particularly important if they oversee nominating or approving trustees. The official hopefully understands the power that comes with the nomination and knows what a trustee does, so they can appoint excellent people. It is still important to build that same strong relationship with your trustees. It is crucial that they understand their role and how it fits within the library's governance. They must have a clear knowledge of the mission of the library. Start early with their orientation by providing them with everything they may need to know alongside a tour of the building. But take a step beyond this by arranging for training for the full board. It is likely that your state library offers this, but there are also consultants you could hire.

Meet your trustees on their level. You are the subject-matter expert for the library, but take the time to see where they are coming from. What are their experiences? What expectations do they have about being a trustee and for the library? You increase their knowledge with training and resources, but you gain their trust by listening to their perspectives. In the experiences I outlined above, certain trustees did not seek us out for conversation. They acted. They spoke out. They sought information and sent it to other trustees in a manner that likely violated open meeting laws. They wrote and proposed policies to the board. They did all this, but they did not take the time to talk with the library administrators. I have often asked myself why that is. It is likely that they did not have a good understanding of their role or the administrator's roles. Possibly they did not think that we were willing to have an informal conversation about their concerns. Instead, these conversations were conducted in public meetings where posturing seemed more valuable than listening. If there is a problem, do not hesitate to pick up the phone and have that hard conversation. Be professional and avoid dancing around an issue; ensure clarity by restating what you understand about the matter.

The advocacy that libraries spread among their public is crucial. We want the public to know what we have to offer, and we want it to be accessible to them. A wealth of advocacy resources already exists through materials on public relations, marketing, and more. What I want to address here is the value of identifying key library supporters. Strong supporters were a major source of strength for our library.

It is helpful to be embedded within your community. You can join civic groups, such as Rotary or Lions, to talk about the library and gain connections. If there are any groups that use the library for meeting spaces or refer people to your services, those are usually excellent groups to know. Aside from this, get to know your patrons. Who comes into the library? Who interacts with the library's social media accounts? Who attends board meetings or is willing to seek out meetings with local officials to talk about how much they care about the library? These are powerful advocates within your community. They may speak to news media to discuss the value in the library's mission. Their inclusion in news stories is beneficial as it shows the community's love for the library. If feasible, talk with them about what might benefit the library and its staff.

Obscenity

Throughout my experiences and after, while following news stories, I heard the same refrain. "How dare libraries expose children to sexually explicit books!" From a practical standpoint, I agree. Children should not be exposed to sexually explicit or graphic materials. They do not understand what they are seeing or how to process that information. It is terrible to expose a child to sexual content. My issue with this refrain is simple—I disagree with their definition of sexually explicit. I contend that the books in question are not sexually explicit or pornographic.

In discussing what it means for a material to be considered obscene, many librarians use the Miller Test, from the 1973 Supreme Court case. This states that a material is considered obscene if three criteria are met. First, the average person applying contemporary community standards would find the work, taken as a whole, appeals to the prurient interest. Second, the work depicts or describes, in a patently offensive way, sexual conduct specifically defined by the applicable state law. Third, and finally, the work, taken as a whole, lacks serious literary, artistic, political, or scientific value.

In our instance, there was disagreement about the test. There were many who felt that the books in question did not meet some, or any, of the criteria: the book was not wholly appealing to prurient interest, was not depicting sexual conduct defined by Arkansas law, and did not lack literary, artistic, or scientific value. Yet, there were some who disagreed and believed the books did meet the criteria. A primary argument made hinged on what "sexually explicit" means.

I often heard the complaint that the library did not have a definition of "sexually explicit" or "pornography." These people argued that not having a definition allowed those items to be purchased. I could not imagine trying to define those terms. Every possible definition lands on shaky ground that could have long-term consequences for the average resident. Perhaps it is any instance of a description of sex, but would that include any type of sex? Would it include masturbation? What about overtly sexual descriptions of other people? Maybe it is any description of an event that causes a feeling of sexual arousal? Then how would we define that? Is it the reader or a character within a book? Would that even include a preteen developing a crush on another character? Why not? What about non-overtly sexual depictions that evoke arousal? Would we have to ask people if they experienced arousal while reading it?

Even if we landed on an excellent definition, how do we apply it? Those arguing against this content initially say that it should not be available for children. Slowly, they edge to saying that children should not be able to stumble across it at all, meaning not even in the adult section. Well, there goes the James Patterson shelf! Specifically, I heard this argument leveled against *Gender Queer* (2020) by Maia Kobabe, located in our adult graphic novel section. Our reconsideration committee decided to retain this title in its current location; the patron argued that it should not be in the library where a child can find it. Interestingly, he also argued with a staff member about where the book was shelved, insisting that it was in the area where teen graphic novels were located. (An amusing yet depressing aside: a previously mentioned trustee later said that another title should be moved to the adult graphic novels because that is where the library kept "graphic" novels.)

Returning to the Miller Test, notably, the three prongs focus on the item *as a whole*. It is unclear if some who challenge books, in fact, read the item in its entirety—and what impact the full context might have on their view. In recent months, groups have been sharing "reviews" of titles for local folks to post and share online (Jensen, 2022). These reviews could be used to generate challenges. This spreads their message without the person reading the entire book and seeing the "controversial" sections in context. Knowing the context might risk the person realizing that perhaps this book is not filth, the way another person on Facebook said it was.

Context is key when determining if a material is explicit or, in other words, if it is solely intended to appeal to prurient interests. It also provides validation of the appropriate age group for the book in question. It is easier to fret about a six-year-old stumbling across an "obscene" teen book than it is for that child to read that worrisome title. Even at the appropriate reading and comprehension level, context still rules the day. An average reader is reasonably intelligent; they would be able to consider the situation. The plot leading to the questionable scene includes valuable information about the characters. The reader would be able to understand why a situation went a certain way. They are smart enough to think how they could apply that lesson to their own lives. Not every book must present a morality tale or be a textbook to provide the reader with insight or personal growth. A book may include the experiences of a character living a risky lifestyle, but the reader adds value to the story by adding their own insights to the plot. How can a person pass judgment on an entire book based on a few paragraphs when a book is open to interpretations owing to the knowledge and imagination of each reader? Of course, a book may also be read simply for entertainment.

It is worth mentioning that our current wave of book bans center on sexuality and gender identity. Race has also been included in the challenges of other libraries, although it was not as explicitly referenced during the challenges received by the CCJPL during my time there. Other censorship waves dealt with politics, religion, witchcraft, and more. This concern over what it means to be sexually explicit, for example, did not happen with *Animal Farm* by George Orwell (1945) or any Harry Potter title.

Benefits of Reading

There are numerous studies and explorations of the lifelong impacts of exposure to various media types, content, and exposure time frames. Here, we will explore the impacts on mental well-being and reading. To center on the concerns recently at hand, I will focus on books that discuss sexual education, lived experiences, and teen fiction, as these were themes in our book challenges.

There is a real impact of reading about others' lived experiences and fictionalized literature. Reading helps us feel less isolated and more connected to those around us and even to our own experiences (Dowrick et al., 2012). While paradoxical to some, reading about the harsh experiences in many well-known, beloved titles (Toni Morrison's *The Bluest Eye* [1970], Laurie Halse Anderson's *Speak* [1999], and Maya Angelou's *I Know Why the Caged Bird Sings* [1969], to name only a few) can be cathartic. Those who have not experienced a similar situation can have greater compassion and empathy for others, as they see through the eyes of someone with that experience, through reading (Blackburn et al., 2015). Reading can improve the mental health of the reader and assist them in building stronger relationships with those around them through building capacity for offering support (Lewis, 2015). Interwoven into this is the importance of representation.

No one person could truly understand the lived experiences of everyone they meet. Throughout our lives, we experience incredibly different things. Those with siblings likely understand this: even growing up in the same household and having (seemingly) similar childhoods, you can have very different experiences and very different perspectives on the same events. For a voracious reader, it becomes second nature to read about experiences faced by those dissimilar from us. We can take that for granted. We might forget that others are not accustomed to reading books from dissimilar perspectives. When confronted by the perspective of an "outsider" to that person's social group, that perspective can seem outrageous. I believe many of the challenges to titles such as *All Boys Aren't Blue* (2022) by George M. Johnson and *Gender Queer* come from those who do not often engage with representations of people beyond their comfort zone. Knowing these are true stories depicting the author as a teen may cause this to be more egregious. They may wonder why anyone would want to read a description of a non-heteronormative sexual encounter. None of this should preclude a teenager from access to books that discuss these "uncomfortable" topics and having the intellectual freedom to know more about themselves and those around them.

This could become a cyclical issue. The teen readers of today become the adult readers, and parents, of tomorrow. Recognizing others for who they are and having empathy toward them goes a long way in later years, particularly if people find a love of reading early and continue reading while exploring new literary territory into adulthood. Feeling emotionally transported by a book and, consequently, gaining empathy (Bal & Veltkamp, 2013) may be more common among frequent readers.

Any librarian can tell you the impact a single book can have on a kid. Finding that right fit, even if it is not of "literary merit" or teaching morality, helps a kid to realize that reading is worthwhile and fun (Jaffee, 2016). When reading is an enjoyable pastime, literacy skills become far easier to grow. Relying on school reading assignments, including homeschooling, limits the child's introduction to books that spark a love of reading and lead them to becoming a lifelong reader. Do not begrudge a title for lacking literary merit; no one has gone from reading textbooks to *War and Peace* (by Tolstoy; 1867) without a lot of fun and relaxing books in between. As reading can improve mental well-being (Sima, 2022) and brain health (Berns et al., 2013), librarians celebrate the kids (and adults!) picking up *Goosebumps* or *Twilight*, knowing that one book is a small step in their lives.

Conclusion

Of course, you may note that I did not conclude my part of this story. It can be very trying to summarize my experiences. In the eight months that I worked during this onslaught, many incidents occurred. There is a certain amount of self-care that comes from being able to give advice to other librarians about how to handle this at a strategic, policy level but nothing can prepare you for the experience. It is a deeply painful thing when you love your job, but are told, time and again, directly and indirectly, that you are falling short and failing children. As a manager, it is sobering to see your staff upset and facing public ridicule for providing access to books that inspire tolerance and acceptance. To hear comments from the public about how the library has touched their lives and what it would have meant for them, their child, their sibling to see a Pride display and to know that the library was a safe place is one of the most bittersweet moments a librarian can have—hearing the good we do, wrapped in the context of a hateful, sometimes dangerous, world.

Ultimately, I decided to leave my job. It was a difficult, painful decision that I still struggle with. I loved my job at CCJPL, but my decision was based on two points. First, I felt that a clean slate would be better for my library. Our director had also resigned and, with me leaving, new administration could come in and, hopefully, be able to settle the matter. I did not believe I stood a chance at settling the issue as I was not listened to by certain people. Our library also received many public record requests from a local elected official, backed by two other people. I hoped that, with the new administration, this issue would settle down and they would stop attempting to prove nonexistent fraud.

Second, I felt a lack of support from some people and did not see an end to the issue. I felt support from my fellow library staffers, spouse, friends, and staff at the Arkansas State Library. Despite this, I ultimately believed that certain elected officials were intent on harming the library, in part by appointing trustees who were focused on their agendas. Released public records requests indicate that the county judge sought to defund the library. While I felt support from most of the trustees, I thought it likely that the scale would slowly tip in the other direction. I had been micromanaged by certain trustees and my professional opinion discounted too many times to continue with confidence that I would again someday feel comfortable at work. Further, even if all other appointees were well-qualified and intentionally supportive of the goals of the library, I knew I was looking at five to ten more years with those trustees.

I also felt very uncomfortable continuing to live in the town. While I recognize that those arguing against the library were a minority and that I had the support of a larger community, I did not feel safe to take a walk around the block. I was also made to feel that some of those involved were interested in tarnishing my professional reputation. There were some who made efforts to belittle me and my work to trustees, in the newspaper and on social media. Notably, one person responded to my resignation letter with a public records request that demanded I turn over evidence of my harassment. It seemed that it would eventually do more harm to myself than good to my community and staff for me to stay.

The initial incident has now been more than a year ago. As of this writing, the beat goes on. During my time, we received material reconsideration requests for multiple titles: *All Boys Aren't Blue, And Tango Makes Three* (by Justin Richardson and Peter Parnell; 2007), *Gender Queer, It's Perfectly Normal* (by Robie Harris; 1994), *This Day in June* (by Gayle E. Pitman and K. Litten; 2014), *The GayBCs* (by M. L. Webb; 2021), *LGBTQ Rights and Activism* (by Stephen Currie; 2020), *L8r G8r* (by Lauren Myracle; 2014), and *People of Pride* (by Little Bee Books; 2020). All titles were retained. *It's Perfectly Normal* had previously been moved to the "Parent/Teacher Section" (a section for parenting and educator books); the committee returned it to juvenile nonfiction. The committee determined that no older versions of *The GayBCs* would be retained or purchased as older versions were less inclusive and viewed as demeaning to the LGBTQIA+ community. Appeals were issued for the recommendation made for *All Boys Aren't Blue* and *L8r G8r*; the former was retained, and the latter was removed along with the two preceding titles in its series.

By my final board meeting, two trustees had submitted four policies that would restrict the library's collection development, programming, and displays. Those policies were rejected by the board. One trustee seems to have signaled their intention to continue submitting such policies.

At the end of the day, the library is continuing to do an excellent job. Even from afar, I see their well-attended events, filled with smiling patrons. I hear from my friends how the library continues to be a welcoming place. I am hopeful that the community can move beyond this and support one another and the library.

Finally, and in conclusion, an oft-stated librarian refrain: not every book is for everyone. Behaving like this is the case insists that every title be appropriate for everyone. It does not work. No one would go to the library if every book had to be acceptable for a four-year-old. Add in arguments that every book should include a lesson, telling us how to be good, upstanding, moral people, and that is a recipe to send people hurtling to a bookstore. Not every book is for every person, but every reader has a book that is for them. Water will seek its own level, and people will read the stories that appeal to their reading skills and views. Those books may be poetry, prose, graphic novels, nonfiction, or written like a text exchange, but everyone has a right to say what books are right for them.

References

Bal, P. M., & Veltkamp, M. (2013, January 30). How does fiction reading influence empathy? An experimental investigation on the role of emotional transportation. *PLOS ONE*. https://journals.plos.org/plosone/article?id=10.1371%2Fjournal.pone.0055341

Berns, G. S., Blaine, K., Prietula, M. J., & Pye, B. E. (2013, December 1). *Short- and long-term effects of a novel on connectivity in the brain*. Brain Connectivity. https://www.ncbi.nlm.nih.gov/pmc/articles/PMC3868356/

Blackburn, M. V., Clark, C. T., & Nemeth, E. A. (2015). Examining queer elements and ideologies in LGBT-themed literature: What queer literature can offer young adult readers. *Journal of Literacy Research*, 47(1), 11–48.

Dowrick, C., Billington, J., Robinson, J., Hamer, A., & Williams, C. (2012, June 1). *Get into reading as an intervention for common mental health problems: Exploring catalysts for change*. Medical Humanities. https://mh.bmj.com/content/38/1/15.short

Jaffee, C. (2016, January 14). *Raising a lifelong reader: Tips for reading with your child*. PBS. https://www.pbs.org/parents/thrive/raising-a-lifelong-reader-tips-for-reading-with-your-child

Jensen, K. (2022, May 19). *BookLooks, framed as "objective" book rating resource: A moms for liberty joint*. BOOK RIOT. https://bookriot.com/moms-for-liberty-booklooks/

Kline, P. M., Rose, E. K., & Walters, C. R. (2021, July 26). *Systemic discrimination among large U.S. employers*. NBER. https://www.nber.org/papers/w29053

Lewis, C. (2015, April). *How far have we come? A critical look at LGBTQ identity in young adult literature*. https://scholarworks.gvsu.edu/cgi/viewcontent.cgi?article=2072&context=lajm

Sima, R. (2022, March 16). The mental health benefits of reading. *Psychology Today*. https://www.psychologytoday.com/us/blog/the-art-effect/202203/the-mental-health-benefits-reading

Strand, K. (2019). *Disrupting whiteness in libraries and librarianship: A reading list*. The Office of the Gender and Women's Studies Librarian. https://www.library.wisc.edu/gwslibrarian/bibliographies/disrupting-whiteness-in-libraries/

Books Discussed in This Chapter

Anderson, L. H. (1999). *Speak*. Square Fish.
Angelou, M. (1969). *I know why the caged bird sings*. Random House.
Currie, S. (2020). *LGBTQ rights and activism*. ReferencePoint Press.
Harris, R. H., & Emberley, M. (1994). *It's perfectly normal: A book about changing bodies, growing up, sex, and sexual health*. Candlewick Press.
Johnson, G. M. (2022). *All boys aren't blue: A memoir-manifesto*. Farrar, Straus and Giroux.
Kobabe, M. (2020). *Gender queer: A memoir*. Oni Press.
Little Bee Books. (2020). *People of pride: RuPaul Charles*. Little Bee Books.
Morrison, T. (1970). *The bluest eye*. Knopf Doubleday.
Myracle, L. (2014). *L8r, g8r*. Amulet Books.
Orwell, G. (1945). *Animal farm*. Signet.
Pitman, G. E., & Litten, K. (2014). *This day in June*. Magination Press.
Richardson, J., & Parnell, P. (2007). *And Tango makes three*. Simon & Schuster Children's Books.
Tolstoy, L. (1867). *War and peace*. Charles Scribner's Sons.
Webb, M. L. (2021). *The GayBCs*. Quick Books.

About the Editor and Contributors

Editor

Shannon M. Oltmann (she/her) is an associate professor in the School of Information Science at the University of Kentucky. She obtained her PhD from Indiana University. Her research interests include information ethics, censorship, intellectual freedom, public libraries, privacy, and qualitative research methods. Oltmann is the past editor of the *Journal of Intellectual Freedom and Privacy* and associate editor of *Library Quarterly*. She recently published a book titled *Practicing Intellectual Freedom in Libraries* (in 2019). Oltmann's work has been funded by the American Library Association and the Institute of Museum & Library Services. She has presented her research at numerous academic conferences. Her work has been published in *Library Quarterly*, *Journal of the Society for Information Science and Technology*, *Public Libraries Quarterly*, *Collection Management*, *Libri*, and *Library and Information Science Research*.

Contributors

Moni Barrette (she/hers) is a sixteen-year public librarian who expanded her expertise in libraries, comics, and relationship building through her role at LibraryPass as the director of content management and publisher relations, where her interest in teaching grew. As cofounder of the nonprofit Creators, Assemble!, president of the American Library Association's Graphic Novel & Comics Round Table, and adjunct lecturer at San Diego State University, she became dedicated to promoting learning through the use of comics and popular culture. Outside of professional endeavors, Moni spends her time with her family (two human babies, two fur babies, and her husband), watches scary movies, and hunts for ghosts against her better judgment.

Glen J. Benedict is the access services librarian at the University of the District of Columbia, a historically Black land-grant university and the only public university in Washington, DC. He has been working in libraries for eight years. An avid advocate for freedom of speech and intellectual freedom, he has served on the American Library Association's (ALA) Committees on Legislation and Intellectual Freedom and has presented on book bans and challenges at diverse gatherings, including ALA's inaugural LibLearnX, the Washington Research Library Consortium's Annual Meeting, and Flame Con (all in 2022). In his free time, Glen can be found creating imaginary worlds and exploring our real one.

Rene Burress is a department chair and associate professor at the University of Central Missouri where she has worked for the past ten years. Prior to moving to higher education, Dr. Burress was a kindergarten teacher and elementary school librarian. When she is free, she spends time with her family, and she loves to travel (she has recently made it to all fifty U.S. states).

Becky Calzada is a thirty-five-year Texas educator and is currently the district library coordinator in Leander Independent School District, which is located northwest of Austin, Texas. She was recently selected to the fourth cohort of the American Library Association's (ALA) Policy Corps, a group of library professionals dedicated to advocacy of library goals and values. She is a member of the ALA Intellectual Freedom Committee, a member of the ALA Center for the Future of Libraries Advisory Group, on the Legislative Committee for the Texas Library Association, past chair for the Texas Association of School Librarian division, and cofounder of #FReadom Fighters. Becky can be followed on Twitter @becalzada.

Rhona Campbell, MLS (she/her), is currently the high school librarian at Georgetown Day School in Washington, DC. So far in her twenty-three years as a librarian, she has worked in public library youth services and schools, helping teachers, administrators, nannies, other librarians, parents, and students from ages two to nineteen. A former reviewer and writer for *School Library Journal* and *Capitol Choices*, Rhona has also published in the *Washington Post* and on blogs for Georgetown Day School and the Office for Intellectual Freedom of the American Library Association. This chapter could not have been written without the support of my colleague Lisa Fall.

Carolyn Foote is a thirty-nine-year-old Texas educator and is currently a library consultant and freelance librarian. Recognized as a White House Champion of Change in 2013, she served as a school librarian for twenty-nine years for a school district in the Austin area. Her work has centered on collaboration, technology use in libraries, library design, and advocacy.

Foote is a cofounder of #FReadom Fighters. She has been the recipient of the AASL Library Collaboration Award, the AASL Intellectual Freedom Award, the ALA Robert Downs Intellectual Freedom Award, and the TLA Libraries Serve Communities Award. She has previously served as an advisory member on several boards, including the ALA Center for the Future of Libraries Advisory Board. She is a frequent contributor to library magazines and a frequent conference presenter.

Jamie Gregory has been an educator for seventeen years, serving as a high school English teacher for eight years and finishing her ninth year in 2022 as a high school librarian, all in South Carolina. She is currently the upper school librarian and journalism/newspaper teacher at Christ Church Episcopal School in Greenville, SC, and has blogged for the American Library Association's Office for Intellectual Freedom Blog since 2019. She achieved National Board Certification in Library Media in 2017 and the PBS Media Literacy Educator Certification in 2021. She is the 2022 South Carolina School Librarian of the Year, the 2022 News Literacy Project Alan C. Miller Educator of the Year, a 2022 *Library Journal* Mover & Shaker, the 2022 recipient of the Intellectual Freedom Round Table's Eli M. Oboler Memorial Award for intellectual freedom writing, and the recipient of the 2021 NAMLE Media Literacy Teacher Award.

Dorcas Hand retired in 2016 after more than forty years in independent school libraries in Houston, Texas: St. John's School, Episcopal High School, and Annunciation Orthodox School. She has been active in the American Library Association (ALA) and Texas Library Association (TLA) since 1978, and cofounded the Houston Area Independent School Library Network (HAISLN) around 1984 and their annual Recommended Reading List in the early 1990s. She currently serves as the TLA chapter councilor to ALA Council (2021–24) and as a board member of the Freedom to Read Foundation (2021–24). She is one of three coordinators of the TLA IF Helpline. She chaired the COLA Ecosystem Task Group (2018–20), which wrote the Toolkit and Continuum, and she cochairs the COLA Ecosystem Subcommittee (2020–present).

Amanda Harrison worked for fifteen years in PreK–12 education and fourteen as a school librarian. She was part of the 2006 Teach for America, Chicago cohort, and has worked in schools in Illinois, Missouri, and Kansas. She completed her PhD in 2020 from Emporia State University with a dissertation titled "The Impact of the Network Society on the Professional Identity of Serbian Librarians." She is currently an assistant professor at the University of Central Missouri's Library Science program and has served on numerous professional committees and boards, including the Kansas Association of

School Librarians, the American Library Association's International Relations Round Table Reception Committee, and the Beta Phi Mu, Beta Epsilon Chapter. Current and ongoing interests include school libraries, librarians connecting globally, and the development of librarians' professional identities.

Martha Hickson has been a high school librarian since 2005. A graduate of the Rutgers University School of Communication & Information, Martha has written for *School Library Journal*, *Booklist*, *KnowledgeQuest*, the American Library Association Intellectual Freedom Blog, *NJEA Review*, and *School Librarian's Workshop*. She has been a presenter at conferences and webinars, including the American Association of School Librarians, Future Ready Librarians, the New Jersey Library Association, and the New Jersey Association of School Librarians. Her defense of intellectual freedom has been recognized with awards from the New Jersey Association of School Librarians, the New Jersey Library Association, the American Association of School Librarians, and the National Council of Teachers of English. In 2022, the National Coalition Against Censorship presented Martha with the Judith Krug Outstanding Librarian Award and the American Library Association presented her with the Lemony Snicket Prize for Noble Librarians Faced with Adversity in recognition of her "energy and bravery in the face of . . . persistent and ongoing hostility," while advocating for students' First Amendment right to read.

Julie N. Hornick is a senior instructional services librarian at Florida Southern College (FSC) in Lakeland, Florida, a post she has held since 2016. At FSC, she liaises with the Art & Art History and Science Departments as well as the Schools of Education, Nursing & Health Sciences, and Physical Therapy. She enjoys planning and participating in outreach events and activities designed to bring students into the library outside of their regular curricular needs. Prior to joining the faculty at FSC, she worked for seventeen years in the public school system in South Carolina, where she spent two years as a high school French teacher and then fifteen years in elementary and middle school libraries. She holds an MA in French from Penn State University and an MLIS from the University of South Carolina. Her current research interests include incorporating new technologies into instruction, instructional design, and the ways in which academic libraries enrich the campus experience of college students.

Andrea Jamison is an assistant professor of librarianship at Illinois State University. She has more than seventeen years of experience working in the field of education and libraries. She speaks internationally on library inclusivity, intellectual freedom, and the interplay of race, power, and privilege in children's books. Her research involves examining equity issues in library services and the role that libraries play in either perpetuating or mitigating systems of inequity. Andrea has conducted content analyses on hundreds of collection development policies to determine how policies address diversity and how they align with the American Library Association's (ALA) Library Bill of Rights. She has written articles on these topics for *Knowledge Quest*, *American Libraries Magazine*, the Library Assessment Conference, and ALA's Office of Intellectual Freedom Blog. Currently, she is under contract to write a book for Beta Phi Mu's International Honor Society's Scholars Series on leverage equity in libraries. Andrea received her master's degree in teaching from Concordia University and her master of library science and PhD in information studies from Dominican University School of Library and Information Science in River Forest, Illinois. Currently, she is the immediate past chair for ALA's Ethnic & Multicultural Information Exchange Roundtable, which promotes multiculturalism in librarianship and a library ambassador for Lee and Low Books. She also chaired the 2018 working group that revised ALA's Library Bill of Rights for Diverse Library Collections.

Jenna Kammer, PhD, is an associate professor at the University of Central Missouri in Warrensburg, Missouri. She teaches in the library science and information services program. Prior to working as a professor, she has worked as an instructional designer, reference librarian, and paraprofessional.

Kerrie Lattari is in her ninth year as a Maine middle school library media specialist. She is passionate about media literacy, middle grade literature, and baked goods.

Terri L. Lesley, a lifetime Wyoming resident, has worked at a public library for twenty-six years, including nine years as the executive director. She and her husband have three grown children and a dog. In addition to having a passion for reading and writing, she enjoys traveling, hiking in the Big Horn Mountains and Black Hills, and photography. She has a degree in business administration from the University of Wyoming and a master's in library and information science from the University of North Texas. She is the 2022 recipient of the John Phillip Immroth Memorial Award from the American Library Association's Intellectual Freedom Round Table.

Mernie Maestas is a PhD candidate in the School of Library and Information Management at Emporia State University and the lead librarian for the Wentzville School District (WSD) in Wentzville, Missouri, where she has worked as a school librarian for eighteen years. Prior to that, she was a classroom teacher in WSD. She has taught library courses as an adjunct professor at the University of Central Missouri and Missouri Baptist University. She is also the past president of the Missouri Association of School Librarians.

Kelly Mayfield holds a master of arts in theology from St. Meinrad Seminary and School of Theology. She is the author of *Mine in China* (2016), a guidebook to adoption from China. Following her three years of working as a paraprofessional school librarian at a private elementary school, she began to pursue an MSLS from the University of Kentucky. A native of Kentucky, Kelly currently resides in Ohio with her family, where she works in collection services at Columbus Metropolitan Library.

Matthew Noe (he/his) is the lead collection and knowledge management librarian at Countway Library, Harvard Medical School, and a part-time instructor at the University of Kentucky in the School of Information Science. He is most well-known for his work in comics librarianship, health sciences librarianship, and, in particular, graphic medicine. Matthew was the 2021–22 president of the American Library Association's Graphic Novels and Comics Round Table. He is a founding board member, website editor, and treasurer for the Graphic Medicine International Collective. You will find his comics reviews in both *Booklist* and *Diamond Bookshelf*. At the local level, he is the treasurer on the Worcester Public Library's board of directors. You can often find him overcaffeinated, ranting about all manner of things on Twitter, or curled up with two dogs, a book, and not enough hands.

Kristin Pekoll is a former YA librarian from Wisconsin. For eight years, she provided professional and emotional support to library workers experiencing bans and challenges as the assistant director of the American Library Association's (ALA) Office for Intellectual Freedom. She is the author of *Beyond Banned Books: Defending Intellectual Freedom throughout Your Library,* published by ALA Editions in 2019.

Tonya Ryals has worked in public libraries for over fourteen years, with seven years spent in library administration. She currently resides in Vermont and is a consultant with a government library.

Joe Schweiss is currently the associate director of the Portland Public Library in Portland, Maine. He has worked in public libraries since 2006, including fifteen years as a director. He knows that he would not have accomplished much without the amazing people that he has had the pleasure of leading and working with over the years, nor will he ever forget that fact.

Dee Ann Venuto was introduced to the behind-the-scenes world of libraries, including their code of ethics, while working as a student assistant during high school. This experience led her to pursue an undergraduate degree in English education and library science from Shippensburg University and an MLIS from the University of Texas in 1991. Later, she earned a supervisor certificate from Rutgers University. A New Jersey public educator for over thirty years, Dee Ann has been the high school librarian at a county vocational school and most recently media center coordinator at her alma mater. She has served as vice president of the county school librarians' association and board member of the local and state library cooperatives and is a member of the American Library Association's (ALA) Intellectual Freedom Committee. Most recently, her library was selected for a television commercial by the state teachers' education association. The challenges discussed here brought several accolades, including the NJ Librarians' Association and the American Association of School Librarians' Intellectual Freedom Awards, and the National Coalition Against Censorship's Intellectual Freedom Fighter honor. Dee Ann seeks to educate others about challenges by writing, participating in research, and speaking at library science programs and library conferences.

Cindy C. Welch is a clinical professor in the School of Information Sciences (SIS), College of Communication & Information (CCI), at the University of Tennessee (UT-Knoxville). Before joining SIS in 2008, she provided youth services in public libraries in North Carolina and Illinois. She also worked at the American Library Association, serving as the last deputy director for both the Young Adult Library Services Association and the American Association of School Librarians. She oversees the school library program at UT-Knoxville and teaches classes in storytelling, youth services, youth literature, and collection development.

Angie Wiegers is the library coordinator for the North Kansas City School District in Kansas City, Missouri. She has worked as the coordinator for four years. Angie has been an educator for twenty-three years and a public school librarian for fourteen of those years. During her free time, she likes to hang out with her amazing family, go hiking with her big pup, and read, read, READ!

Amie Wright (she/her/hers) is a public history PhD student at Carleton University (Ottawa, Canada). Her SSHRC-funded doctoral research explores the understudied legacy of comics censorship in Canada and its impact on vocational practice and norms in schools and libraries. Other research interests include the teaching of history, visual and popular culture, critical librarianship, and the history of education. Amie is the former manager of school outreach at the New York Public Library and the past inaugural president of the American Library Association's (ALA) Graphic Novels and Comics Round Table (GNCRT). Currently, she chairs the GNCRT's Preparing For and Addressing Challenges to Comics in the Library Committee. Find her at @librarylandia for sporadic tweets on embracing public history, decolonizing GLAMs, fighting vocational awe, and reveling in all things comics (and animal memes) related.

Index